Trout Fishing

(Originally published as *Trout and How to Catch Them*)

Kenneth Mansfield was born in 1902 and joined the regular army in 1920, where he served in the Army Educational Corps, the Intelligence Corps and the Burma Intelligence Corps. He retired in 1950 a Lieutenant Colonel.

After retirement he went into general journalism, but his subjects soon became canalized into angling and associated matters. He has contributed to all the major angling magazines and periodicals and was for ten years 'Coridon' in *Anglers' News*. He has written several books on angling and has edited others, notably *The Art of Angling*, *The Fisherman's Companion*, and the *How to Catch Them* series. He was also editor of the magazine *Angling* for eight years.

He is married and his hobbies are stamp collecting, travelling, natural history, military history and, of course, angling.

GW00601109

Pan Anglers' Library

Trout Fishing

Edited by Kenneth Mansfield
(Originally published as *Trout and How to Catch Them*)

Pan Books London and Sydney

First published 1970 as *Trout and How to Catch Them*
by Barrie & Jenkins Ltd
This revised edition published 1974 by Pan Books Ltd.
Cavaye Place, London SW10 9PG
2nd printing 1977
© Barrie & Jenkins Ltd 1970
ISBN 0 330 23901 5
Printed and bound in Great Britain by
Cox & Wyman Ltd, London, Reading and Fakenham

CONTENTS

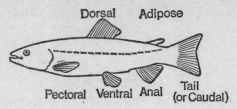

FIG 1. The fins of a trout.

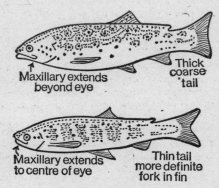

FIG 2. *Above:* Trout. *Below:* Salmon Parr.

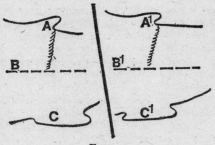

FIG 3.

Salmon   Trout
12 scales   14 scales

AA¹ – Adipose Fin
BB¹ – Lateral Line
CC¹ – Anal Fin

L. BAVERSTOCK

River Fly Fishing

(For notes on rods, reels, lines, etc, see Appendix)

1 CASTING A FLY

THE ideal way to begin is to have a few lessons at a good casting school where you will be under the care of a skilled instructor who will see that the only habits you form are good ones.

It is by no means essential to go to a casting school but, if you decide to learn on your own or with the assistance of an angling friend, you must know what you are trying to do before you even think of picking up a rod.

As a newcomer to fly fishing you may rely far too much on what your friend says and unless he is a first-class fisherman the chances are that you will pick up all his faults and add a few of your own.

Early lessons

The first few lessons are most important because as soon as you get a rod in your hand you start to form habits and if you are to cast really well the habits must be good ones.

An experienced fisherman can be of great help in assisting a beginner to cast because, in many ways, practical tuition is more effective than theory. But the written word is invaluable for indicating the path this tuition should follow and if the beginner applies the following notes to his practice he should have no trouble in mastering casting quite quickly.

The essential requirement for good casting is accurate timing of the movements of the rod so that they are begun and finished at the correct moment for developing full power in the rod and a good speed in the line.

For very long casting the angler has to learn to manipulate the line with the left hand while the cast is being made and this rather complicates matters, because the movements of the left hand have to be timed correctly too so that they fit in with the action of the rod.

It is the perfect combination of hand and rod which produce the outstanding caster, and the distances these men can throw a fly have to be seen to be believed.

Fortunately we do not have to aspire to such heights and our task is, therefore, much easier.

Once a sound basis has been laid, the fisherman is free to develop his technique in the direction which best suits the fishing he does. For example, if he fishes wide rivers he will probably want to develop his distance cast as much as possible while, if his sport is obtained on small overgrown streams, accuracy will be his goal. At the start, however, don't worry about any of this. Just make sure that you have the essentials right and everything else will follow gradually.

Try to make a start on a calm day so that you do not have to make compensations in your casting for sudden gusts of wind or the behaviour of an unruly line. These can make things difficult for the most experienced of fishermen and they rob the beginner of the necessary feel of his equipment which he must have if he is to progress quickly. A rod and line feel entirely different on a windy day, so much so that a beginner may find them unmanageable.

It is also a great help if you can begin practice on a river or, at least, over water. Here again there is an entirely different feel to the equipment when it is used as it is intended to be used.

The old idea of starting by taking the rod out on to the lawn should only be adopted as a last resort in cases where it is difficult to get to suitable water.

On water you immediately get the feel of the line as it comes off the surface and you get the atmosphere of the whole thing so much better. The behaviour of the line on moving water cannot be reproduced on dry land, so you have to go to the water to learn how it helps and handicaps your casting.

Before we pick up the rod let's have a look at the most important parts of a cast so that when the rod starts to bend in our hand we will have some idea of what we are trying to achieve.

8

Grip

I think the best way is to begin with the thumb on top of the grip, as shown in the diagram. This is not quite as comfortable as the more natural way of holding the rod which is achieved more or less by just picking it up, but it has the important advantage that it greatly assists in preventing the wrist from turning over too far as the rod is brought back. You can easily prove this for yourself by moving the wrist with the knuckles held upwards, then trying to do the same with the thumb on top (Fig 4).

Later on you may find that a different grip comes more easily to you and once you are casting moderately well there is no

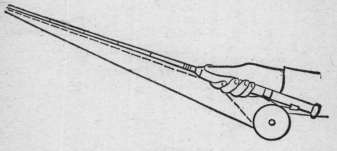

FIG 4.

reason why you should not adopt the grip you prefer. By that time you will know just how far back the rod should go and will check your wrist movement accordingly.

But for the present keep the thumb on top of the grip. If the rod is allowed to go far past the vertical the line drops much too low as it extends behind and the chances of it getting caught up or even lashing the ground are greatly increased.

This is one of the points about good casting which is so important that I think I can be excused for calling it a rule. The rod must not be allowed to go far past the vertical on the back cast.

The beginning of the cast is most important too and you always want to aim at getting the line nice and straight, so that

9

as soon as the rod begins its lift it starts the whole of the line moving off the water.

When this happens the rod takes the weight of the line at once and starts flexing quickly so that it develops plenty of power.

Back cast

If the cast is begun when the line is lying raggedly on the water, a considerable part of the energy imparted by the rod goes towards straightening out the line instead of moving it all off the water. The full weight of the line does not begin to pull on the rod until the line has straightened and by that time the rod may be well towards the end of its backwards movement.

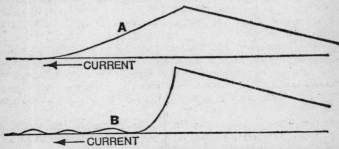

FIG 5. Start of Cast. A, Before casting straighten line or allow current to do it for you. B, If line is ragged on the water like this, casting is made more difficult.

Failure to remember this point and put it into practice will cause endless bother and poor casting. It is especially important at the start because most of a beginner's casts will end raggedly so that, unless steps are taken to straighten the line, the next cast is spoiled before it has begun.

There are two main ways of straightening the line. It can be done by waiting until the current pulls the line taut or it can be done by the angler himself. All he has to do is to pull in a couple of feet of line with his left hand and leave it hanging in a loop between the bottom ring and the reel. This will take the curves out of the line and often saves time because you do not have to wait for the current to do its work (Fig 5).

I think that at this stage it would be as well always to keep the line passing over the first finger of the right hand when fishing. When you want to draw in line with the left hand just ease the grip of the finger and pull the line through.

The loop of line will then be readily available for shooting, a device we will examine later.

By keeping the line firmly under the finger you will keep everything tight as the cast is made and avoid loose line between the rings which will cause poor and sloppy casting.

Let us now see what happens when the line has been pulled smartly off the water and disappears behind the angler. This is one of the critical moments in any cast and the beginner may easily fall into the trap of throwing the line back and just hoping that it will behave itself until he makes the forward cast.

It has often been said that if you make a good back cast it is impossible to make a thoroughly bad forward cast and there is a great deal of truth in this.

What, then, are the requirements of a good back cast? We have already shown that the line must be straight at the start of the cast so that it flexes the rod quickly. This enables the rod to speed the line into the back cast but this, alone, is not sufficient; the line must travel in a proper path behind the angler for the best results.

The best tip I can give for this is to imagine that you are throwing the line backwards, but at the same time UPWARDS. If you do this you will not go far wrong and the beginner would be well advised to make this a rule too.

Having got the line travelling into the back cast properly, we are rapidly approaching another critical moment of timing for we now have to decide when to begin the forward cast.

Forward cast

I think most beginners are inclined to commence the forward cast a little too soon and many would certainly improve their casting if they hesitated a moment longer before starting the forward thrust (Fig 6).

There has to be a happy medium, of course, and to leave the line in the air too long is just as bad as starting the forward cast too soon because both cause power to be lost at a crucial moment.

The problem is something similar to the one we discussed

when we were talking about the start of the cast and it simply means that we have to begin developing full power in the rod as quickly as possible.

This will be achieved if the forward thrust is begun just as the line is coming up to its peak extension and is pulling well on the rod. If the forward cast is made too soon there will be a big loop of line in the air which the rod will have to straighten out before it develops much power. If it is begun too late the line will have fully extended behind and the pull on the rod will be considerably reduced as the line begins to fall to the ground.

We have now covered the main points necessary for good fly casting but before beginning operations put up the rod, without

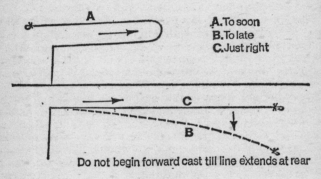

A. To soon
B. To late
C. Just right

Do not begin forward cast till line extends at rear

FIG 6.

putting a line on it, and go through the motions of each part of a cast.

Note how the rod feels in the hand when it gets upright; it will not travel far past this position in actual casting. When the rod comes forward do not drop the point low towards the water otherwise there will be a tendency for the line and cast to slap down on the surface instead of falling gently.

Having done this you will have noticed that, even without a line, the rod automatically flexes into the back cast once the swift lift has been made. It will be obvious that it is quite impossible to separate the different stages of a cast into little watertight compartments and this is exactly as it should be.

You do not say, 'The lift stops here and now I am doing the back cast', these things take care of themselves. What the angler has to concentrate on is the blending of the various stages one into the other so that the whole thing is a smoothly progressive action.

It is, however, best to divide the different stages clearly at the start so that the beginner can pinpoint the stage which is causing him trouble and see what he must do to correct the trouble.

Demonstration

I see no reason to delay the representation of real fly fishing so we will mount a short nylon cast and any old fly at once. See that the line is well greased before you begin so that it floats well and is, therefore, easier to pick off the water. Pick a place where the bank is clear, or even wade out into the stream before starting. There will be plenty to do controlling and watching what is happening to the line without having to guide it around trees and bushes as well.

One of the easiest ways of learning to cast is to fish a wet-fly downstream. The line will be pulled straight out below you by the current and the lift can be made easily back over the shoulder because there is no need to change the direction of the moving line in mid-air. The line comes straight off the water back over the shoulder and comes forward in exactly the same way.

Avoid mid-air changes of direction in the line at the start and concentrate on getting out a moderate length smooth cast. Once you get the rhythm there will be little difficulty in picking the line off the water below you and then completing the cast by dropping the fly at an angle across stream.

When there is a considerable change in direction do not try to complete the cast in one movement. It often helps to make several false casts, keeping the line moving backwards and forwards in the air, without letting it touch the water, and gradually altering the direction of the line until casts are being made towards the spot you intend dropping the fly.

False casting is necessary when you are estimating the distance of a fish. Keep the line moving in the air until you have got out what you think is sufficient, then make the final forward thrust and drop the fly slightly above the rising fish.

To get out line when you are starting to cast, pull a few yards off the reel and move the rod briskly backwards and forwards. This will pull the line through the rings and it can be allowed to lie on the water between throws until there is sufficient line out to start working the rod.

The line is nothing more than an extremely long weight which is cast by the rod, and the rod will not begin to bend well until enough line has been drawn through the rings and past the top ring.

The length of line needed to do this properly varies from rod to rod but all rods have one length of line which they will handle particularly well. Increase this by much and the action takes on a strained uneasiness, decrease it by much and the rod goes dead.

When you have gained some experience you will sense the point at which your own rod performs best. Try to keep somewhere near this in your actual fishing distances and you won't go far wrong. Once the required length of line is out, adjustments to suit individual casts can be made by pulling excess line through the rings with the left hand and allowing it to hang in a loop until it is required.

Naturally, if you have just made a very long cast and wish to return to the fishing of a shorter line you will not let the loose line hang but will wind it back on to the reel.

Casts will have to vary enormously in distance to suit conditions and the type of water but always keep at the back of your mind the intention to use the length of line which best suits your rod. Don't creep right up to fish and make ridiculously short casts when it is not necessary, nor make enormously long casts just for the fun of it. If you persist in this you will waste time and catch fewer fish.

Casting into the wind

A windy day can prove most troublesome to the best of anglers, especially if they are using light lines, so don't worry if you run into trouble on these days, it happens to all of us.

There are a few tips which will improve casting in a wind and they are as follows. When the forward cast is made INTO a strong wind bring the rod point down smartly and quite a bit lower than you would for a normal cast. The extra bit of punch put into the stroke helps to extend the line better before the wind has much of a chance to get hold of it and the fly reaches the water sooner. The presentation of the fly may not be as delicate as we would wish but fish are not as fussy during rough weather as they are when everything is bright and still.

Generally, when casting into a wind you need not use quite so much power in the back cast because you have the wind to help you. Save the beef for the forward cast.

If the wind is at your back the reverse will be the drill, hefty back cast and a rather more gentle forward cast.

Sometimes there is a gusty cross wind when the fly does its best to embed itself in your head as it sails past. This gives you a most uncomfortable feeling but the tendency for this to happen can be greatly reduced by holding the rod slightly off the vertical, with the butt tucked in towards the side, as the cast is made.

On rough days it often pays to keep the travel of the line as low as possible, even to the extent of holding the rod out from the side almost parallel to the ground. The line is brought smartly back in a slightly upwards plane and the finish to the forward stroke is a definite roll of the wrist which keeps the forward extension of the line low.

The ability to shoot line is invaluable to the fly fisherman and it is essential to be able to do it reasonably well if only from the point of convenience.

When you are fishing there will be any number of occasions when you find yourself with a yard or so of line hanging in a loop from the right forefinger. To avoid reeling this line up it can be added to the next cast by shooting it at the right moment.

Shooting line

Shooting line consists of releasing the slack on the forward cast so that it is dragged through the rings by the pull of the extending line. The shoot enables the average angler to add a yard or two to the length of line in the air with his rod. It is also useful when fishing from a position where there is a strictly limited amount of space behind so that the required length of line cannot be put into the back cast.

Good timing is needed for good shooting and you have to judge the moment for releasing the slack to coincide with the moment of peak pull in the forward moving line.

You know at once if you have timed the release correctly. A good shoot will make the line slap against the handle as it is pulled tight. If the slack is released too soon it will not be drawn properly through the rings and a bad cast is likely to be the result. A somewhat similar result will occur if the release is delayed too long.

Remember that when you are fly fishing you must ensure that the rod works properly and does its job well. To do this it may at times be necessary to use a fair amount of power but it should never be necessary to use force. In fact we can go further than this and say that force should not be used. If you feel that you cannot cast well enough to satisfy yourself and resort to force in an attempt to improve matters, it is a sure sign that there is a fault in your technique and you should take steps at once to find out where the fault lies.

The use of force cannot improve your casting because it deadens your sense of timing and aggravates the trouble you are trying to overcome.

2 DRY-FLY FISHING

Rods

THE usual length for a dry-fly rod is between 8 and 9 ft and split cane is by far the most popular material for its construction.

A true dry-fly rod has a slightly stiffish action although this is smoothed out considerably when the correct line is added.

A general-purpose rod has a rather softer action, somewhere between stiff dry-fly and soft wet-fly and very many anglers manage admirably with a rod of this type for both wet and dry fishing.

Rod actions vary considerably, even among so-called dry-fly rods, and the one for you will be the rod with which you feel happiest and which takes care of your particular fishing problems.

If you approach fly fishing with a delicate touch you may prefer a medium-action rod while a more robust angler would want a good stiff action.

The answer is to try as many rods as you can so that you learn what each will do.

16

Casts

Nylon monofilament casts have almost universally superseded the gut casts of earlier years. The advantage is that they do not have to be wetted before knotting and are not noticeably affected in strength by light or exposure in the atmosphere for considerable periods. They can be obtained in continuous tapers without knots too.

The cast should end in a good fine point and for all ordinary fishing you can come down to about 1·8 lb with advantage. A point of this strength will take astonishing strains as long as they are applied carefully.

The only risk with them is when the strike is made, for this puts a sudden severe strain on the nylon and the beginner may have several breakages in a row before he learns to tighten rather than strike.

Striking is a bad term because it inevitably conjures up visions of an angler using considerable force and this is not what is needed. If you are naturally heavy handed use slightly stronger points until you get used to the excitement of seeing the fly taken and learn to react more gently.

Don't increase the thickness too much, otherwise you will find that the fish object and will refuse to take the fly, especially if the water is clear and the weather calm. The finer you can safely fish the better.

Seasons

Generally speaking dry-fly comes into its own in April, May and June, probably declines towards the end of July and hits rock bottom in August. This is a notoriously bad month for dry-fly fishermen, but September may show better sport and the season often ends quite well.

The foregoing can only give an idea of what may happen. Some rivers are earlier than others and the fish regain condition more quickly in these waters. Find what the pattern is in your district and when other anglers reckon to get their best sport.

Early in the year trout will be found on the easy flowing flats and quieter streams where they can get a maximum of food with a minimum of effort. They have not yet recovered from their spawning exertions and are not strong enough to face the turbulent and highly oxygenated water of the rough streams.

At the beginning of April the wet-fly may be the best bet but, if you are determined to get in some practice with dry-fly, concentrate on the quieter water.

Trout are wary, even in the early part of the year and you have to move carefully and make as little disturbance as you can. This is especially so when you are fishing the flats where the surface is frequently glassy.

Sport is often limited to an hour or so each side of mid-day at this time of the year. Things are usually quiet in the morning until about eleven o'clock when there may be short periods of hectic activity which go on until about one. Then, as the short day begins to go, cold clamps down again and the best of the fun will be over. There are exceptions to this and you must be ready to take advantage of mild days and warm spells which can have a magical effect on sport.

It is much easier to see fish rising on the flats than in the streams and the persistent rings may lure you from the quiet streams to try your luck.

Placing the flies

Keep as far back from the rises as you can comfortably cast and you will greatly increase your chances of success.

One thing is in your favour at this time of year: the fish are hungry, and if you can get the fly travelling down over them without them sensing danger you are almost certain to have good sport. Fish are by no means as fussy about their food as they will be later on but they will still not tolerate clumsiness on the part of the angler.

Whenever you can, avoid putting the line slap over the fish as you finish the cast. It is far better to make the cast slightly to one side so that the fish sees only a few inches of the fine cast, if that. Many fish are put down by the sight of yards of line floating over them like a ship's hawser before the fly arrives.

Drag

Up and across is the usual way of casting, but it is by no means the only way in which a fly may be used. Sometimes you have to cast straight downstream or across stream to cover a fish but when you do this you immediately run slap into the fly fisherman's nightmare, drag.

Drag is the effect produced when the current bellies the line and compels the fly to move in a different direction to that in which it should travel. The result is usually a tugboat wake which makes the fly appear extremely unnatural and reduces to almost nil the chances of a fish taking it.

Some fishermen avoid drag by not casting to positions which produce it but by doing so they pass much fishable water and put themselves at a serious disadvantage.

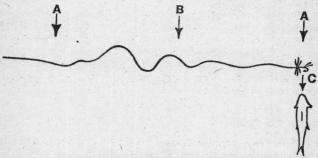

FIG 7. A, Moderate current. B, Fast current. Drag on fly avoided by slack line. C, Fly travels naturally to fish.

There is no magic formula for avoidance of drag, but it can be held off sufficiently long to enable the fly to pass over a rising fish in a normal manner.

If you make a cast across stream you are likely to find that the middle water of the river or part of it will be flowing faster than the water where the fly lands. The faster water immediately starts to put a downstream belly in the line and this quickly shows itself by creating drag on the fly.

In this case drag can be avoided by making a deliberately ragged cast so that when the fly lands there is quite a bit of slack line left on the water. The current will have to take out this slack before it can form a belly in the line and exert drag on the fly and by that time the fly will have passed over the fish and can be recovered ready for the next cast (Figs 7 and 8).

One of the easiest ways of making a deliberately ragged cast is to get out a yard or two more line than you need to reach the rising fish then, just before the fly hits the water some distance above it, give a little twitch on the line with the left hand. This will deposit several good slack coils on the water which is just what you want.

When casting downstream, the same dodge can be used but the extra length of line should be increased and the line given a rather harder pull. This is because the current straightens the line more quickly when it has a straight pull on it and you need more slack on the water to delay the drag. A little extra grace can be obtained by lowering the rod point and pushing it forward. Keep a watchful eye out for drag, it may be the reason why your fly is ignored by fish although it passes over or close to them.

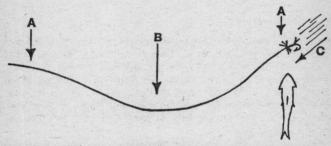

Fig 8. A, Moderate current. B, Fast current bellies straight line, causes drag. C, Fly dragged unnaturally across fish.

Striking

Because of the fine point which the fly fisherman uses he has to be careful in striking otherwise he will leave behind a trail of broken casts and lost flies. If you really strike a pound trout or chub you will almost certainly cause a break where the fly is tied on.

When you cast over a rising fish you inevitably experience a sense of excitement and anticipation as the fly nears the fish and it is easy to become so keyed up that when the fly is taken you strike as though you were trying to hook a shark.

Whether you strike slow or fast the movement must always be controlled and in relation to the strength of the equipment in use.

Carry a reel of fine nylon with you so that if you have a few accidents you can put on a new point in a matter of moments. Don't make the point too long or you will find that the last part of the cast does not extend cleanly on the water.

Fish lies

As the days warm up and lengthen, the trout take up their summer quarters in the streams and as the season progresses it is here that we will get most of our sport. There are certain exceptions to this which we will talk about later.

There are still plenty of fish on the flats but, in conditions of low clear water and bright weather, they are virtually impossible to catch.

Fishing the streams

Now we need every bit of cover we can get because the fish have regained condition and are no longer ravenous, so that they become more difficult to tempt and much more wary.

This is one of the best reasons for fishing the streams. The broken water goes a long way towards masking our movements and also helps to conceal the line and cast. The speed of the water helps too by forcing fish to decide quickly whether or not they want the fly.

There is only one drawback to fishing the streams which bothers many beginners, this is the difficulty of seeing the fly and what is happening to it in the rough water.

This can be largely overcome by using hackle flies made of first-quality cock hackles and slightly on the bushy side so that they stand up well and float for a long time on the rough water. Ginger is a good colour to show up and makes a first-class fly as well.

You have to be on the alert all the time when fishing the streams otherwise you will miss many rises, not because you strike incorrectly, but because you do not strike at all. Rises are not easy to spot at the start and you have to watch the popply water carefully for the tiny flicker or disturbance around the fly which shows that a fish is there. Tighten at once.

Keeping track of the progress of the fly is a knack which comes with experience and is not necessarily related to super eyesight. I know several anglers whose eyesight is below average who use drab little flies which look exactly like the flecks of foam which are so abundant on the streams. They watch where the fly lands and follow it down by gauging the speed of the water. They hook nine rises out of ten so don't be dismayed if you experience difficulty at the start; persevere and the knack will come.

When you catch a fish don't be in too much of a hurry to get started again. The fly must float well and it will only do this if you dry it thoroughly and re-oil it before returning to the stream.

An old soft handkerchief is excellent for absorbing the moisture from the fly and it should be squeezed firmly in the folds for several seconds to take as much moisture as possible out of the body.

Ensure that the fly is clean before it is dried. If there is any blood or slime on it, give it a swill in the river first.

When the fly has been thoroughly dried give it a good oiling, then blow into the back of the hackle to bring it back into shape after the drying. You are now ready to carry on.

Don't stay on any one stream too long or you greatly reduce your chances of catching fish. Persevere if you see fish rising but otherwise keep moving from place to place and cover as much water as you can.

You may not see many rises because they are not easy to spot in the disturbed water but do not let this worry you. Trout often rise to an artificial when there is no sign of any natural fly about.

Whatever you do don't be sidetracked by the rises you will see on the smooth surface of the flats, they come later. Once the brightness goes out of the sky and there is a hint of dusk you can finish with the streams and move on to the quieter water.

Now is the time to search out the flats which you ignored earlier on. Move quietly up to the tail of one of them, where the smooth water starts to break into the runs, and you are almost sure to see the rings made by feeding fish.

Don't let the gentle dimples on the surface mislead you into thinking that there are only small fish rising. Large trout will feed in this manner towards dusk and fish of three-quarters of a pound or more rise so quietly that they sometimes deceive experienced anglers.

Evening fishing

The hour before dusk goes like lightning when you are fishing and it is essential, if you are to take full advantage of the chances it offers, to be well prepared.

The same fly will do but put on a heavier cast; one with a point of about 3 lb breaking strain should be about right. As the light begins to fail you lose some of the assistance which your eyes have been giving you and are much more likely to break on striking or allow a fish to snag you. The heavier cast takes care of this for you and allows you to make more mistakes without having to pay the penalty for them.

It is a considerable help to have a couple of spare casts ready so that when tangles occur you need not waste valuable time trying to sort out the mess. Just take off the tangled cast and replace it, fly and all, with a new one.

Exercise care now and you will have some wonderful sport. Move with great caution and do not wade unless it becomes absolutely necessary. Whenever possible cover the fish near in from the bank before venturing into the water.

This is because the rings made by your wading will spread right across a small river and may stop fish rising over a wide area. When you have to wade, edge quietly and gently upstream so that you make as little disturbance as possible. Your care will be richly rewarded.

There are fish rising all over the flat now. There's one, right in the tail immediately above you, he has no idea you are there and is feeding quietly but confidently. There he is again. Measure the distance by false casting in his direction then drop the fly a couple of feet above him. Here comes the fly, down towards the rough water, but before it can disappear in the rough a gentle dimple surrounds it and you tighten. A short scuffle and there you are, a nice half-pounder.

As long as you move quietly you will go on catching fish until it gets too dark to see the fly.

Whenever I think of this kind of fishing a certain flat on the Usk comes to mind where I can stand in one spot and catch half a dozen good trout in the dusk. They rise all around and sometimes, when a particularly lusty fish takes hold, it feels for a moment as though I have hooked a moving rock.

The more open the flat is the longer you will be able to fish it in the evening for it will gather every speck of light. Tall trees prevent the light from reaching the water so avoid these places if you intend fishing late.

Never miss the chance of this evening fishing for it is undoubtedly the deadliest part of the day for catching trout and, whatever you do, don't go packing up just because it is getting dusk.

Windy days

I mentioned earlier that the flats were almost useless to the dry-fly fisherman during the summer except at dusk. There are, however, a couple of exceptions to this when it is possible to get first-class fishing in these places during the day.

The most important of these occurs on blustery windy days when the surface of the water is broken and ruffled. If you are out on such a day go straight to the flats for conditions are as near perfect for good sport as you will ever get.

On these days trout often take almost as well as they do at dusk and the rare opportunities which come your way should be accepted with open arms.

The buzzy hackle-fly will do admirably for these occasions and it is an astonishing sight to see it bobbing up and down like a tiny tugboat in a rough sea. It doesn't seem possible that there is a fish within miles on such a day but suddenly the fly is gone, and if you recover from your surprise quickly enough to tighten, you will have learned a valuable lesson about where and when you can catch fish with a fly.

You can even wade the flats when the weather is rough without causing much disturbance, and can thus get the fly to places which have been out of reach or easily disturbed since the early part of the season.

Fish lying in these favoured places have been immune to the attentions of anglers and have probably not seen another fly that year so that they become careless. This is all to your advantage, for you stand to pick up some good fish with the help of your ally the wind.

After floods

The only other chance to do good execution on the flats during summer comes after a flood when the river is getting well back to normal level but still has a tinge of colour in it. This has the same effect, from the angler's point of view, as the wind, concealing the movements of the fisherman and making the fish less suspicious.

Both wind and flood bring extra delicacies into the water, blown from tree or bank or washed out of the earth, and the fish await them eagerly.

The choice of which fly to use at any particular time is something which causes a lot of argument among anglers. Broadly speaking there are two schools of thought. The one says that the angler should ascertain which fly is on the water and is being taken by the fish so that he may use an artificial which resembles it as closely as possible.

The other method is to carry a selection of flies which give an overall impression of the flies likely to be found in the waters being fished and to persevere with these.

From what I have previously said about hackle-flies you will have gathered that I favour the latter method and I find that it works in a highly efficient manner.

Whichever method you favour, please don't become one of those poor harassed creatures who has so little confidence in his fly that he feels impelled to change it every other cast. The saying that you don't catch fish unless your fly is on the water is only too true, and if you are constantly changing flies you waste valuable fishing time.

If you feel that your own idea of the most pleasant way to fish consists of using the exact imitation method, do not hesitate to adopt it. The only guidance I want to give here is to remind you that, at the start, you will follow the hackle-fly much more easily in broken water and this is a formidable advantage.

Otherwise it is a matter of personal preference and there is so much room for individual ideas that I would not dream of being dogmatic. If we all had to conform to a rigid set of rules fishing would cease to become a sport.

Greased line

Whatever fish you are after, make sure that the line is kept well greased. This is an important point in dry-fly fishing because it makes casting and striking so much easier. When the line is floating well it picks off the water smoothly and without any fuss. A waterlogged line feels like lead and is sometimes quite difficult to pick off the water as it has to be brought to the surface first.

The same points apply to striking. If the line is floating nicely the strike goes quickly and cleanly to the fly but if the line has sunk there will be a noise like ripping paper when you tighten, caused by the line coming up through the water and the resulting strike will be sluggish.

To ensure that the line floats well see that it is well greased before you start fishing. Run it out between two trees and rub in some Mucilin gently with the fingers. Polish with a soft cloth and you are ready to begin fishing.

Greasing a line when it is wet is not very satisfactory so, if your line starts sinking during a day's fishing try and dry it before applying grease. If the day is warm there will not be much difficulty in doing this, but if it is a cold wet day the best thing to do is to rub the line down with a soft absorbent cloth before greasing.

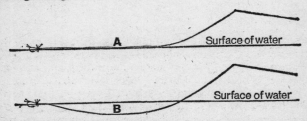

FIG 9. The effect of a well-greased line. A, Line well greased, floats and easy to lift from water. B, Ungreased line sinks, making it difficult to strike.

3 WET-FLY FISHING

RODS built for wet-fly fishing have a softer action than those designed for purely dry-fly work but, as we have already seen, a single medium-action rod can be made to do for both methods.

There is no doubt that it is better to have two rods if this can be managed because it is often better to use a longer rod for wet-fly than would be used for dry-fly.

We need not go into much detail about the rest of the kit

needed for wet-fly fishing, as much of what has already been said about dry-fly tackle applies also to wet-fly.

Lines are expensive things and many fishermen use the one line for both methods. This works out all right as long as the rods have somewhere near the same action.

Where one line has to suffice, choose it with the dry-fly rod in mind. Delicacy of casting is not of such paramount importance with wet-fly and you can afford to make allowances for this.

The cream of the wet-fly fisherman's sport comes in the spring and very exciting it can be too. Early in the year the wet-fly is superior to the dry-fly and it accounts for some terrific baskets of trout. Your chances of success with the wet-fly are above average because, according to the pattern of fly you use, they may be taken as flies, nymphs or even tiny fish.

There are three distinct ways of using a wet-fly. It can be cast upstream, downstream or square across. The upstream method is often used during the summer but more of that later; let us concentrate on the spring at present.

Number of flies

Unless the river is large I would not advise the use of more than two flies and these can be mounted on a cast of about 6 ft. On small waters three flies are quite unnecessary and can be a confounded nuisance and the loose flies have a habit of getting caught up in the net just when you are trying to land a fish.

The flats are the places to start operations with the wet-fly and they are the perfect places for spring fishing. Remember this and lose no opportunity to get to the waterside because the best of the fun is over in a few precious weeks.

Fishing downstream

If you intend fishing downstream make casts at an angle of about forty-five degrees and allow the flies to swing round in the current.

You will find it quite a help to drag in a couple of feet of line as soon as the flies enter the water. This puts you in direct contact with them immediately so that you feel every movement and know the instant a fish takes.

Search the water thoroughly and move steadily downstream

27

so that you are constantly covering new water. Don't waste time hammering away in one place, the essence of the game is keeping on the move so that as many fish as possible see the flies.

If the flies skate across the surface once they get below you, hold the point of the rod down low. This sometimes does the trick but it may be that there is grease on the cast or flies which prevents them from sinking properly.

The odd thing about this is that all fishermen do their best to avoid drag in any form on the assumption that it makes the flies' action appear unnatural and yet you will often get fish tugging at the flies as they come skirting round.

Another moment when you may expect a take is just as you begin to lift the line ready for the next cast.

A fairly long rod is most useful in the spring because it enables you to search large areas of water with comfortable casts and there is a lot to be said for a rod of about 11 ft. There is the added advantage that the longer rod helps to keep you out of sight of the fish.

Hooking

There is one drawback to the downstream method of fishing which makes me avoid it whenever I can. When the flies are fished below you it is often difficult to hook fish securely and quite a lot of fish are lost in this way. What happens is that you feel a good pull and tighten only to find that the fish gives a few strong wriggles and it is free. The only way I know to combat this is to hold the fish very hard as soon as it is hooked and keep up a strong pressure all the time. A moment's slack line and the fish may escape and this can happen right at the mouth of the net.

I find it much more satisfactory to cast square across and recommend that you give this method a try.

The idea is to fish the water in overlapping segments but to avoid letting the flies get immediately below you at any time. As soon as they begin to swing around, a fresh cast is made. Don't let the moment when you lift the flies out get later every cast, otherwise you might as well fish the downstream method.

The great advantage of this method is that the flies are fished in an area where fish can be easily and securely hooked and there will be few losses through lightly hooking or pricking fish.

Hooking is simplicity itself, all you have to do is to raise the rod gently but firmly when you feel a fish. There is no need to hurry; in fact, it is better not to.

Indications of takes

It is always a help, when wet-fly fishing, to watch the line because you will frequently get advance warning of a taking fish. There are also occasions when an unusual movement of the line is the only indication of a taking fish and if you do not

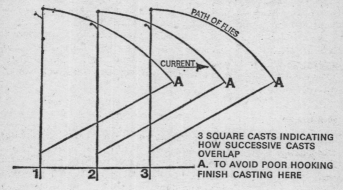

PATH OF FLIES

CURRENT

A   A   A

3 SQUARE CASTS INDICATING
HOW SUCCESSIVE CASTS
OVERLAP
A. TO AVOID POOR HOOKING
FINISH CASTING HERE

1   2   3

FIG 10.

keep an eye on the line's behaviour you will inevitably miss fish. There are few obstructions which will stop a wet-fly cast from moving downstream and you will not go far wrong if you assume that any odd movement or stoppage of the line is due to a fish.

Flats are often exposed places and there will undoubtedly be times when the wind is very troublesome. This is one of the problems of spring fishing which has to be overcome and it is a disadvantage which can be turned to account. A wind may make casting more difficult but it also ruffles the surface of the water and helps to conceal your movements from the fish. The knowledge gained will stand you in good stead whenever you have to fish fly in a wind.

We have already seen how much of the difficulty of casting into a wind can be overcome by finishing the cast with a downwards cut and bringing the rod point lower than on an ordinary cast.

But even when the cast has been made the wind can still play havoc with it unless you are careful. One of the most annoying things which can happen is when the wind gets under the line and forms a great belly in it. This drags the flies all over the place and makes them uncontrollable, but the nuisance can be combated by keeping the rod point held well down all the time so that there is nothing for the wind to get hold of. When conditions get really bad some anglers go as far as to put the rod point in the water.

A most useful advantage which comes with fishing square across is that it is possible to fish the flies at different levels in the water with a considerable amount of control. When the principle is understood one can go after the fish at the level at which they are feeding rather than heave the cast out and hope that the odd fish will take an interest.

Sinking the cast

Sometimes there will be no signs of a rising fish so that, if we are to stand the best chance of catching fish, we will want the flies to keep close to the bottom where we assume the fish will be more likely to take an interest in them. To achieve this it will be necessary to use glycerine or something else which will help the cast and flies to sink quickly. Nylon floats persistently and you will have to treat it with something to get it to sink fast. Remember the flies as well, of course, and you may even find it necessary to do a yard or so of the line too.

Big hatches

There are periods of hectic activity during the spring, often around midday, when fish rise extremely well. Some rivers have terrific hatches of March browns and when these are on the trout go mad, slashing wildly all around them as though they know that the feast will be short lived. These spectacular occasions afford an excellent opportunity for getting an accurate idea of the number of fish in any stretch, for nearly all of them will be on the feed and visible.

Oddly enough, exciting though they are, these wild rises do not seem to increase the angler's chances of success, in fact I have frequently found that the periods of greatest visible activity among the fish coincide with my own periods of slower sport.

I usually do best when the surface of the water is comparatively quiet but is broken here and there by rising trout. Dry-fly is often useless during peak activity, the fish rising all around the artificial and swamping it in their eagerness to get at the real thing. My favourite tactics now are to oil the cast and a little of the line so that the wet-flies swim well up in the water where they are often taken by the feeding fish.

The spring rises can be most difficult things to deal with and there is not much more that I can say about them. Once you know that the flies are suitable for the time of year and are of the size used by anglers familiar with the river, don't waste time chopping and changing them about. If you do not catch fish for a while it is more likely to be due to the fish themselves rather than the flies.

Artificial flies

As a wide generalization, if you are in doubt as to which flies to use, and cannot get immediate advice, try using two which are complete opposites, one dark, one light, and not too heavily dressed. Trout can see and will take the most lightly dressed flies even in rough water so there need be no fear on this score. As soon as the fish show a preference for one or other of the flies it may be worth replacing the unsuccessful fly with a pattern nearer that which is catching fish.

There is far too much dressing on many flies and wet-flies are no exception. A fly dressed in this manner looks solid and quite lifeless in the water and does not appear anywhere near as attractive as a lightly dressed pattern.

A most useful fly, which is easily tied, consists of nothing more than an ordinary tying-silk body, primrose coloured, a couple of fine whisks tied in at the tail and about three turns of the same soft pale blue hackle at the head. I have seen these flies so shredded by the teeth of feeding trout that the already sparse dressing was reduced to a few hairs, but still they caught fish.

Rather similar in construction, but even less complicated, are the deadly spiders whose soft fibres work so realistically in the current. Both these and the soft-fibred hackle-flies are general

31

representations of fish food rather than exact imitations but they are, nevertheless, very successful.

Fishing upstream

When the warmer weather comes along the upstream wet-fly is a good method. It is fished in a similar manner to the dry-fly and the techniques are not very different.

As soon as the fly is in the water the fisherman begins raising the rod point so that he keeps in close contact with the fly as it

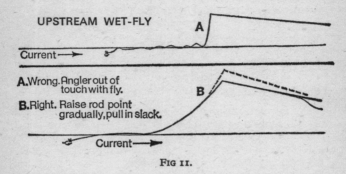

UPSTREAM WET-FLY

Current ⟶

A. Wrong. Angler out of touch with fly.

B. Right. Raise rod point gradually, pull in slack.

Current ⟶

Fig 11.

comes towards him. Apart from raising the rod it will be necessary to draw in the line with the left hand too. This enables you to respond to any bite immediately because the point of the rod must not go too high if hooking is to be done with ease.

Rather short casts are usual and they have to be made very frequently because of the speed with which the fly comes back to the angler. Any line drawn in with the left hand is shot on the next cast and the length of line is limited to that which will work the rod but is easily manageable.

Detecting the take

It is best to avoid long casting, at least until you become proficient at the game, because the hooking of taking fish is not so easy as it is with dry-fly.

This is the stumbling block for many beginners and even

competent performers at the more usual downstream method. There is no tell-tale surface rise and you may fish for quite a time without feeling a thing. For real success at this method you have to completely reject the idea that when a fish takes you will feel a pull. Now you must concentrate on the line and strike when anything happens to it which is in any way unusual.

This may appear to be a difficult thing to do but don't despair, it is different but not difficult and only takes a short time to learn. Remember that the hooking position is excellent, in fact it is probably as good as any and once the initial strangeness has gone this will be proved time and time again.

Just to elaborate on the technique for a moment it might help you to get the feel of the method more quickly if you imagine that you are pulling the fly gently back down to you rather than letting the current carry it down. If you digest this point and put it carefully into practice you will keep beautifully in touch with the fly and hooking will be almost automatic.

Precautions

One further tip, do be careful with your wading and move about as quietly as you can. This is especially necessary because of the short distance of the casts which means that you will be quite close to the fish you hope to catch. The water is likely to be low and clear and stealth must be the watchword at every step. The most perfect presentation of the fly will fail if you have already frightened the fish.

Needless to say, fine tackle is a must and it is as well to use a single fly on a fine tapered cast. Cover as many runs and stickles as you can and do not be afraid to experiment. If there is no sign of rising fish it may pay you to glycerine the cast in order to get the fly well down in the water. This dodge has been the means of preventing a blank day for me on numerous occasions.

4 NIGHT FISHING

NIGHT fishing is not allowed on some rivers, but where it is allowed the long warm nights can provide fishing of a kind which does not occur during the day.

Night fishing is a great developer of vocabulary for no one can deny that the weirdest things seem to happen to the line and cast at the start. But once you admit to yourself that there is no hope of seeing what is happening to the line, however hard you peer, you are on the road to success. Instead of 'blindly looking' start to feel the action of the rod in your hand and notice how it comes to life when it starts to work. This will tell you how much line is out for you know how much line is needed to work the rod properly.

Let your ears help too. Listen to the sound of the line in the air as the rod works it backwards and forwards. If you hear noises which remind you of a whip in use you will not need me to remind you that your timing is all wrong for it will not be long before you get a good tangle.

Once you make a real effort to allow your senses of touch and hearing to come to your aid, progress will be rapid. There are few more satisfying sounds than the gentle hiss of a well-timed line being cast in the dark.

To come back to the practice of night fishing. It is probably wisest to carry a torch but pretend that you do not have it with you, using it only when absolutely necessary. On a good summer night there is usually a faint glimmer of light which will show up trees and bushes sufficiently well for you to avoid them if you move carefully. If you use a torch frequently you blind yourself for a while after it has been put out and the chances of a fall are greatly increased. Avoid using the torch near the water too. If you must use it make sure that it does not point at the river.

The best places to fish will be the shallow, quiet corners; the flats are excellent. Until you have experienced it a number of times you will be surprised how close in trout come at night when they are feeding. Short casts are usually all that is required and you may catch fish almost 'on the stones'.

I would strongly recommend that you do not wade at night unless you are familiar with the particular stretch of river, for you lose much of your sense of direction in the dark and you may be fishing a place where a few steps in the wrong direction make all the difference between 6 in of water and 6 ft. Quite apart from this, wading creates a great disturbance in the quiet water.

Naturally, it will help a lot if you can find a place where

the bank is free from obstructions so that you can concentrate on your casting without having to worry about anything else.

Make short casts, draw in just a little line with the left hand to keep you in touch with the fly, then let it work round. Lift the rod point gently at the end of the cast and hold it quietly for a moment. A fish often chooses this instant to take, so be prepared.

It is important to keep well in touch with the fly because you have to rely on what you feel on the line to tell you when a fish is there. This will cause no bother when the fish are really on the feed because they take with a bang. You cannot tell whether you are striking at a small fish or a big one so be prepared by using stronger casts for night work. A nylon cast of 4 or 5 lb breaking strain will see you through most emergencies and don't forget to carry a couple of spares. Put a fly on each one and wind them on to a small wooden carrier or piece of card so that they may be brought into use without the possibility of getting them tangled right at the start.

Keep kit to a minimum on these night jaunts. Requirements are quite small and the more you lumber yourself with unnecessary tackle the more you will have to search to find what you want.

As to flies, any of the orthodox sea trout flies will do and you only have to make a few inquiries of local anglers to find the names of favourite patterns for your own waters. Experience may well make you favour one particular fly and if this happens, stick to the one which brings you sport.

Some of the ordinary trout wet-flies are good for night fishing but, generally, they should be a little larger than the size you would use during the day.

It is a mistake to move about much, not only because of the increased danger of bumping into things but also because it is unnecessary. Trout congregate at their favoured feeding places at night and you will get all the sport you want without moving more than once or twice. If this is not so, the reason is likely to be that conditions are not suitable for night fishing.

There is a lot to be said for having a companion on night trips as long as you keep a reasonable distance apart when fishing. It is safer to have someone at hand in case of accident.

Just as there are nights when trout seem to go mad and will

slash at anything, there are infuriating times when they just follow the fly and knock gently at it.

One of my first steps on these difficult nights is to replace the fly with a smaller one which I find helps to encourage a bolder approach.

This helps to defeat the stealthy attack and, coupled with the smaller fly, often leads to improved sport. It is best to modify your fishing too. When you feel a fish, resist the urge to strike and drop the point of the rod until you feel a definite movement. There will often be several knocks before the fish takes firmly and you should wait for the proper take before striking. This is something that can only really be learned by experience but it does not take long to learn when a fish means business as opposed to merely playing with the fly. When a trout is playing with the fly you can strike as slowly or as fast as you like, you won't hook one in twenty.

I just don't know why trout react like this on some nights. It may be that some trick of fractional light, often present on a summer night, shows up the line and cast and gives the fish warning. Something is obviously wrong but as we could do little about it in any case, we have to adjust our methods to get sport in spite of it.

Once the first chills come to the nights, sport starts to decline and although you may still catch fish you will have to work much harder for them. With the arrival of the nippy evenings much of the charm of night fishing vanishes. The time during which it is worth while is limited, so make the most of it.

OLIVER KITE

Elements of Nymph Fishing

1 NATURAL NYMPHS

What is a nymph?

THE term 'Nymph' is often loosely applied to the underwater larval forms of various aquatic insects such as Dragon-flies and Stone-flies, but to the nymph fisherman its meaning is altogether more precise. To make this meaning quite clear, let us first establish just where and how nymphs fit in among the 20,000-odd named British species of insects.

Insects are invertebrate creatures which have six legs, and they may be either winged or wingless. Several different kinds of winged insects are of importance to the fly fisher, but one, and one only, concerns the nymph fisherman: this is the order of aquatic Upwinged-flies or *Ephemeroptera*, of which only forty-eight species have so far been recorded in these islands and many of these are rare or local in their distribution.

To these insects alone, at a certain specific and recognizable stage of their underwater development, is the term 'Nymph' applicable. Now at what point in the insects' metamorphosis does this stage occur? To answer this question the following brief description of the life cycle of Upwinged-flies may be found helpful.

Upwinged-flies begin their life cycle as eggs laid over, on or in the water, according to species. These eggs may hatch out in a matter of days or it may be many months before this happens, according to the species and the particular generation within some species.

The tiny creature which first hatches from the egg is termed a larvula. It grows by feeding and periodically shedding its hard-set outer skin to allow for expansion and the gradual development and extension of its numerous small but important physical appendages.

Each stage in growth between these successive moults is called an instar, and after a few such instars, the larvula is properly termed a larva. The larva likewise continues to feed and grow, moulting between each instar.

Superficially the larva living in the water is not very different in appearance from the terrestrial winged insect which it will eventually become, except that it lacks all trace of wings at this stage. *When the larva approaches maturity, however, the wing cases begin to form on its dorsal thorax and to become readily apparent to the observer. It is at this stage that the larva is properly termed a nymph.*

The size of the wing cases determines whether the nymph is *young, half-grown* or *full-grown,* terms which have nothing at all to do with the overall size of the insect.

Full-grown nymphs cease to feed, their jaws atrophy, and they moult for the last time but one, when they change into winged pre-adult insects on the surface of the water and fly off to shelter on land. The pre-adult winged insect is known to fishermen as a dun and to entomologists as a subimago. The name 'dun' derives from the insect's rather drab appearance at this stage. The dun stage is purely transitional, for the insect is no longer capable of feeding and it cannot mate to fulfil its purpose until the final moult of all has taken place a day or so later to release the brilliant iridescent adult insect. Fishermen call this adult a spinner and entomologists know it as an imago.

The spinner's function is to reproduce itself, and in the process of laying their eggs, many female spinners die on or in the water, drifting down on or in the surface film completely at the mercy of feeding fish.

To summarize, Upwinged-flies go through a life cycle consisting of egg, larvula, larva, nymph (all under water), dun and spinner (both winged stages after leaving the water). The dry-fly fisherman is concerned with imitating these flies in the dun and spinner stages. The nymph fisherman is concerned only with representing them in the nymph stage.

A study of the appearance, habitat and behaviour of those natural nymphs which feature significantly in the diet of trout, grayling and other fish is the foundation of modern nymph

38

fishing in the Netheravon style, to the theory and practice of which this section is devoted.

[*Note:* To avoid the repetition of long scientific names, the author refers to some natural species by the names of their artificial representations. A key will be found on pages 74–75 Ed.]

Basic structure of natural nymphs

The basic structure of a natural nymph, whatever its species, is: a small head capsule, a thorax of three segments each supporting a pair of legs, an abdomen of ten segments and, in all British species, three tails.

The head carries two minute antennae, a pair of distinctive eyes and complex mouthparts, enabling the nymph to feed in its chosen environment to which it is usually carefully adapted.

The wing cases forming on the dorsal thorax give the nymph its characteristic humped appearance.

Attached to most of the abdominal segments are fan-like organs along the nymph's flanks. These are popularly known as tracheal gills but their construction, appearance and functions differ considerably from species to species.

Nymphs breathe by extracting oxygen from water taken into their body openings and thereafter diffused. In running water the effect of the current alone is usually sufficient to ensure the presence of sufficient dissolved oxygen in the water. In still waters, however, the nymphs must create their own current around them, using their tracheal gills for the purpose. Many species of considerable importance to the nymph fisherman do not possess adequate organs for this current-fanning, or fail to employ them to this end, and this explains why flies like the six Olives, the Pale Watery and the two Iron Blues do not, indeed cannot, hatch from still water.

Size of nymphs
Nymphs of the different British species of Upwinged-flies vary appreciably in size: the largest, Mayfly nymphs, are about as big as fully grown wasp grubs; the smallest, the nymphs of the tiny Broadwing species, are even smaller than the little maggots of the common house-fly.

39

Feeding

Nymphs feed mainly on detritus, plant remains and minute vegetable organisms and, being mainly herbivorous, their jaws are ill-adapted for defensive purposes. They are therefore obliged to protect themselves by other means. Various adaptations, to which I shall refer in more detail later, enable the different species both to do this and to maintain themselves in their usual environment. Altogether in this country there are six fairly well-defined types of natural nymph.

Type of natural nymph

The six types are:

> Bottom burrowers;
> Silt crawlers;
> Moss creepers;
> Stone clingers;
> Laboured swimmers;
> Agile darters.

A brief description of each of these types is given below. The detailed classification of all known British species within each type is given on pages 74 and 75.

Bottom burrowers

Nymphs of our three Mayfly species are bottom burrowers and as such are specially adapted for tunnelling and for maintaining themselves in the beds of rivers, streams and lakes. They have small pointed heads, powerful mandibles, strong mole-like forelegs for digging and long, slender tube-like bodies, and their tracheal gills are designed to maintain a constant flow of water around them in their burrows, whether these occur in still or running water.

Mature Mayfly nymphs are at least 2 in long. For most of their underwater existence, a period still in some doubt, they are protected from fish by the security afforded by their burrows, but when they finally quit them and rise to the surface to emerge as winged Mayflies, trout may take the big, clumsy nymphs greedily. The use of a large artificial Mayfly nymph to catch them in these circumstances is undoubtedly an effective method of butchering fish but whether it can be considered sport

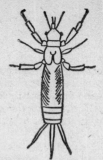

Bottom burrower.

Silt crawler

Moss creeper

Stone clinger

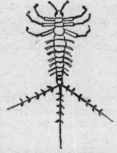

Laboured swimmer

Agile darter

FIG 12.

is another matter which the individual fly fisher should decide for himself.

Silt crawlers

Broadwing nymphs are tiny, slow-moving flea-like creatures inhabiting the surface of silt deposits on the beds of rivers and lakes. Some species, the River Broadwing and the Brook Broadwing, prefer running water, others still water. Some occur in both. Some fly in the early morning at sun-up, others in the evening.

The dense growth of minute hairs on the bodies of these nymphs traps particles of fine silt and detritus which serve to camouflage them most efficiently in what might otherwise be a rather exposed habitat. These nymphs are not often of importance to the nymph fisherman and they are, in any case, almost too small to imitate effectively.

Moss creepers

This group includes only two species, both ponderous, sturdy, stiff-legged nymphs: those of the rather local Yellow Evening dun and of the very common Blue-winged Olive, the nymphs of which occur in rivers and streams in many parts of these islands.

Moss creepers are poor swimmers and they inhabit the mosses on stones on the river bed and also trapped weed and other debris lodged against the banks or caught upstream of bridges, piers, abutments, hatches and other similar obstructions. You can often find one or two skulking in the crevices of old water-logged timbers which have lodged on the bed of the stream.

Unless these nymphs are disturbed, trout see little of them until they rise to the surface to emerge as winged duns, at which time fish may feed on them, especially if attracted to their presence by the duns' struggles to escape from their nymphal shucks.

Stone clingers

These nymphs are specially adapted to cling to stones and boulders on the somewhat unstable bottoms of rough rivers and streams and also the exposed shores of stony lakes where wave action may create rather similar conditions.

Typical stone clingers are the nymphs of the March Brown, the Dusky Yellowstreak and the Yellow May dun. They all have strong, gripping legs and their bodies are distinctly flattened to enable them to offer reduced resistance to water and to cling, limpet-fashion, to smooth surfaces such as pebbles; conditions in which the nymphs of most other species would be swept helplessly away.

Many nymphs of this type do not swim to the surface but crawl out of the water to emerge as winged duns and consequently they are relatively unimportant to the nymph fisherman.

Laboured swimmers

These nymphs crawl about among stones and weed but are capable of swimming with much effort, the action reminding one of a child who has mastered just a few breast strokes. This effort is made necessary by the absence of specially adapted tails to provide an adequate propulsion unit. The tails of laboured swimmers are thread-like, spread arrowhead fashion, and they afford them little drive when they try to swim.

Some laboured swimmers occur in rivers, among the best known being the nymphs of the Turkey Brown and that neglected dark little fly which is still known only by the obscure scientific name of *Habrophlebia fusca*, now called the Ditch dun. They are more often found in lakes, especially those of a peaty nature like the tarns of North Lancashire and Westmorland.

The nymphs of the Claret dun, which I found in the lakes of Castle Howard and Longleat where the Game Fairs of 1960 and 1962 were held, and those of the Sepia dun have a brownish coloration which serves them well for protection in such an environment. In other waters, of course, they are more noticeable to fish to whom they may then fall easy prey.

Agile darters

This is much the largest group of natural nymphs found in these islands and it also includes those species of the greatest significance to the nymph fisherman. Agile darters are strong swimmers, capable of swift acceleration and easy progress in the water. Their streamlined shape and specially adapted tails make this possible. The middle tail filament is thickly fringed with hairs on each side, making it something like a tennis racket in shape. Each outer tail filament is similarly fringed but only on the inner side. These oar-like tails together provide the agile darter nymph with a driving fin of considerable power.

Understandably, therefore, agile darter nymphs appear regularly in open water, moving from feeding place to feeding place and, I suspect, periodically frolicking about for the sheer fun of it. Trout, grayling and other carnivorous fish are familiar with them and their ways and it is these nymphs which the would-be nymph fisherman should study in detail and their behaviour on which he should base his nymph fishing tactics.

Habitat of agile darters

There are four groups of agile darters, one large and three small to medium. The first comprises three large Siphlonurid species not often met with in this country. Nymphs of this kind are of considerable importance to fly fishers in Arctic and sub-Arctic waters, in Northern Scandinavia for example. The other three groups all comprise species smaller in size, including the nymphs of some of our best-known fisherman's flies.

The largest group consists of the nine *Baëtis* species: the nymphs of the six Olive duns, the Pale Watery dun and the two Iron Blue duns. These occur only in running water, for which existence alone their respiratory system is designed. They are all agile, free-ranging, fast-swimming, nymphs capable of sudden darting movements. They are well known to trout and grayling and at times feature prominently in their diet.

The two Spurwing nymphs which are rather more adaptable are among the most rapid swimmers in our waters. The nymphs of the Large Spurwing are rather local in their distribution. The Small Spurwing is probably our most ubiquitous species, the nymphs being found in rivers, streams, lakes and pits. They are most rewarding to study and to simulate, especially if you fish much in still or slow-flowing water.

Three related agile darters are the nymphs of the Slow-water Olive, the superficially similar Deep-water Olive and the Pale Evening dun. Their stout, hair-fringed tails make them exceptionally quick off the mark when disturbed and they also employ a most effective protective trick consisting of sudden rapid movement followed by instant 'freezing'. This can be most deceptive, even to the careful and keen-eyed observer.

The nymphs of the Slow-water Olive are found both in slow-flowing and still waters. They abound in shallow lakes and reservoirs fed by brooks, in ponds and in the sun-warmed

44

backwaters of chalk-stream bends. They are often to be seen in garden pools and I have recorded them in ornamental waters in the parks of great cities both in this country and on the Continent. They were even noted in static water tanks during the last war and full-grown nymphs can be reared to the dun stage in an ordinary aquarium without much difficulty. This nymph is another which the nymph fisherman should study with care, unless he fishes exclusively on swift-flowing waters, in which case he is unlikely to encounter it.

Deep-water Olive nymphs are found mainly in still waters, occurring occasionally in the sluggish pools of slow rivers, living among milfoils and suchlike aquatic vegetation at depths of a fathom or so. In general they are of less importance to the nymph fisherman, except in the deeper lakes and pits, than the common nymphs of the Slow-water Olive but they are sometimes taken freely by trout.

Nymphs of the Pale Evening dun occur in the slow-flowing reaches of the chalk-streams but I have not yet recorded them in still waters, for life in which their respiratory system seems adequate. Indeed they are said to occur in the Irish limestone lakes.

Hatches of Pale Evening duns tend to be concentrated late on warm summer evenings and on these occasions trout tend to take the duns in preference to the nymphs. Since nymph fishing in failing light is far from easy anyway, it is rare, in my experience, for nymphs of this species to be of great significance to the fly fisher during a characteristic dusk hatch of the little white duns.

2 THE ARTIFICIAL NYMPH

Basic requirements

Sinking capability
THE purpose of an artificial nymph is to simulate a natural nymph. Natural nymphs live beneath the surface of the water and the first and most essential requirement of an artificial nymph intended for fishing purposes is that it should sink immediately it comes into contact with the surface. The practice

of sucking nymphs to help them to sink is dangerous and in any case should not be necessary if the nymphs have been constructed to sink. Nymphs which will not sink without first being wetted might as well be rejected out of hand and it is therefore sound practice to test all artificial nymphs before using them for fishing.

To carry out such a test, take a glass of clean water and set it down before you. Then, with the thumb and forefinger, gently place the dry artificial nymph on the surface of the liquid. If the nymph sinks to the bottom at once, smoothly and without dithering, it passes the test, otherwise it fails and should not be used for nymph fishing although it might conceivably be of some use as a dry-fly.

Structure

The nymph fisherman is mainly though not exclusively, concerned in practice with those nymphs which feature largely in the diet of trout and grayling, *Baëtid* nymphs (*Baëtis centroptilum*, *B. cloëon* and *B. procloëon spp*). These all share a common and basically similar physical structure: a small head, humped thorax, tapering abdomen and tails. Logically, therefore, the artificial nymph should be constructed in such a way as to reflect these physical characteristics.

Natural nymphs do not have wings nor, when they swim, do their legs stick out as they do when arranged for examination on an entomologist's slide. It is unnecessary, indeed wholly illogical, to incorporate either wings or hackle in the dressing of the artificial.

Hooking power

The third requirement, and a very important one, is that the artificial must have good hooking power. The choice of hook is obviously mainly a matter of personal opinion but several leading exponents of nymph fishing at the present time use down-eyed Limerick hooks. Other types of hook may conceivably be effective. This one certainly is.

Hook points must be kept sharp. Provided this is done, artificials continue to yield good service in competent hands long after the superficial dressing has become frayed and tattered. As soon as the hook shows any sign of rust or the point or barb becomes damaged, the nymph should be discarded. Do not be

46

tempted to retain nymphs dressed on inefficient hooks. Scrap them.

How many patterns?

It is important to understand that individual natural nymphs of even the same species differ considerably from one another in superficial appearance, especially coloration. The state of development of the wing cases is among the contributory factors and nymphs of the Slow-water Olive, for example, taken at one dip of a nymph net, may be found to range in tone from very light to quite dark, with permutations of combinations of and between these extremes. Because of this, direct imitation of even one species would hardly be feasible, even if it were necessary. In practice, I have not found it necessary at all.

The Sawyer Nymph (very fine copper wire and a reddish-brown cock pheasant's tail feather) tied on 1, 0 or 00 down-turned Limerick hooks, is the only one I use for nymph fishing anywhere in these islands and it has also served me well in Normandy.

The pattern is easy to vary, if so desired, by simply using the herls from a grey goose primary, or heron herls, either undyed or dyed, instead of pheasant tail herls. In practice the herls do not matter much. They are put on to please the fisherman rather than the fish, and even after they have completely worn away, the artificial should continue to deceive if suitably handled in the water, provided that its basic structural outline is unimpaired.

The appeal of an artificial nymph to fish is only partly dependent on its superficial external appearance. To be con-sistently successful, the nymph fisherman must employ his artificials in a lifelike manner, based on the known habits and behaviour of the natural nymphs he is trying to simulate. For some years past I have devoted every available moment to a study of these habits.

There is no point in my recommending patterns for which I neither find nor foresee any requirement, but it is only fair to point out that there are many well-tried wet-fly patterns which can and do prove successful in the hands of those who use them for upstream wet-fly work. To my mind, provided they are fished in the same selective way as the dry-fly or artificial nymph proper, I can see no objection to their use as 'nymphs'. Many

47

of them, I fancy, were created, consciously or unconsciously, as nymphal representations.

Prejudice against wet-fly persists because downstream wet-fly fishing with a team of flies inevitably results in small fish being hooked and possibly harmed. But a single wet-fly, fished selectively either upstream or across, is no more prejudicial to the water than a dry-fly similarly employed. Indeed if the chosen fish is feeding under water, it is less prejudicial since to pester such a trout with dry-flies is tantamount to futile harrying of the creature and to the pointless furthering of its 'education'.

I do not use these wet-fly patterns myself because I am satisfied they would not, indeed could not, prove more effective than the single type of artificial I always employ. Pattern plays little part in nymph fishing, as I understand it.

How to obtain serviceable nymphs

Artificial nymphs of the kind used by the author, many designed by Frank Sawyer, can be obtained from Mrs M. Sawyer, Court Farm House, Netheravon, Salisbury, Wilts. When ordering the size (1, 0 or 00) should be specified.

3 SOME REMARKS ON TACKLE

NYMPH fishing and dry-fly fishing are complementary. There are usually plenty of occasions during the daytime, especially early in the season and perhaps towards the end, as well as during the evening rise, when the nymph fisherman may, if he is so minded, take his fish the easy way, on the dry-fly. Since either or both methods may be used any day during the fishing season the tackle employed should be capable of serving both purposes, unless one is provident enough to take to the waterside a set of specialized tackle for each method, and presumably a lad to carry whichever is not in use at the time.

It is my belief that the tackle necessary for effective nymph fishing is not significantly different to serviceable dry-fly equipment; indeed, a nymph fisherman who understands his art should be able to take fish on any combination of tackle capable of throwing a fly. But there are a few items I should like to discuss and one or two points I should like to stress.

The composition of the cast

Nymph fishing is a three-dimensional art, which is one reason why it is more difficult of accomplishment than two-dimensional dry-fly fishing. The artificial nymph must be presented to the fish at the depth at which it is feeding, anything from a few inches to a few feet beneath the surface. This necessitates pitching the nymph into the water at such a distance upstream of a fish's lie in running water as will give it time to sink to the level of the fish's head by the time it reaches it. The fish may be lying well down in the water. A long, fine-cast point is therefore clearly essential to enable the artificial to be presented effectively.

In practice, I find that this point should be at least a yard long (if its length exceeds 3 ft 6 in your cast will be unbalanced) and this in turn affects the composition of the rest of the cast. For chalk-stream and most still-water nymph fishing I use a point with a breaking strain of 2·9 lb.

I use only nylon for making my casts. Modern nylon is excellent and I have never regretted my decision, taken in 1957, to give up using gut. Nylon is much easier to use, in my opinion more efficient, and a good deal cheaper to buy as well.

When making up a cast for nymph fishing remember that the thickest strand, the butt, should be approximately half the total length of the cast. If the thinnest strand, the point, should be at least 3 ft long, and you know the number of intermediate strands you intended to use, you can easily determine their length. The detailed cast specifications given below will make this clearer.

In this country we tend to use rather short casts, or leaders as they are more appropriately called in some other countries.

[The author points out that, since casts for nymph fishing are ideally 10 ft in length, the rings on rods less than 10 ft long must allow the easy passage of the knot connecting cast and line. Some lines, excellent in other respects, make too big a knot. A stout nylon loop, spliced and whipped to the end of the line, obviates a big knot. He used 8½-ft Milbrolite fibre-glass rods, for chalk-streams and 9-ft ones for lakes and reservoirs. – Ed.]

With them I use a 10-ft nylon cast made up as follows:

Butt:	4 ft 6 in of 0·016 in;
Link:	10 in of 0·012 in;
Link:	10 in of 0·009 in;
Link:	10 in of 0·008 in;
Point:	3 ft of 0·007 in.

Using Continental nylon, this specification may alternatively be expressed as follows:

Butt:	1·50 metres of 0·40 mm;
Link:	0·25 m of 0·32 mm;
Link:	0·25 m of 0·24 mm;
Link:	0·25 m of 0·18 mm;
Point:	1·00 m of 0·16 mm.

It is important to keep the fine cast point free from grease to enable it to sink rapidly behind the artificial nymph. Frequent rubbing down with soft mud helps to ensure this, but if you are fussy about soiling your hands you may prefer to use a detergent powder. I prefer mud.

I usually find it necessary to replace my cast point several times during the course of a day's fishing. For one thing, the point becomes shortened whenever a change is made from nymph to dry-fly and vice versa, and whenever a fly is changed. Although it is not difficult to fish the dry-fly with a 2-ft cast point, with slightly impaired let-down, this is out of the question for nymph fishing where a cast point of less than 2 ft 6 in both feels wrong and is insufficient in practice. Also it is not uncommon for the artificial nymph to catch up in bankside herbage or leaves, especially on a windy day. Reeds, meadowsweet, loosestrife, willow and alder twigs and other snags are present on most fisheries and if a cast catches on any of these, curling round them in the process, it usually develops awkward kinks and the damaged point should be replaced at once.

It is disastrous to find yourself at the waterside without the means of replacing a cast point. I always carry a fairly full spool of point-size (2·9 lb) nylon.

Frequent replacement of cast points (I replace mine from four to six times on average during a fishing day), using the treble blood knot, also tends to eat into the penultimate link, and I also carry spare spools of appropriate strength (3·7 lb) nylon.

Do not throw down lengths of discarded nylon. They can easily cause immense suffering to birds and animals by becoming wound round their legs or bodies, sometimes so tightly as to cause atrophy of limbs or wings. Either take them home with you for subsequent disposal in the dustbin or, less preferably, chop them up into small lengths before discarding them. It is unsafe, too, to leave lengths of nylon lying about on the floor at home. Apart from the danger to your own domestic animals, discarded nylon may be sucked into vacuum cleaners with disastrous effects, both on these contrivances and the tempers of the women using them.

The line

Quick striking is absolutely vital in nymph fishing in which the leisurely strike at times so effective with the dry-fly has no counterpart. A light line helps considerably and, if at all possible, use such a line in conjunction with a rod to match it.

To ensure instant effective striking the line must float. I find nothing beats Mucilin for this purpose. So-called 'floating' lines must really float to be of any use in nymph-fishing.

The reel

We in this country are still most conservative in our choice of reels for fly fishing. The majority of Continental nymph fishermen now use an automatic fly-reel and those I have tried have proved most convenient.

The nymph box

Do not carry nymphs in the same fly-box as dry-flies. To do so inevitably leads to damp being introduced and to the possibility of rusting and deterioration of your dry-flies. Carry your nymphs in a separate box which should be small enough to fit into a pocket but easy to keep a firm grip of with wet, slimy hands on a rough day. I use a small, round, deep box, the lid of which has a serrated edge to give a secure hold. One of my French friends in Normandy has a small sheepskin patch sewn on the outside of the breast pocket of his fishing jacket. Into this he hooks all his wet nymphs, leaving them there to dry in the sun and the wind before he puts them back into his nymph box.

4 WHEN TO FISH THE NYMPH

The significance of nymphs in fly fishing

UPWINGED-FLIES spend a period varying from some days to some weeks as nymphs in the water, during which time those species of the greatest significance to the nymph fisherman are often taken freely by fish, as an examination of their stomach contents readily discloses.

During a hatch of fly, as fishermen refer to a large-scale emergence of duns from the water, the duns themselves usually spend only a short time on the water while their wings strengthen and dry, before taking off and flying ashore to shelter and await their final transposition to the spinner stage. Duns are vulnerable to fish during this relatively short time when they are on the surface of the water.

Most male spinners never return to the water at all, except by chance, perhaps being blown on to the surface by the wind. Female spinners do, of course, return to the water in great numbers to lay their eggs, after which many of them drift down on or in the surface film as spent flies in which helpless condition they fall easy victims to fish.

During the course of its life, therefore, an Upwinged-fly is vulnerable to fish as a nymph for a much longer period than as a dun or spinner (in the case of those species with which we are mainly concerned) and, logically, the fly fisher is justified in regarding dry-fly fishing as an auxiliary method to nymph fishing, rather than the other way round.

The fact is, of course, that much depends on the point of view of the individual fly fisher. Some derive more pleasure from dry-fly fishing than from nymph fishing and such persons may justifiably take the opposite view. Let us content ourselves with saying that the two methods are complementary.

The status of nymph fishing

Although it is usual nowadays for nymph fishing to be permitted on most waters where dry-fly fishing is the basic method employed, there are still some exceptions, in Southern England at any rate. There are certain fisheries, both river and lake, where the use of the artificial nymph is restricted. A few bar it altogether, for one reason or another, and enforce a rigid 'Dry-fly Only' rule. Others allow the nymph to be used but only after a certain date, perhaps 1 July, by which time trout may be rising less freely than in the early part of the season.

Private owners may themselves have reservations about allowing nymph fishing in their waters, especially if fly hatches are consistently good throughout the season and their trout are traditionally free-rising. It therefore behoves the visiting fly fisher to make quite certain that nymph fishing is permitted before he risks infringing the rules of a fishery, or offending his host in the case of private water. Individual owners, syndicates and associations are, after all, entitled to decide for themselves how to order matters on the fisheries over which they exercise control. A sound guide to conduct is: when in doubt, stick to the dry-fly.

Nymph or dry-fly

On waters where both nymph and dry-fly fishing is allowed, the logical course for the fly fisherman is to offer a feeding fish whichever type of artificial (nymph or dry-fly) is appropriate to what it is seen to be taking at the time. If a fish is feeding below the surface, it is only logical to fish for it underwater which, in fly-fishing terms, means using a sunk fly or nymph, and in this book we are concerned only with the employment of the latter.

Trout feed under water on a variety of creatures: freshwater snails, freshwater shrimps, crayfish, caddis, nymphs, fly larvae, minnows and other small fish, including their own kind. The employment of the artificial nymph to take these sub-aqueous feeders will be discussed in later chapters. It is not suggested that nymph fishing is, or would ever necessarily be, more effective for taking such fish than bait or wet-fly fishing but these methods are outside the scope of this work. They are also prohibited on many trout waters anyway and the nymph is then the angler's only hope on days when the fish gorge beneath the surface.

If a fish is feeding on the surface, visibly taking insects floating on the water, it is equally logical to fish for it with a dry-fly. Since dry-fly fishing is the easier method, this seems also a sensible procedure to follow. Observation is always the clue as to which method to use.

It is sound practice to study a feeding fish carefully before you begin to cast to it. The actual cast should be no more than the *coup de grâce*. First make quite certain whether the fish is feeding on or beneath the surface. Because fish can be seen moving freely during a hatch of duns does not necessarily mean that they are all taking the newly emerged winged-flies. Sometimes they are, especially during the early months of the season and perhaps again in September, but sometimes they are taking mainly nymphs just before they reach the surface, and causing considerable surface disturbance as they do so.

On occasions, too, they take both the mature nymphs and the winged duns impartially, especially on moist showery days, and when this happens, both the artificial nymph and the dun pattern dry-fly may prove equally successful.

It sometimes happens that some fish concentrate on the duns and others prefer the nymphs. You see this especially in August when the Small Olive and the Blue-winged Olive hatch all through the long day into the evening, and again in September when seven or eight different species may be hatching simultaneously. You should know that when fish feed mainly on the surface, they can usually be persuaded to accept an artificial nymph but when they feed resolutely underwater, it is damnably difficult to get them to take a floating pattern. To bombard such fish with dry-flies is most illogical. It also leads to fish becoming 'educated' in the ways of fly fishers, and consequently difficult to deceive.

The effects of weather

Certain duns emerge from their nymphal shucks very quickly, giving fish little opportunity to take them without undue expenditure of energy. This is particularly true when the weather is fine and warm, and summer-hatching species such as the Pale Watery, Small Spurwing and Slow-water Olive are all quick off the mark (Spurwings and Slow-water Olives do not hatch only in the summer, they come up throughout the year, and the Pale Watery is on from the end of May to November). This partly explains why the summer months may be regarded as the high season of nymph fishing.

Conversely, on cold days, especially in the early months of the year, duns have some difficulty in extending their wing tips

54

fully. In severe frost they are slow to leave the water, indeed may be unable to leave it at all. In heavy snow, the big flakes settle on the duns' wings pinning the insects to the water. Trout then find them rewarding prey and the fly fisherman can employ the dry-fly to good effect.

On damp showery days, even in high summer, the wings of duns are relatively slow to dry and this factor keeps them on the water longer than in sun-bright conditions, again giving the dry-fly better scope.

If the fly fisherman has learnt to cast, and is equipped with serviceable tackle, as relatively few are, a downstream wind is preferable to an upstream wind. Very strong upstream winds blow surface flies away from feeding fish and cause them much frustration. They may then give up trying to take duns, even Mayflies, in a good hatch during such a wind. In these circumstances the fly fisher can expect to do better with the nymph than with the dry-fly. Bear in mind, however, that few streams run dead straight, and just round the corner you may find quite different conditions obtaining.

Nymph fishing generally affords maximum enjoyment when the water is clear and the quarry is visible. It is easier to achieve accurate presentation, in all three dimensions, the whole process of deception can be readily followed, and the take is more easily observed than when the fish is obscured by reflected light.

If the water becomes discoloured, nymph fishing tends to become less effective. Nymph fishing for trout obscured from direct view by reflected light is, however, most effective once the detection of the take is mastered. This technique is fully discussed later under the heading of 'Nymph Fishing in Reflected Light'.

The sensible approach

In practice, the all-round fly fisher inevitably tends to think in terms of fishing the nymph as a matter of course except to fish feeding visibly on surface food: duns, spinners, sedge-flies, hawthorn-flies, black gnats, ants and so on. Resist this. Keep an open mind. Go to the waterside without preconceived notions of fishing either the nymph or the dry-fly exclusively and be prepared, equipped and competent to use whichever you find

appropriate to each situation which arises during the course of
the day.

5 BASIC TECHNIQUE

What to look for

A NYMPHING trout is recognizable by the little movements it
makes in the water as it intercepts natural nymphs, larvae,
freshwater shrimps and other small food creatures borne to it
by the current of the stream. Nymphing trout, to use a convenient term, look lively in the water, with their tails and fins
moving to enable them quickly to cut off drifting food creatures,
real or artificial.

In favourable conditions of light and background it is often
possible to see a distinct whitening of the trout's mouth as its
jaws open to seize its prey. Even if this cannot be seen when the
fish is viewed from behind, a careful study of its interceptory
movements often makes it possible to deduce the moment when
its jaws are closing on a natural nymph or similar small invertebrate food creature.

The nymph fisherman benefits tremendously from regular
close study of fish feeding in this way, and the knowledge so
gained is of great help when it comes to taking fish on the
artificial nymph in unfavourable conditions when little can be
seen.

Deceiving the trout

The two basic methods of taking trout by underwater fly fishing
may conveniently be termed attraction and deception. The basis
of modern nymph-fishing technique is deception, but attraction
is not ruled out when its employment is considered necessary
to aid deception. If this attraction is of a sufficiently lifelike
nature, it straightaway becomes deception.

*Deceive your fish by offering it an imitation resembling in size
and structural outline the natural nymph it is expecting to see in
the water at the level where it is expecting to see it and behaving
as it expects it to behave.* This is the simple dogma of the Netheravon creed.

56

Having deceived your fish, it is also vital for you to know when your deception has succeeded so that you can set your hook in its jaw before it discovers the deception and ejects your artificial.

The basic technique of nymph fishing therefore comprises the following four cardinal elements:

    (*a*) Presentation of the artificial.
    (*b*) Simulation of the natural.
    (*c*) Detection of the take.
    (*d*) Effective striking.

Once the hook is pulled home, the procedure in no way differs from fly fishing. Let us now examine each of these elements in detail.

Presentation

The artificial nymph must be presented to the trout both accurately for line and at the appropriate level in the water, which may be anything from 1 or 2 in below the surface to 5 or 6 ft down. Many nymphing trout lie well up in the water and, in the majority of cases, the depth at which the artificial should

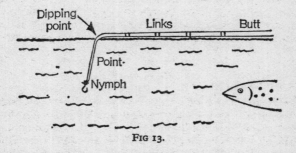

FIG 13.

reach the trout does not exceed a foot or so. It must be pitched in such a way as to arc over and enter the water without disturbing the surface or otherwise alarming the fish.

The action of nymph pitching is quite different to the action of casting a dry-fly. In dry-fly work the main aim is to achieve a let-down capable of deceiving the fish. That let-down fails if

57

immediate drag sets in. Consequently the dry-fly cast is not only aimed at an imaginary point 3 or 4 ft above the surface of the water but also at least 1 ft beyond the fish's lie, and with sufficient force to cause a slight recoil to relax the nylon cast before the fly begins its let-down. Unless you cast a dry-fly in this way, your chances of deceiving much-educated trout in awkward lies is much diminished.

In nymph fishing the drag you must guard against is lateral drag, and you do that quite effectively by fishing directly

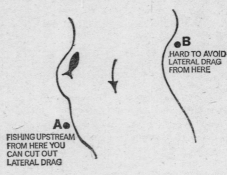

●B
HARD TO AVOID
LATERAL DRAG
FROM HERE

A●
FISHING UPSTREAM
FROM HERE YOU
CAN CUT OUT
LATERAL DRAG

FIG 14.

upstream whenever possible. Far from a floating, parachute-like let-down, you want a smooth direct, otter's entry into the water for your artificial and you do not aim so high as in dry-fly fishing but use the same bit of extra force in the cast to pull the nymph back and down into the water. With practice you can measure your fish to perfection and drop your nymph at the appropriate distance upstream.

If you are new to the art, it will pay you to practise nymph fishing and the technique of presenting the artificial at a given level in the water, still correct for line. Circumstances vary in different streams and even in different parts of the same river, and careful judgement is called for to assess the relative influence of such variable factors as the strength and speed of the current, the precise depth at which the fish is feeding and the sinking capability of the artificial nymph selected for use. It may only be necessary to pitch the nymph a few inches upstream of the fish if it is feeding in slow-flowing water. In a swift current or if a fish is lying well down, it may be necessary to cast much farther upstream.

Never be ashamed to practise. Indeed you cannot hope to do well, much less aspire to mastery, without it. I reckon to be out of practice if I go three days without fishing. If you can't get to a river, try the local canal, duck-pond, swimming bath, or, failing all else, dry land, a lawn, garage, hangar or other open space. At least you can go through the motions and keep your wrist in trim. People who say they haven't time to practise are convincing only when they never go to bed.

Simulation

The handling of the artificial nymph in the water will be discussed in some detail later. The first requirement is, of course, to employ an artificial of relevant size. It is impossible to lay down hard and fast rules but it may be of help to review very briefly the nymphal activity likely to occur in trout streams during each month of the fishing season.

March

Only one Upwinged-fly is likely to be emerging in quantity during the opening weeks of the season on the earliest rivers, the Large Olive, for which the nymph should be dressed on size 1 hooks. When the duns hatch freely, as they may regardless of severe weather conditions, trout rise to take them on the surface and nymph fishing is usually unnecessary in these conditions. It is a useful stand-by in the event of no surface activity being apparent, though in my experience the rewards fall short of what may be expected during a good hatch of duns using the dry-fly, say my Imperial, the dressing of which is

Hook: 1;
Silk: purple;
Hackle: honey dun;
Whisks: greyish-brown;
Body and thorax: heron herls from a dark blue primary (undyed);
Ribbing: gold wire.

When freshly dressed, and before oil and water have darkened it to a most realistic-looking shade, this fly, in the purple and gold from which its name derives, is a very pretty pattern. In practice it serves well enough to imitate both the Dark Olive of autumn and winter and the Large Olive in spring when, on cold days, it comes up very dark indeed. As a result it is sometimes called the Large Dark Olive. The Large Dark Olive (*Baëtis gemellus*) does not occur in these islands though it is plentiful on the Continent on mountainous streams and rivers.

April

Early in the month the Large Olive is still the predominant fly on the water, but towards the end various other species may be seen. On some rivers the March Brown hatches well and hungry trout, feeding up after winter spawning, may take the duns greedily. This fly does not occur on the chalk-streams and even on the rivers where I see it hatch well, the nymphs do not seem to receive as much attention from the trout as those of the Large Olive, Olive and Iron Blue.

The nymphs of the Olive Dun may, at this time of the year, be represented by artificials dressed on hooks as large as No 1 and those of the Iron Blue (either species) may be simulated by artificials on size 0 hooks.

May

Nymphs maturing in May include those of the Olive Dun, both Iron Blues, the Slow-water Olive and the two Spurwings, of which latter the Small Spurwing is much the most important. You will not go far wrong in May with nymphs dressed on size 0 hooks.

You will not go far wrong, in my opinion, if you think of most of your fly-fishing up to the end of May as being dry-fly fishing, keeping the nymph up your sleeve for emergencies or exceptional circumstances.

June

One of the most predominant species on running water in June is the Pale Watery, and when this little fly is coming up in quantity, trout often prefer the nymph to the dun. I then recommend artificials dressed on 00 hooks, though you may be able to get away with size 0 with naïve fish.

July and August

This is the peak season of nymph fishing, at which time a great many different species may be attracting the attention of feeding trout. If none are especially predominant, use nymphs on a 0 hook. If there are many Blue-winged Olives coming up, as is often the case on these long summer days, use a No 1. And in August when the Small Olive is on, use artificials dressed small on oo hooks.

September

Those species which have both spring and autumn generations reappear this month, including the Large Olive and the two Iron Blues, the latter rather smaller than the spring versions. When they are present in abundance, use a oo nymph. Late in the month when the Large Olive, or the Dark Olive is on, use a No 1.

Detecting the take

A fish may take an artificial nymph voluntarily, in which case we call it a *voluntary take*, or it may be induced to take by calculated action on the part of the nymph fisherman, in which case it is known as an *induced take*.

The significant point about the voluntary take is that the nymph fisherman remains passive, apart from gathering in slack line, until it occurs and then strikes the moment he detects it.

The induced take is used when the fish disregards the artificial until attention is drawn to it by some deliberate action by the angler, usually with a short sideways movement of the rod-tip causing the nymph to lift or swim in the water in a lifelike manner, impelling the fish to react by taking it, perhaps involuntarily.

In very fast water in which the artificial nymph travels so swiftly that even if the fish is seen to take it, the nymph fisherman scarcely has time to react, it may be necessary to assume the nymph will be taken and to time the strike accordingly. This is the *presumed take*.

In certain circumstances, especially when fishing directly across to a trout in favourable conditions of background and visibility, the take is obvious because the trout's mouth is seen to open and shut. Usually, too, a fish lifts slightly to take and levels out the moment it has done so, this slight lowering of the head end of the fish being another signal to strike.

When fishing from behind, neither of these indications may be received and the drift of the nymph must be carefully judged and a strike made when it reaches the position of the fish. This is the *proximity take*.

I shall have more to say on this important subject later.

Effective striking

Intelligent and informed anticipation is the key to effective striking. Try to picture in your mind what is going on under the surface of the water, whether your quarry is visible to you or not, and in the induced take what you intend to cause to happen beneath the surface. Remember that the time to strike, and the only time the strike is likely to be effective, is the precise moment when the fish closes its jaws over your artificial. As soon as it discovers the deception, a wild trout usually ejects the nymph immediately and the chance of hooking it is lost, perhaps the whole of that day.

Palm all slack line in the usual way as the nymph is drifting down with the current so that when you want to use your rod tip to set the hook, there will be no delay in the transmission of the strike.

Striking in nymph fishing is quite different to striking in dry-fly fishing. In the latter, it is necessary to give a trout time to put its head down, the levelling-out process described on Page 61, and to close its jaws over the dry-fly. This period varies from river to river, especially according to the size of the fish and may be anything from one to eight seconds. In nymph fishing, however, you cannot afford to wait even one second.

Any obvious movement, lift, twitch, dart or turn by a fish close to the assumed position of your drifting nymph may or may not be a take but if you wait and wonder you may lose the only opportunity you will get of hooking it, if it really was a take. The first-class nymph fisherman inevitably takes the majority of his fish first cast basing his strike on the proximity take, thereby acquiring a reputation for some subtle communion with his quarry. The proximity take is, however, plain common sense and unless you act on it, you will not find nymph fishing half as rewarding as it should be.

When you are unable to observe your fish directly, and so to detect any act or movement by it which might reveal the take to you, you must rely on the indication disclosed at your *dipping point*. This is the place where the floating part of your leader or cast turns down into the water as it is gradually drawn beneath the surface by the sinking artificial. It is not a static position on the cast but should be thought of as a tiny hole in the water through which the floating part of the cast is gradually disappearing and through which it will, in fact, accelerate to some extent in the event of a take. You must watch carefully for such acceleration, should a voluntary take occur, and you must key yourself up for it when you employ the induced take.

Dipping point indications will be discussed in greater detail in the following section, which deals with nymph fishing for trout obscured from direct observation by reflected light.

6 NYMPH FISHING IN REFLECTED LIGHT

Indications of a take

WHEN a fish is concealed from his direct observation by reflected light from the water, the nymph fisherman can detect a take in one of two main ways by dipping point indications, and by miscellaneous surface indications. At all times the nymph fisherman should try to visualize what is going on out of sight beneath the water so that these indications, some of which are extremely slight, can be anticipated and instantly acted upon when they do occur.

The dipping point is the primary indicator of a take in nymph fishing in reflected light and, indeed, in all circumstances in which direct visual observations of the fish itself is impracticable.

Dipping point indications can be made more visible by carefully greasing the butt of the cast, and perhaps the intermediate links as well, to act as an eye-guide to the dipping point in rough water or poor light. The cast point itself should, of course, be kept scrupulously free of grease and made to sink freely by regular rubbing down with soft mud.

If you study a nymphing trout which is visible in the water, you often notice it move forward eagerly to take a natural which it has seen coming towards it. Trout may take an artificial

63

nymph in the same way and this forward momentum of the fish causes a slight tug to be imparted to the floating part of the cast which is duly registered at the dipping point.

When a trout takes a natural nymph just beneath the surface, it usually tilts, tail down and head up to do so. As the trout levels out, its head dips down. If it takes an artificial just beneath the surface, this dip down with the nymph gripped between the trout's jaws pulls the fine point of the cast causing slight acceleration to be registered at the dipping point. Such an indication is only trifling in itself but if you are expecting it, you notice it immediately and react sharply to strike effectively before the trout can eject your artificial.

Bulging trout

Trout feeding actively on nymphs and freshwater shrimps over beds of water-celery and ranunculus disclose their position in reflected light by their frequent movements to intercept food creatures in the thin water over the weed. These movements give rise to bulging, crinkly swirls on the surface. Bulging trout are a most rewarding quarry for the nymph fisherman and if you find fish behaving in this way over weed-beds on a bright summer morning, the best of them, with care and persuasion, should be yours for the taking.

A feature of bulging trout is the eagerness with which they feed and a small artificial nymph may attract their attention while it is still some feet upstream of them, causing them to shoot forward to take it. Be careful not to be caught off guard by the speed of their reaction. This will be clearly indicated at the dipping point by a short but pronounced forward and downwards tug.

If the artificial nymph pitches or drifts down on the flank of a bulging trout, the fish may turn sharply aside to intercept it with some violence. In such a case the take is indicated by a sharp sideways tug on the floating part of the cast, caused by the fish turning back with the nymph gripped between its jaws.

A preliminary indication is sometimes given in these cases for as the fish turns aside to begin its move towards the nymph on its flank, it creates a swirl visible as a crinkle on the surface.

In thin water over a weed-bed, this initial swirl may be followed by a bow-wave on the surface, tracing the course of the trout invisible in the water directly beneath the head of the wave. This bow-wave ends abruptly at the moment of the take, after which the trout goes about and thereby creates a second crinkling swirl. To be effective, your strike must coincide with the check of the bow-wave. If you wait until the second swirl shows on the surface, you will probably be too late as by the time your strike is made, the trout will almost certainly have ejected your artificial.

In a hard-flogged fishery, a fair description for most of the water open to the majority of fly fishers, the trout surviving by, say, August, have probably been deceived on several occasions and owe their lives to the slow reactions of nymph fishers and their own ability to eject their artificial nymphs promptly.

Trout under cover

Your study of visible fish feeding well up in the water will reveal the readiness of some trout to turn and pursue food creatures which they become aware of when they appear behind

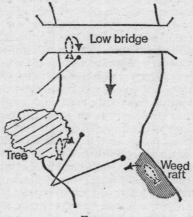

FIG 15.

them. Often, too, a trout will turn and pursue an artificial nymph which has dropped slightly short and entered the water a little way downstream of their lie. This readiness of a feeding fish to turn and pursue can be the undoing of trout which occupy covered lies under the protection of low bridges, culverts, overhanging tree branches and the like. Unfortunately in reflected light there is scarcely any dipping point indication when a trout takes an artificial nymph as it is swimming downstream, especially if it is travelling on a fairly even keel and ejects the nymph before turning round and swimming back to its hidden lie.

It may, indeed, be difficult to establish whether the trout is pursuing the nymph unless its initial reaction creates a swirl or its track causes surface disturbance. This explains why, very occasionally, trout are hooked 'by accident' when nymph fishing.

Some induced take tactics

An induced take often succeeds when an expected voluntary take has failed to materialize. When it is considered necessary, pitch the nymph sufficiently far upstream of the fish's assumed lie, according to the strength and speed of the current, to enable it to sink to the fish's level by the time it reaches a point just upstream of it. To induce the fish to take, movement should then be imparted to the artificial with the rod-tip. If the timing is correct and the imparted movement is sufficiently lifelike, both trout and grayling seem impelled to take the animated nymph.

The technique of the induced take and the subsequent strike calls for much practice and if you have access to water where grayling are plentiful, these will enable you to obtain this. Small grayling, especially, react very quickly to inducement and enable you to sharpen up your own reactions.

It sometimes happens that a trout known to be in a certain lie is invisible to the nymph fisherman from the point where he is to cast but that it is possible to see into the water a little way to one side or the other. In such cases, the induced take can be employed to fetch the fish across into the water where it will be visible to the angler and, consequently, where it will be easier to detect the take when it occurs.

7 SLOW-WATER TACTICS

How trout take slow-water nymphs

THE nymphs which generally occur in the slower-flowing reaches of rivers include those of the Small Spurwing, the Slow-water Olive and the Pale Evening dun. They are all fast swimmers.

Trout take these nymphs in three main ways:

(a) Close to the surface, a moment before they emerge as winged duns.
(b) In mid-water.
(c) Near the bottom.

Sub-surface tactics

Small Spurwings and Slow-water Olive duns both hatch well at times during the day, especially in the summer months. On dry sunny days, both species emerge rapidly and quickly take wing. Slow-water Olive nymphs select launching sites on weed or lumps of chalk close beneath the surface and when they finally emerge, they may appear to do so by shooting straight through the surface like a missile fired from a submarine.

Trout feeding near the surface understandably find it more profitable to intercept the nymphs before they emerge rather than to try to snatch the quick-escaping duns, a method of feeding calculated to use up more calories than the fish could gain.

To take these trout, cast precisely, pitching the nymph into the water only a little distance upstream of the feeding fish so that it will reach it accurately for line and at the appropriate depth, a mere few inches beneath the surface. Little movement need be imparted to the artificial except slight upwards lift to simulate the natural nymph rising to emerge as a winged dun.

Unlike the previous two species, the Pale Evening dun is not often seen emerging in the daytime. It is a crepuscular species, most often encountered late on warm summer evenings in July and August. The duns, too, are slower to leave their nymphal shucks and during a good hatch, trout take them freely, even neglecting Blue-winged Olives when these are also present on the water in good numbers. In these circumstances, a suitable dry-fly pattern is necessary to take trout feeding on them. My own dressing can be thoroughly recommended:

Hook: 0;
Silk: white;
Hackle: cream cock;
Whisks: cream cock, trimmed short;
Body: three herls from a grey goose primary;
Thorax: same herls, doubled and re-doubled in the usual way.

Apart from the fact that when trout take the duns freely, nymph fishing is less likely to be profitable, nymph fishing in the failing light of late evening is always something of a strain, although there are times when it pays dividends.

Mid-water tactics

Trout feeding in mid-water may be either stationary or cruisers but in either case they are usually most alert for any movement which may disclose the presence of food creatures in their vicinity, among the possibilities being the nymphs of slow-water species which have swum into mid-water either from the bottom or from the surrounding weeds where they graze.

Slow-water Olive nymphs spend a lot of time among weed, and the closely related Deep-water Olives mostly live among such waterweeds as milfoils, though mainly in still waters. Spurwing nymphs, too, climb about in the shelter of weed. Between the weed clumps there is often a good deal of coming and going, both voluntary and involuntary, and trout intercept nymphs in mid-water, when they are moving from feeding place to feeding place, and also chivvy them out of the weeds and seize them in mid-water when they succeed in their aim.

Present your artificial to a mid-water trout to reach it at the appropriate depth and not more than a few feet away. Then attract the fish's attention to the nymph, employing the induced take technique to simulate a natural nymph darting from weed clump to weed clump. This should only be necessary if the trout fails to respond with a voluntary take, accepting the sinking artificial as a natural nymph settling back into the deeps after a mid-water frolic.

If, in the hope of a voluntary take, you allow your artificial to sink well below the trout's depth without eliciting the expected response, impart slow, smooth lift to it with the rod tip, simulating a natural nymph rising into mid-water on a characteristic frolic. Such movement, although appearing slow, will cause the artificial to swim through the water at characteristic darting speed and will almost always attract the fish's attention. It may follow the artificial downstream in an unhurried manner before taking it, and it takes steady nerves to await such a take and react in the approved manner.

Deep-water tactics

Trout may take Slow-water Olive, Deep-water Olive, Spurwing and sometimes laboured swimmer nymphs in the deeper, sluggish reaches close to the bottom. The latter, especially, fall easy prey to trout and grayling attracted by their jerky, swimming action, on the relatively few occasions when they quit their usual cover and fish see them in open water.

When trout are feeding several feet below the surface, their activity and position can only be detected in favourable conditions of light and background, for in reflected light no surface movement can be expected to disclose their presence.

In such cases it may be necessary to cast the nymph anything up to 15 yards upstream to give it a chance to sink to the fish's level by the time it reaches its lie. At these depths, I have found the induced take is usually necessary to achieve deception.

The imparted movement may be of two kinds:

(a) Upwards, to simulate a nymph rising into mid-water after feeding among leaves and suchlike debris on the bottom.
(b) Sideways and upwards, smartly, to suggest the well-known rapid dart of a natural Slow-water Olive or Small Spurwing nymph.

In either case, the artificial should move at least 1 ft through the water as a result of the action of the rod tip. If properly timed, such movement should be almost automatically followed by the induced take itself as the trout, perhaps involuntarily, reacts to the lifelike behaviour of the artificial it sees gliding through the water. You must therefore be keyed up, ready in all respects to react in turn, and set your hook in the jaws of the fish at the moment of the take you have so artfully induced.

Weed-cutting effects

Weed-cutting operations give rise to unpleasant and somewhat difficult fishing conditions, certainly on the reaches immediately downstream of where they are taking place. The water becomes discoloured to a greater or lesser extent, according to the amount of silt disturbed during cutting, and great rafts of shorn weed tresses follow one another downstream in a continuous procession, making casting difficult and the landing of a hooked fish most hazardous.

It is important to appreciate that these drifting weed masses contain many creatures on which trout prey freely, nymphs among them, and many of these do not allow themselves to be borne away on the current until they reach the sea. Food creatures are constantly deserting the weed masses as they drift with the stream to seek a new habitat without delay. Trout are well aware of this and are on the watch to intercept them. At weed-cutting time, therefore, the shrewd nymph fisherman is present to minister to their needs, to his own profit.

Weed rafts

Drifting weed tends to lodge here and there along the river, usually against some obstruction such as a bridge pier, a low overhanging tree branch, projecting roots or old timber piles. Although such trapped weed may periodically be freed and moved on by the keepers, it is often quickly replaced by more weed drifting down from cutting operations or weed-rack clearance on reaches higher up.

These weed rafts may provide a welcome habitat for many nymphs, shrimps and other trout food creatures, and also shelter for the fish themselves who understand their double significance as potential larders and alternative covered lies to previously occupied lies now exposed by the weed-cutting.

Such trout may thrive and fatten in these sheltered lies but

70

rarely show themselves to the angler by surface movement. In time the nymph fisherman comes to know both the most likely places for weed to lodge and rafts to form and the most productive rafts in terms of fish-holding potential. Some of the best rafts are so popular with trout that they may continue to yield good fish time and again throughout the rest of the season.

Only by practical experience can such profitable local knowledge be acquired, but the ability to appreciate and weigh up the possibilities of weed rafts observed on strange waters should stand the visiting nymph fisherman in good stead. If you run a nymph down the side of a weed raft two or three times without any sign of a voluntary take being registered at your dipping point, or otherwise being disclosed, try again using the induced take.

A warning

Whenever you are nymph fishing in the presence of drifting weed, be sure to check your artificial frequently, to make sure that it has not fouled some weed stem or leaf. This often happens and unless the point of the hook is cleared regularly, your nymph is unlikely to deceive fish as it should.

8 NYMPH FISHING IN LAKES AND PITS

Natural nymphs in still waters

NATURAL nymphs of many species inhabit still waters, among them those of the Mayflies, certain Broadwings, various stone clingers and some of the best-known laboured swimmers. The true Olives, the Pale Watery and the Iron Blues are not found in still waters, for life in which their respiratory system is unsuitable, but some of the more robust Baëtid species thrive in ponds, lakes, gravel pits, reservoirs and suchlike still waters.

The most important of these to the nymph fisherman are the nymphs of the Small Spurwing, the Slow-water Olive and the Deep-water Olive.

The Small Spurwing is a remarkably ubiquitous species, occurring in rivers, streams and lakes in many parts of these islands. The nymphs live among water weeds close to the surface where trout sometimes cruise in search of them. They are fast swimmers and from time to time they appear in open water between the weed growths, either in transit or frolicking in play, and there too the attention of feeding trout may be attracted to them.

Slow-water Olive nymphs live mainly in shallow, sun-warmed waters around the edges of lakes, pits and small ponds, as well as in those parts of streams where a high summer temperature obtains. Here the nymphs feed on vascular plant tissue, algae, detritus and the excreta of water-lice. They are to be found in the water in every month of the year and no species differs so much in coloration from individual to individual. Growth is largely suspended from November to March, and the main emergence period is from May to September, with quite a few appearing before and after this time.

Deep-water Olive nymphs which superficially resemble the last species may be distinguished from them by their rounded gills: those of the Slow-water Olive are heart-shaped. They also prefer to live in deeper water, rarely occurring near the shallow edges of lakes and pits. There they live among weed growths beneath the surface. The duns emerge in early summer and again in September.

In waters holding any or all of these three species, trout are almost certain both to be aware of them and to prey on them when the chance to do so arises. In other waters, however, nymphs may play a relatively insignificant part in the diet of trout, in contrast with other food, creatures such as corixidae, snails, sticklebacks and so on. In such waters, the fisherman is likely to do better with lures such as the 'flies', 'nymphs' and 'bugs' which are usually recommended by the local fishery authorities themselves. Equally, in waters holding a good population of natural nymphs, nymph fishing may itself be a rewarding as well as an artistic method of taking trout.

Suitable waters for nymph fishing

I consider that nymph fishing in lakes and pits is most likely to be effective when they are of limited extent, partially sheltered, contain some weed and support a population of natural nymphs of the kind on which trout prey.

Nymphs of the three species just described in detail are all agile darters and it would be illogical to expect to find them on the exposed shores of stony lakes and big reservoirs. Fish the artificial to trout cruising near the surface over weed growths, and use a stronger point than you would for river fishing. If the trout themselves are visible, you stand a better chance of presenting your artificial accurately for line, although lake trout often weave about considerably as they cruise to feed.

The speed of a cruising lake trout often makes it easier to hook than its counterpart lying stationary in a stream. When hooked, lake trout often run hard and fast and you must have plenty of backing on your reel to allow for this.

Pockets of open water between weed masses often repay exploration with the nymph, especially in late summer, and if there is a little ripple on the water fish may take with great freedom. A touch of grease on the butt of the cast makes it easier to detect the take in these circumstances.

If the lake shores are thickly weeded, it may be an advantage to fish from a boat and it helps if you have a companion to row and to enable you to concentrate on the job in hand. I have enjoyed some rewarding evenings using the nymph on a variety of lakes of this kind since I devoted serious study to the natural nymphs occurring in still waters.

Lake trout cruising to feed generally take the nymph not more than 1 or 2 ft beneath the surface. If the nymph has sunk 3 or 4 ft down without a voluntary take resulting, try the induced take, imparting slow, smooth lift which will bring the artificial steadily up to within inches of the surface.

This method often proves deadly for big rainbow trout and most of those which I catch are taken in this way. You may or may not see the curious grey-green shadow of the fish in the water as it lifts to take savagely, according to the degree of clarity at the time, but if your eyes are good you often see the slight whitening under water which is caused by the rainbow's mouth opening, and is the signal to hold back with the rod to set the hook.

9 CLASSIFICATION OF NATURAL NYMPHS BY TYPES

(British Species Only)

Serial	Species	English Name of dun	

Bottom Burrowers *(Ephemerids)*

1	*Ephemera danica*	Mayfly	
2	*Ephemera vulgata*	Mayfly	
3	*Ephemera lineata*	Mayfly	Rare

Silt Crawlers *(Caenids)*

4	*Brachycercus harrisella*	—	Local
5	*Caenis horaria*	Yellow Broadwing	
6	*Caenis macrura*	River Broadwing	
7	*Caenis moesta*	Black Broadwing	
8	*Caenis robusta*	Dusky Broadwing	Local
9	*Caenis rivulorum*	Brook Broadwing	
		A minute species	

Moss Creepers *(Ephemerellids)*

10	*Ephemerella ignita*	Blue-winged Olive
11	*Ephemerella notata*	Yellow Evening dun

Stone Clingers – Class I *(Ecdyonurids)*

12	*Arthroplea congener*	—	Nymph unrecorded
13	*Ecdyonurus insignis*	—	
14	*Ecdyonurus dispar*	Autumn dun	
15	*Ecdyonurus torrentis*	Large Brook dun	
16	*Ecdyonurus venosus*	Late March Brown	
17	*Ecdyonurus forcipula*	—	Only one record
18	*Rhithrogena haarupi*	March Brown	
19	*Rhithrogena semicolorata*	Olive Upright	
20	*Heptagenia longicauda*	—	
21	*Heptagenia lateralis*	Dusky Yellowstreak	
22	*Heptagenia fuscogrisea*	Brown May dun	
23	*Heptagenia sulphurea*	Yellow May dun	

Stone Clingers – Class II (*Potamanthid*)

24	*Potamanthus luteus*	Large Brown-backed Yellow dun	Local

Laboured Swimmers (*Leptophlebiids*)

25	*Habrophlebia fusca*	Ditch dun	
26	*Leptophlebia vespertina*	Claret dun	
27	*Leptophlebia marginata*	Sepia dun	
28	*Paraleptophlebia sub marginata*	Turkey Brown	
29	*Paraleptophlebia tumida*	—	Rare
30	*Paraleptophlebia cincta*	Purple dun	

Agile Darters – Class I (*Large Siphlonurids*)

31	*Ameletus inopinatus*	Brown Mountain dun	
32	*Siphlonurus linneanus*	Large Summer dun	
33	*Siphlonurus lacustris*	Large Summer dun	
34	*Siphlonurus armatus*	Large Summer dun	Rare

Agile Darters – Class II (*Small Baëtids*)

35	*Baëtis niger*	Iron Blue	
36	*Baëtis pumilus*	Iron Blue	
37	*Baëtis atrebatinus*	Dark Olive	
38	*Baëtis rhodani*	Large Olive	
39	*Baëtis buceratus*	—	Local
40	*Baëtis vernus*	Olive dun	
41	*Baëtis tenax*	—	Like *B. vernus*
42	*Baëtis scambus*	Small Olive	
43	*Baëtis bioculatus*	Pale Watery dun	
44	*Centroptilum luteolum*	Small Spurwing	
45	*Centroptilum pennulatum*	Large Spurwing	
46	*Cloëon dipterum*	Slow-water Olive or Pond Olive	
47	*Cloëon simile*	Deep-water Olive or Lake Olive	
48	*Procloëon pseudorufulum*	Pale Evening dun	

R. C. BRIDGETT

Loch Fishing

[*Note*: Later editions of this book were revised by C. F. Walker. His footnotes to the text are followed by the initials C.F.W. to distinguish them from comments made by the present editor, which are followed by the letters 'Ed.']

From C. F. Walker's Introduction.

When this work first appeared, every conceivable aspect of the subject was covered with commendable thoroughness. There is, however, one department in which our knowledge has increased since Bridgett's day; namely, the entomology of still water. It was not, in fact, until the publication of J. R. Harris's invaluable work, *An Angler's Entomology*, in 1952, that the lake fisher had anything to guide him in the recognition of the various insects he encountered at the water-side. Bridgett . . . was not nor did he claim to be, an expert entomologist, though he had a rough working knowledge of fly-life which he applied in practice with satisfactory results.* He did not, for example, quite appreciate that many of the flies he found on lakes were not the same species as he had been accustomed to see on rivers, particularly those of the order Ephemeroptera, in which the nymphs of certain species are specially adapted for life in still water, while others can only exist where there is a current. Useful though his chapter is, therefore, in drawing the lake angler's attention to the value of studying the natural insects and their relation to his artificials, the reader would do well to supplement it with a perusal of Harris's book, in which more detailed and accurate information on the subject is to be found.

* His observations have been supplemented by footnotes – C.F.W.

1 A CHARGE AGAINST THE LOCH

A VERY serious reproach has been cast against the loch fisher. It has been declared that loch fishing is only a game of chuck-and-chance-it, not at all entitled to the dignity of the name of sport. In very many cases the charge is deserved, but loch fishing is not necessarily such a poor game, any more than river fishing must needs be scientific.

Many anglers, when they propose to spend a day on the loch, procure a cast of flies or a number of casts for the occasion; a few take some interest in the selection of patterns and their positions, but the majority accept without question whatever is offered, provided that the assortment shows a sufficient variety of colours and includes at least one long-established favourite. On arriving at the loch-side the angler is accustomed to put on a cast of small flies if the breeze is gentle and the day bright, or a quartet of larger size if a big wave rolls along and the sky is clouded.

He sets out and, when the boat is laid on the drift, he casts on and on with persistence and perseverance, every cast delivered more or less in the same fashion. He may for sake of variety change the direction of his cast from time to time, subject the flies to slow, rapid or jerking movements, test their luring power at various depths, but on the whole there is little expenditure of thought; the labour is generally dull, tiresome and uninteresting.

Such is loch fishing, as commonly understood and as practised by a large number of anglers; but it may be readily elevated into something far greater, something really commendable and scientific, something capable of giving pleasure to any man.

To understand how such a great result can be brought about, and to realize how it is that the loch can be of such engrossing interest to a few anglers who, refusing to be content with unvarying methods and fortuitous successes, have discovered its possibilities, it will be necessary to examine in detail the lures classed together under the term 'loch-flies'.

The name 'fly' is somewhat misleading, because it suggests that the artificial is a representation of a winged insect, whereas it may imitate also various kinds of creatures, and may even be merely the product of someone's imagination. Those of the last type, a numerous company, that still survive as the result of a long process of elimination, have been found by experiment to be frequently acceptable. None can tell when they will prove useful – and that is one great objection to them – but it is not difficult to find a reason why they meet with success, even though it is the case that they bear little or no resemblance to any form of life known to the trout.

Probably everyone has seen in a river-pool a trout in close proximity to a shoal of minnows; the latter appear perfectly regardless of the presence of a potential enemy, which in turn pays not the slightest attention to them. Should, however, one of the minnows begin to twist and turn about, as will often happen, or should an angler draw a spinning bait through the shoal, the trout will rush open-mouthed upon the offender. I have not witnessed such an occurrence, but others have declared it to be quite common; I should expect it to happen and see no reason for doubt in the matter. Obviously there is aroused within the trout the lust to kill rather than a desire to eat. It is well known that some trout repair to the shallows, when night falls, in order to satisfy their appetites with a dish of minnows, but at other times, when they accept a spinning lure, they are actuated by a totally different impulse. The occasional success of a 'fancy fly' is similarly explained.

The artificial 'fly' may attract a trout in many ways; it may appeal to its appetite by reason of a similarity to something which the trout is at the time partaking of, or which it is accustomed to receive; it may arouse curiosity, anger or the passion for destruction.

Which of these impelling forces should it be the angler's endeavour to set in motion? Clearly it should be the first, for, if he can find the correct means by observation, experiment or deduction, he will command general attention, whereas, if his lure represents nothing familiar, he can at best supply an impetus only to an occasional individual. The desire to eat affects many trout simultaneously; curiosity and the desire to kill must be differently aroused in different fish, and must, moreover, be awakened specially in every particular case. When the trout for any reason are abstaining from food altogether, or taking some form that does not admit of imitation owing to its nature or size, then, but only then, should the angler attempt their capture by means of lures, the success of which is only accidental.

It will be agreed that the general procedure on a loch is exactly as follows. The angler throws out his cast down the wind. If the fish are rising, that is to say, feeding on flies floating on the surface, or are taking nymphs resting or swimming high, he is almost certain to have good sport by fishing his 'flies' high in the water. If, however, the trout are not feeding at the surface, nor inclined to take his 'flies' so worked, he still uses the self-same cast, but sinks it deeply, pulls it towards the boat or bank, and probably secures a fish or two.

The least consideration should convince him that, if his 'flies' are suitable lures for the first set of conditions, they cannot possibly be thoroughly satisfactory for the second, and vice versa. They cannot represent surface insects and subaqueous creatures equally well. Yet the same cast will kill whether it is fished at the surface or deeply sunk, but that does not prove that the methods and lures are good. It shows rather that, had a more judicious selection been made, sport would undoubtedly have been very much better than that actually obtained.

Very frequently the angler, when about to set out for some loch, asks his tackle-dealer or a friend to recommend him a cast suitable for the time and place. Such a request suggests that the person addressed is able to foretell how the trout will behave, what they will accept in the way of food, and that they are going to confine themselves exclusively to some particular form throughout the day. As a refusal might be misconstrued, a cast is supplied; it is necessarily a compromise, an attempt to meet every possible contingency, but not succeeding conspicuously in any respect. That is one reason why the cast generally carries as many as four flies. The probability is that every type of 'fly' will be represented, for, by increasing the number of types, the chance of providing something acceptable are likewise increased.

If, only in the absence of any clear indication from the waters, every loch fisher used such a cast merely for the purpose of finding out the type of food at the time welcomed and, the discovery made, thereupon prepared another cast bearing representations of that type exclusively, the objection to loch fishing would cease to exist. Four lures on the cast would then become not only unnecessary but inadvisable; two will suffice, and perhaps the angler will find cause to reduce the number still further.

The angler ought to know the various forms of life that his

79

lures are designed to imitate; he should know regarding each form accepted by trout, its distinguishing characteristics, its habits and principally its favourite position in the strata of the waters. If he is unable to find out what a certain 'fly' represents, he may safely put it down as a 'fancy' pattern, which cannot be expected to have much attraction for a feeding trout.

The angler, who uses such a cast, kills a trout now and then, and does not make any modifications on his lures and methods, is either unable or too lazy to connect cause and effect. He may have certain conclusions forced upon him, but, afraid to interrupt the sequence of successes, he lets well alone, and so misses much of the pleasure that the loch is well able to provide. On some days, in fact the cast should not be used at all.

If a rise is in progress when he reaches the fishing-ground or occurs at any part of the day, such a quartet of flies, or any other, would be quite unsuitable. In the first place, he must be able to distinguish between a true rise and an apparent rise. The trout may be pursuing ascending nymphs* and taking them very near the surface; in that case a fish will cause a distinctly visible boil. Or, again, flies may be plainly seen riding the wave and trout may be noticed taking them. He must make sure that the fish are really taking flies, for it is when the surface is well supplied with winged insects that a mistake is most easily made. He sees the flies and he expects that the trout are feeding on them, whereas it may be the nymphs that are still causing the commotion. A few minutes spent in careful watching will determine what is occurring, and on the conclusion depends the choice of lure.

If the trout are accepting the fully fledged insects, there is not the slightest doubt that a dry-fly, or a pair of them of correct pattern will prove to be the means of ensuring the most interesting sport. There are anglers who refuse to believe in the efficacy of, or necessity for, a floating fly, and there are lochs where that lure is not held in high repute. I have not yet seen a loch, the trout of which abstained from surface-food, and such unbelieving anglers must be easily pleased when they consider a fourfold appeal to fortune superior to a carefully planned direct attack upon an individual trout. They will, however, give their luck great assistance if they will use wet-flies intended to represent or suggest the flies on the water; that is to say, their lures

* Or pupae – C.F.W.

80

should be precisely similar to the floating variety in every respect, save one, viz, that they are allowed to sink. These should be carefully laid over the rise, and they will meet with a fair response, not because they are wet or the angler skilful, but simply because a trout is not able to tell whether a fly is slightly above, just below or on the surface.

In the absence of a rise, the determination of the correct lure is more difficult, but one fact should be obvious, viz, that it is not the floating fly. Possibly the only feasible method will consist of a trial with the experimental cast, which of course must be chosen, after the manner of the one mentioned above, for this express purpose. In other words it must carry different types, so that it will make deductions possible. The angler would do well to remember that, if he fished that cast with the order of the flies reversed, the amount of sport obtained at any time would be infinitesimal. The realization of this fact will assist him to an understanding of the problem.

An examination of the mouth or stomach of the first trout caught will tell him all he desires to know; the fly that effected the capture, the depth at which it was taken, the manner in which it was accepted, may all suggest certain conclusions, but the inspection will remove all doubt. It will probably reveal no mature flies at all; more likely it will show a miscellaneous assortment of nymphs or perhaps a number all of the same variety; there may be a complete absence of food.

In the last case fishing may be postponed until a more auspicious period of the day arrives; but as such inaction is not at all attractive, the alternative is to play for a fluke with the cast already on the line or with another carrying patterns like Peter Ross, Dunkeld, Cinnamon and Gold, Butcher, something with a touch of jungle-cock, Colonel Downman for example, so these are calculated to arouse within a trout curiosity, jealousy, the love of destruction or whatever it is that causes so many fish to rush upon their doom. As a form of sport this may fail to satisfy the scientific angler, but if these lures are used only when all else fails or by way of experiment, and not, as is rather general, under all sorts of conditions, the gravest charge against the loch is removed.

If the post-mortem examination indicates that nymphs have been in favour, a new cast should be immediately made ready, fitted with two specimens of artificial nymphs of the most abundant varieties disclosed. Such lures are now easily procurable; if the angler does not possess patterns, he should note that, by pinching off the wings of some wet-flies, such as Blae and Black, Rough Olive, Woodcock and Yellow, Blae and Harelug, etc, very passable imitations of the commoner nymphs result.

If the loch fisher goes about his sport on these lines, discovering, by means of observation or by the help of an autopsy made possible by a more or less lucky capture, what it is that the trout desire, having a definite object in view rather than making himself the sport of fortune, changing his lures and methods from hour to hour not in haphazard fashion but as the fish decree, he will extract far greater pleasure from his days on the loch.

2 HABITS OF THE LOCH-TROUT

THE loch-trout lives a far more secluded life than does his relative of the river; it is difficult, generally quite impossible, to keep him under observation, and the conclusions arrived at below may be considered based on totally insufficient evidence. Accuracy is unattainable, or seems to be, therefore conjecture must content.

One, and perhaps the greatest, point of difference between loch-trout and river-trout is that, while the latter has much of his food brought direct to him, the former is compelled to go in search of all but an insignificant part of it. The river carries along on its current myriads of flies and, in times of flood, a large and varied mixture of worms, slugs and grubs; every trout, according to his luck or power, takes up his station to intercept the feast. There are times, of course, when he must move about if he would receive a share of what is available; at night he roams the shallows in quest of minnows and sedges; in stone-fly time he pushes into the necks of pools; at periods of nymphal activity he would fare badly if he remained at his post. It is unnecessary to make a long list of examples for, however long it might be, it would not affect the fact that a river-trout has a well-defined feeding-station which he occupies and, when called upon, defends, but which he leaves without regrets when it loses for a time its advantages.

In a loch, on the other hand, there is an absence of current, perhaps not quite complete, but barely perceptible except in a few clearly marked localities. A certain number of trout will collect round the mouths of tributary streams and across an out-flowing river, but these fish will form a relatively small portion of the total stock, and will rather resemble river-trout in habits and general characteristics. Wind does waft along the floating ephemeridae* and other flies, a fact of which the fish seem to be aware, but the quantity of food obtainable through these means is infinitesimal. The loch-trout must be a roamer.

A fish may take up a definite post, such as a clump of weed or rocky corner. While the abode may not be exactly permanent, occupancy is retained for quite a long part of the fishing season. Of that I have no doubt, for, not in one loch but in many, I have seen day after day a trout rising steadily in the same spot, clearly defined and obviously desirable, and have made attempts at his capture.

Just as there are in a loch some peculiarly desirable points, so there are certainly highly popular areas. Some of these regions may be quite small, far separated from the shores of mainland or island, difficult to locate from description, but well worth marking down clearly when discovered; there may be nothing to betray their presence excepting repeated acceptance of the lures, and therefore accident first disclosed them; but, if the bottom of the loch could be inspected at these parts, the reason for their excellence would be at once revealed. Others are large, being perhaps long, broad shallows containing weeds that encourage and sustain certain sub-aqueous creatures, or stretches of submerged rocks which are preferred merely because they afford adequate shelter and a convenient resting-place in proximity to a feeding-ground.

A few areas are good only under exceptional conditions. For example, when gales are out and the loch is very wild, the lee of a wood, besides being the only comfortable part, is capable of making the hours pass pleasantly. Flies and caterpillars are blown off the trees, and the trout soon learn that something is being provided for their sustenance. The boat moves quietly along the calm belt; the angler is sheltered from the gale; the flies search the edge of the troubled waters, and not in vain. I have happy recollections of successful days on three separate

* Now known as *Ephemeroptera*. See also pp. 91 and 95 – C.F.W.

83

lochs, when the only difficulty was to get the boat through the turmoil of wind and wave into the protection of the trees.

The angler may easily be induced by his experiences to arrive at false conclusions. Anyone is liable to expect good sport where he has before obtained it; but it does not follow that, because a certain area is good on one occasion, it will continue so invariably, even after making due allowance for different conditions. Should it sometime fail to come up to his expectations, he probably decides that the weather or some influence is at the moment unfavourable, and that, by remaining in the vicinity, he will in course be greeted with attention. Such a decision may have a happy result, but it may as easily bring him regrets.

A bay or shallow is not likely to maintain the same standard of excellence at all times. Its merit is due to the fact that it is productive of trout-food. The latter consists of a large variety of forms, but these do not all rejoice in the same type of surroundings. Fly-larvae, to consider them exclusively by way of example, select a bottom which suits them; some hide under gravel, some burrow in mud, some crawl over sand, some lurk among weeds. It is not to be expected that one bay can be suitable for all. In addition, these creatures are not always available to the trout; when they leave their hiding-places, that is when they are actively preparing for the transformation to the winged state, they fall ready victims to the pursuing fish, but at other times they are comparatively safe. It is scarcely necessary to add, however highly significant it is, that the activity with its attendant perils does not arrive for different species all at the same time.

Larvae of one species comes to maturity more or less all together, and move upwards to the surface; another species inhabiting quite different surroundings develop at a later date. So the sequence is continued down the year. The fact that flies of one kind emerge in relays or detachments does not affect the case beyond introducing complications and rendering the angler's problem more difficult to solve. Any one bay, therefore, has a kind of intermittent popularity, times of plenty alternating with days of scarcity, the dull periods being of varying duration, relieved, perhaps, only by some lucky windfall.

Another and equally important point clearly demonstrated is that the trout in still water undertake journeys, large or small as the case may be, when they are feeding. No surmise is required; the migration can be and often is witnessed. Of course, if every trout in a loch headed in the same direction at a given time, e.g. up wind, they would ultimately be congregated together off the same shore, a somewhat absurd suggestion and a state of affairs which, it is superfluous to remark, never obtains. The journey is not quite so extensive, and yet it is not necessarily restricted to the confines of one particular bay; one bay may be almost entirely forsaken for another. Moreover, the trout, as is often quite apparent, act as individuals; that is, independently of one another.

The angler would do well to remember this habit of the loch-trout. When he sees a rise he very sensibly attempts to cover it; if it occurs in the vicinity of weeds or over rocks he may fish out the cast already made before aiming at the mark, but in open water the sooner his fly reaches the centre of the rings the better. Anyone of experience will agree that promptness in the cast is the supreme essential; if delay is incurred, inaccuracy in direction has actually a better chance of success than the most delicate precision. These are undoubted facts capable of verification on many days, but facts are not always remembered when they would prove of most service. The angler must see far more than the mere rise; he must decide whether the trout is at rest at the observed point or travelling; if it is not stationary, he must note, or failing that, guess in what direction it is heading.

We all know that trout will remain together in place where the food-supply is abundant, why should they not leave it together when the stock is exhausted and search for another kindly region? Some forms that spend their whole existence under water, for example, shrimps, water-boatmen and so forth, render certain bays always desirable, moderately or exceedingly, as the case may be, and in these delectable regions the labours of the rod continually meet with reward; but even these places are invaded by questing trout and, in consequence, are periodically better than they generally are.

An angler resident on the shores of a loch, and accustomed to fish it day after day, is sure to have remarked how sport falls off in one bay and revives again, and that in other bays the reverse holds. The fact is readily noticeable in small lochs in which it is possible to search thoroughly every part several times in the course of a day.

It is obvious that, if a shoal of loch-trout set out for a destination presumably not predetermined but dependent upon circumstances, the objective being not a place so much as the presence of food, they must likewise have a point of departure. The previous feeding-ground is the most likely to be suggested, but it is to be noted that trout occasionally rest and abstain from food; most of us would be tempted to declare that it is seldom that they do feed. They select as resting-places stony and weedy tracks, in which they may sometimes be caught, though they are not at the moment very interested in food. The river-trout have their feeding-stations and their resting-quarters: large fish especially have these sometimes quite a long distance apart. From a bridge one may see plenty of trout alert and eager, rising at everything that comes along, and some time later not a single fish is in sight. The trout in lochs likewise have their chosen corners, where they remain under cover, and from which they come in answer to the demands of appetite.

We have all heard an angler declare that the trout were rising all over the loch. His language is picturesque rather than strictly truthful; the slight exaggeration may be pardoned. When a hatch of flies occurs, the trout, if they happen to want them, will scatter, the better to obtain an equitable share of the spoils. The flies may spread, but rising trout will not be equally numerous in all parts of the loch, and some places will be totally undisturbed. In the river, so in the loch, a hatch is local, confined to a small area; but wind may drive the flies over almost its whole breadth, so that in small weedy lochs like Loch Dochart rising trout may be seen in nearly every direction; the calm belt, however, along the sheltered shore will not be disturbed.

Of what assistance is all this discussion to the loch fisher? The facts are: (1) different parts of a loch produce different forms of food, and (2) these forms are not available all at the same time. A certain consequence is that one area may be bare while another is plenteously furnished. There is one assumption made which, however, has been shown to be not altogether groundless – viz, that trout are not content with alternating wealth and want, but that they, collectively as well as individually, move from an exhausted area in quest of one more hospitable. Since it cannot for a moment be granted that trout are aware of what is occurring at a distance, they must set out not for a place but for a purpose; the desire to eat drives them away from that region which has temporarily lost the power to satisfy it. The loch fisher would do well to remember the facts and to accept the hypothesis as another.

While he is on the loch he may see a fine general rise, or only an occasional rise, or not the slightest sign of a rise. In the first case the procedure is obvious; he should require no directions; the flies are there for his guide, and good patterns, fair imitations of the insects on the water, will bring him sport in full measure. They should be fished dry if the greatest response is desired, but wet-flies will, in spite of the handicap under which they labour, sometimes yield a good return.

The second case may be more difficult to solve correctly. Why are the rising fish so few in number? The trout may be all willing to rise, but few flies are available, or there may be abundance of flies and the fish either indifferent or still in active pursuit of the ascending nymphs. A floating fly will soon decide whether the trout are eagerly scanning the surface, and, if it fails, a cast of nymphs will determine whether or not they are feeding below. Few anglers can have failed to observe that, when such conditions obtain, casting out from the boat as it is being rowed along is frequently very successful. The lures gradually sink where they alight, but, as the line tightens to the movement of the boat, they are suddenly swept upwards and towards the wake; at the beginning of this change of direction the action of the lure probably resembles that of a nymph. Perhaps success is due to a totally different cause – viz, that the lures come before the notice of travelling trout, but that cannot be more than a partial reason, because the response is sometimes long continued.

Should there be no indication from the surface that trout inhabit the loch, fishing loses much of its interest, but it does not follow that it will be unprofitable. The loch-trout obtains by far the greater portion of his food beneath the surface, so that on the great majority of days no rising fish are to be seen. Dry-fly fishing at a venture on the loch is rather dreary, and usually but ill-rewarded; moreover, it is not sensible to offer the trout what they obviously are not taking. The angler should provide himself with a cast of lures imitating subaqueous forms, a mixture comprising the species of nymphs about due a change of scene or those just passed away, as well as shrimps or other creatures that spend all their lives under water. Beginning with a well-chosen cast, he should be content to fish it for a time, and instead of changing a lure now and then he should rather change his ground: the cast will do its duty when he discovers the trout. He should fish water shallow and deep, in the vicinity of rocks and weeds, and over sand and gravel. If nothing results, he may safely conclude that the trout are not meanwhile interested in food, and that, if any are to be caught, it will be by appealing to an impulse other than appetite; a cast of ordinary loch-patterns used over likely places will perhaps then bring a fish or two to the net.

Acting on these principles I have had some interesting days on various lochs, and have always felt inclined to conclude that the success was due to the system suggested and not to accident.

3 THE MOODS OF LOCH-TROUT

THE loch-trout is a creature of many moods, a few of them pleasing to the angler, many of them irritating, some of them tantalizing, and these moods vary from day to day, from hour to hour it may be, so that none can predict with certainty or even hope of being correct what their inclinations and humours will be at any given time.

Much discussion has taken place on the question as to what causes trout to feed. Such discussions are quite harmless. Should a desire to eat and a supply of food be present at the same time, trout will feed until appetite is satisfied or supplies are exhausted, and they will not feed if either requirement is a-wanting. It does seem ridiculous to debate at length on such a subject, for there is nothing more in it. Weather conditions may stifle or stimulate the desire to eat; they may affect certain forms of trout food by rousing them to activity or condemning them for the time being to quiescence and imprisonment. Managers of trout farms inform us that in very cold weather fish have no inclination to eat, and will ignore the food thrown to them; and, as in the hatchery, so in the loch.

On the loch it is no uncommon thing to see even in the middle of the season the surface covered here and there with flies of one or of many species, and yet there is not a single welcoming rise. The temperature may be neither higher nor lower than that at which trout become eagerly inclined for food, and the angler should make sure that the inactivity is not only apparent. In spite of the undisturbed surface, the fish may be exceedingly alert, pursuing and swallowing with the greatest keenness nymphs ascending to change their state and, of course, they may not. Instead they are perhaps picking up molluscs from among low-lying weeds, scooping up midge-larvae from the surface of the mud, or hunting out shrimps from their retreats. And it may be that they are perfectly heedless of the flies and of everything else; but, if this is the case, the angler's opportunity is sure to come at some period of the day, for trout have appetites hard to appease, and they will, therefore, not continue obdurate.

To the tantalizing moods of loch-trout belongs their period-ical indulgence in short-rising, as it is termed. The angler is continually having his hopes raised by the sight of a fish breaking the surface beside his flies, or of a heavy boil in the water, or by a sudden but slight arrestment of the lures, as he brings them towards him. His greatest desire is frequently on the point of being realized, but just as often fulfilment is denied. This humour is not quite so often in evidence as the angler endeavours to persuade himself and others that it is, but, nevertheless, it is often enough on exhibition. Sometimes the eye and hand refuse to work harmoniously together; the strike is administered too slowly; it may occasionally be performed too quickly, but generally slowness is to blame for non-acceptance of well-intentioned offers. The angler may, on the other hand, be merely the victim of bad luck. The fact that a very large proportion of trout caught are hooked in the corner of the mouth shows that the hook must have travelled a considerable distance from the first moment of contact to the final securing of a hold; there are many chances of failure, against which the angler, after he has taken care to provide himself with the most serviceable hooks available, is powerless to guard. However, there is not the slightest doubt that often it is the trout, and not the angler, that prevents success.

The fact is that at times the fish delight in toying with the fly, taking hold of it by the feathers of the wing or by the hackle, but never closing their mouths over the hook. The angler receives an apparently excellent offer, strikes and meets with a fine resistance; the fish is to all appearance securely hooked. It runs out a few yards of line while the reel sings cheerily, and then the line falls limp and woefully slack. The disappointment is intense, and when the same sort of thing is repeated at short intervals the exasperation becomes too great for endurance.

This playful humour of loch-trout is quite commonly displayed. Moreover, the angler on such occasions is very unwilling to change his tactics or lures because offers are frequent, and he feels that no matter how often he is disappointed, the next one is sure to be an earnest endeavour. Hope does not readily die within him. In fact, he is rather afraid to change his cast, lest, by so doing, the offers should cease altogether, and they, after all, are worth something. The cure does not invariably consist of a reduction in the size of lure; that is generally recommended, but sometimes it will not be effective. Most of us have known instances of large flies, that is, a little larger than the standard size for the particular loch, alone procuring response of this annoying nature though it be, and of small flies being totally ignored. Seeing that the trout are obviously not anxious to feed, but are not unwilling to be interested, I think that a number, sufficient to bring satisfaction on a difficult day, would be induced to seize and hold lightly dressed patterns which are conspicuous without being large, but I have not had the experience often enough to enable me to reach a definite conclusion as to the most efficient remedy.

There are other occasions when loch-trout are generally declared to be rising short, whereas they are indulging in a totally different, but equally irritating, practice. Time after time a fish will come at the fly, splutter over it or near it, and retire without touching it. It cannot for a moment be entertained that the trout act thus unanimously with malice aforethought; there must be some reason underlying the sudden abandonment of intention, for, it must be agreed, they set out for the express purpose of securing food, of acquiring that which from a distance appears to be food, but which at closer range arouses suspicion.

Trout very seldom miss a natural fly; an individual now and then may, but on the whole it is correct to say that they make no mistake in aim. Deceived by erratic movements, variously caused, of the artificial fly, a trout quite often fails to secure the object of its earnest attack, but in very many cases the failure is intentional; the fish has had its suspicions suddenly aroused and quickly turns off its course. Something creates distrust; it may be the lifelessness of the lure, or some error in its shade, size or shape, and it may be, and generally is, the gut.* Stout, opaque gut, fine glittering gut, dark-stained gut will alarm the most eager fish; not always to the same extent will it deny the angler sport, but when the light is of a quality which renders the cast conspicuous, gut having any of these faults will produce complete failure. I consider that there is no part of the equipment more important than the cast to which the flies are attached; it should be of a faint, misty shade, and nothing stouter than 2x is ever really necessary in trout fishing. A finer quality still would generally suffice, provided always that it was equally inconspicuous, but invisibility is not an invariable concomitant of fineness. I think that in the strength suggested is found the best combination of the qualities required by the angler.

This missing of the fly is not a mood of loch-trout at all; they never are inclined to miss, but seeing that the instinct of self-preservation has not been withheld from them, they are enabled, under certain circumstances, to distinguish between real and unreal, and in consequence they refuse at the last moment what they hoped and expected to find acceptable. The journey from the depths is performed deliberately and with confidence; the movement at the surface is eloquent of alarm; the final retirement is precipitate.

We are accustomed to class as moods what are really not moods at all. The trout in our lochs have to take what is provided, whether it agrees with their inclinations or not. Hence we find them smutting, tailing and bulging, not so much because they are in the humour to indulge in these practices, but simply because there is nothing else for them to do. They might prefer a few substantial sedges to a myriad of tiny diptera, but they would rather feed than go hungry: so they take what comes. When they are scooping up the swarms of the Watery dun† or the hosts of smuts, when they grub among mud and weeds in search of larvae and snails, when they pursue the elusive nymphs, sport may not be so fast and furious as it is when they are sucking down the drifting ephemeridae or fluttering caddis-flies, but it can be highly interesting.

Too often loch-trout maintain an attitude of complete indifference towards food; they have the valuable faculty of being able to do without. In winter when for many days on end

* In the author's day only silkworm gut was available for casts – Ed.
† See footnote on page 96 – C.F.W.

91

supplies may be altogether withheld, it must be very comforting to possess such a power, but to exercise it during the fishing season means the defeat of the angler. Sometimes the weather conditions seem to promise great events; flies are numerous and not too abundant, and in all likelihood a variety of subaqueous forms is also available, but the trout will have none of them; no sign of life comes from the waters; in vain is all labour; the day drags on to its weary and welcome end, and not the slightest encouragement has been given to reward patience or recompense perseverance. There must, it would seem, continue to be some mystery inherent in fishing, something totally inexplicable. And what would it help us to know the cause when we must ever be unable to remove it? It is some consolation to know that the unhappy period must end sooner or later, perhaps at the approach of evening, and that is worth waiting for, the hopeful gloaming, for seldom indeed can the trout resist the appeal of blundering sedges or exhausted spinners. However, patience may have to be exercised still longer, because a chill wind may arise which forbids these flies to venture forth. Still the weary time must pass, but there is nothing we can do to speed its going.

Let us turn from these dull, uninteresting days, which are, after all, relatively infrequent, to the happiest times when the trout are in their most responsive mood. I mean the days, and the evenings, when duns emerge in little companies all over the loch, here and there, each a small centre of excitement. A fair breeze is blowing, just enough to keep the boat drifting slowly and steadily; a few strokes with the oars bring us within reach of another clump of rises, whenever one has been exhausted. Then the carefully anointed fly is delicately laid among the new-fledged insects, and the eye must mark it well to distinguish it from its competitors and to know when it is sucked below. The strike succeeds, for, of course, this is a lucky day; the trout fights well, but, this being a day of no failures, it in due course glides over the net.

I mean also those wonderful days when no flies, or very few, are in sight, when no rising fish are about, and the wet-fly cast is in use, those days when, the moment the lures alight, the water parts. These are great days. We do not know which cast is to succeed, nor when the sudden break is to come, but it comes often and suddenly. We expect it every cast, and yet it always comes unexpectedly. It is glorious sport, and though every success is really only an accident for which the angler can claim no great credit, still I like, and I think everyone must like, the loch-trout to be in that mood.

There are all sorts of days on the loch and many moods of the trout, and we need them all, the bad days and the irritating, tantalizing moods especially, for without them we could not appreciate at their true worth the crowded hours which do come to all of us now and then.

4 ENTOMOLOGY OF THE LOCH

IT is somewhat difficult to decide to what extent the angler should be versed in the entomology of the loch, but I think that most will agree that a little knowledge at least of the subject is essential. My own opinion is that the slow advance in the science and art of loch fishing is largely accounted for by the lack of interest displayed in the food of loch-trout. The loch used to be looked upon as the duffer's paradise; now it is often the expert's despair. Haphazard methods will no longer suffice. To go to extremes in the study of insect life would be very easy; nothing could be simpler than to overwhelm the angler with scientific nomenclature, and nothing could be more unnecessary. All that seems to be advisable for him meantime to know amounts to very little, but that little is important.

I consider that all should want to know what an imitative lure represents, for only then can they fish it properly. Should it represent no living creature and yet prove acceptable, certainly it would be interesting to learn to what special property its effectiveness is due. Why should one fly be quite ignored for an hour or two, while its rivals are excelling, and then suddenly begin to attract all attention to itself? Such a thing can be observed, the reason for it may be determined, and the lesson remembered and applied with effect on some future occasion. In fact, the more one thinks about the sport the greater is the pleasure derived from it. Those who fish the same set of flies on the cast the whole year through are, in my opinion, denying themselves a great pleasure, and that I would still assert, even although they could show that they catch quite as many trout as do other anglers who have much more respect for the sport. It is not possible for one to estimate the enjoyment of another, yet I feel sure that some study to find out what the trout want, and an endeavour, whether it results in success or failure, to satisfy their particular desires, will produce an increase of interest.

Consequently I believe that some acquaintance with the entomology of the loch is required. The angler, however, desires only so much, enough to enable him to fish intelligently, and, as a necessary consequence, with greater success. He has no wish, and he has no need, to become an expert entomologist. He wants to catch trout, not to acquire, after much laborious study, a multitude of scientific names, not to trouble himself with microscopic distinctions. He wants, for example, to be able to recognize at a glance, and name the different families of flies and know their characteristics, so that he may compare notes with his friends, and, in so doing, avoid confusion, which meantime, though simple to avoid, is very prevalent. In addition to that, acquaintance with a few species of each family will assist him considerably.

Loch flies may be divided, well enough for the angler's purpose, into three classes, viz, duns, caddis-flies and two-winged flies. They are readily distinguished from one another. (See *Trout Flies*, page 162 *et seq*, for detailed descriptions – Ed.)

I am convinced that it is owing principally to the lack of really satisfactory imitations of the larvae of duns and midges and also, to a smaller extent, to the fact that loch fishers have been rather easy to please with representations of winged flies, that there are so many comparatively poor days on the loch. As soon as artificials bearing a closer resemblance to the living creatures are available, all that remains to ensure a great increase of sport is a general knowledge of the method of using them. The river fisher has beautiful, lifelike copies of flies to use. Why is the loch fisher so easily satisfied? There are many days on the loch on which not a trout is seen breaking the surface, and flies on such occasions may be present and they may not; some of these days are quite good from an angling point of view and some are bad. Those that are good would be very much better if we could make and use the right type of lure, while the blank days would become very exceptional.

Let us examine now the most important species, importance

94

being determined by their abundance, distribution and the welcome accorded them by the trout. I have fished and caught fish on the fly in nearly a hundred Scottish lochs, and in all but a very few of them I have found one member of the ephemeridae or duns represented, viz the Olive dun. This is all the more remarkable in that I have visited these lochs just as opportunity offered, and not at any special time, not for the purpose of, or in expectation of, finding Olive duns, but with the intention of fishing.

I have almost come to the conclusion that this fly is native to every loch in Scotland. How often is it represented on the fly-cast? I think very seldom. Yet from the beginning of May, and sometimes before that, down to the end of the season, the fly may be on the surface, or its nymph may be active beneath the surface, any day and on most lochs. The entomologist will probably say that under the title of Olive dun I am including a dozen, or perhaps more, different species of duns,* but the trout have not learned that yet. Until they do, what is known as the Medium Olive on the river will in most cases prove sufficient for the loch. Sometimes and in some places a hatch of dark-coloured Olives occurs, and a large, handsome fly it is, a favourite, too, with the trout. It is well worth knowing and imitating with greater approach to exactness than is aimed at in Greenwell's Glory. In summer a pale variety appears in some lochs, and, wherever plentiful, it should be attended to also.

For dry-fly fishing on the river, beautiful dressings have been devised. These will serve equally well on the loch for the same purpose; the size may be left unaltered, or it may be slightly increased as the angler decides. I do not think that any change is necessary. For wet-fly fishing there will be required a certain modification to ensure a good entry into the water, an easy undisturbing passage through it, and a tendency to sink slightly. If the upright wings of the floating pattern are tied down, all that is needed is at once accomplished. There is another alternative. The material for the wing may be tied on in a bunch, split, and then well thrown back with the tying silk. The fly should then be used as a bob-fly. That is, I think, the best method of winging a bob-fly and, so dressed, the Olive would prove a serviceable substitute for the Butcher, which, however, still remains my favourite for that important position.

* There are only two lake species: the pond and lake Olives – C.F.W.

There is another member of the family of duns which is indigenous to many lochs and reservoirs, a fly which comes out on calm, warm evenings of June and July, sometimes in myriads. I refer to the Pale Watery dun. I have heard it often spoken of as the White Moth. It is, of course, not a moth at all, nor has it any resemblance to one. These mistakes lead to great confusion, and render necessary at least some slight knowledge of insect life.

Few can have missed seeing the Pale Watery dun,* and no insect gives one a better opportunity of witnessing the transformation from one winged state to another. The little creatures are fond of choosing the angler's clothes as the place whereon to effect the change; that is not so bad, but when they select his hands or his face, there is certainly some discomfort, for they have to take a grip with their feet before they can succeed in extricating themselves.

My experience is that the trout pay little heed to the duns, which appear only on hot days when the fish are apt to be indifferent to food, surface-food at any rate. When the sun sets, the trout begin to move more freely about; at the same time the dying spinners crowd the water. Consequently the angler should imitate the spinner, which he can do fairly well by means of a wingless fly dressed with a very soft hackle; and he must fish it dry. The trout swim close to the surface, scooping up the flies as they go, until the water may, with some reason, be said to be 'boiling'. As the flies lie with their wings outstretched and flat on the surface, they are difficult to see, unless one looks vertically down upon them.

I think that the Olives and the Pale Watery duns are all of that family that the angler need attend to meantime. That may seem very little, but seeing that up to the present no attention has been paid to them except by an angler here and there, it amounts to a great deal, and they have provided us with several patterns whose capabilities can be depended upon, or the reason for whose existence has been suggested. These patterns are Medium Olive, Greenwell's Glory, Blae and Yellow, and to represent the Pale Watery dun, the Blue Hen Hackle. To these I should add the Rough Olive. It is a superb fly, serving a double purpose; it represents a dun very well, and is at the same time an excellent imitation of one of the smaller caddis-flies.

* Evidently refers to *Caenis* spp mistaken for P.W.D.s – C.F.W.

There must also be included a reproduction of the Olive nymph.

When we come to consider the great family of caddis-flies, two difficulties are met. In the first place it is not easy to decide which species should be omitted and which selected; secondly, for several deserving of being chosen, satisfactory names, known to the general body of anglers, seem to be a-wanting. The members of the family are very numerous; more than 200 species, it is said, are known in this country, and these are spread over every type of clean water, running and still. Trout must, therefore, know them very well, and some of the favourite loch-patterns are, it is clear, based on caddis-flies. The scientific names of the various species would prove of little benefit to the angler, who, therefore, must use another method. Some he recognizes by the shade of wing in the natural insect, eg the Cinnamon Sedge; others he names and knows from the artificials and the materials used in their manufacture. The latter is perhaps a curious method to adopt, but it suffices for the purpose; it may sound absurd to hear that there was a fine hatch of Grouse and Greens on the loch, but an angler will know quite well what is meant. A similar use of some common names would be still more ridiculous.

Probably the best-known species is the large caddis-fly, which no fisher who stays late on the loch in June can have failed to see. It seems to be known also on every reservoir. Unfortunately it is commonly, but erroneously, called the stone-fly by club members and others. In size, perhaps, but in no other particular does it resemble the great stone-fly (*Perla maxima*) of the river. Stone-flies are only of slight importance to the loch fisher, as the natural insects will be found only off the mouths of tributary streams. This caddis-fly rises straight from the bed of the loch,* and many a one is gulped down just as it reaches the surface; probably more, therefore, are seized in the depths; others again live to flutter about on the water for a time, but their career is apt to be cut short. Quite early in the evening an occasional specimen may arrive, towards the gloaming they become more plentiful, and during the darkness heavy plops far out on the loch tell that fine trout, which would look well in the basket, are busy welcoming the latecomers.

A caddis-fly that I have seen on many lochs is well imitated by the Woodcock and Black. It seems to prefer the vicinity of

* In the pupal state. The adult emerges on the surface – C.F.W.

old wooden piers and ancient boats. The Corncrake Sedge, Cinnamon Sedge, Woodcock and Yellow, Grouse and Green are all good. Cinnamon and Gold, a favourite fly with many, is probably modelled on a caddis-fly, but it lacks one of the principal characteristics – viz, a stout, hairy body; the likelihood, therefore, is that the pattern owes its deadliness to some other property, perhaps the glittering, arresting gold.

Of two-winged flies the most important is that known as the Blae and Black. I have found it on every loch and throughout the whole of the fishing season. There must be many species included under the one title, differing only in minute particulars.* They are all the same in colouring; the wings vary much in length and the flies in size. I have seen a hatch which had long, substantial bodies and, to all appearance, wholly inadequate wings. The artificials, Black Midge, Black Gnat, Colonel Downman, Lord Saltoun, are all representations of the same insect. They sometimes hatch out very strongly and very early in the year. I have seen Loch Fad in Bute and Loch Ard absolutely covered in places with the empty shucks of the flies, and in various lochs I have caught trout filled to the teeth with the nymphs.† Couligartan Bay in Loch Ard seems to be particularly well adapted to the development of these flies. I think that the nymph should receive most of our attention, as the fly after emergence takes to the air; some species are very retiring, clinging to the leaves of bushes round the loch-side; others sport high under trees; and I have met them often, true water-born flies, a long distance away from the loch where they were hatched. To the water, however, they return to lay their eggs, and therefore the perfect fly is also worthy of imitation.

There is another member of this group deserving of notice, and, as my introduction to it was somewhat curious, I may be permitted to go into details. Once on Loch Leven at the beginning of June I found the water most plentifully supplied with a small, bright, green beetle, which the trout took freely. The creatures were all over the place; they came from the trees in Cavilstone Strip. I determined to make an imitation in readiness for the following year, and I did so, giving it a body of green wool and finishing with a small red hackle to float it, for my intention was to fish it dry. Unfortunately the next year, when

* This no doubt refers to the family Chironomidae – C.F.W.
† He is probably referring to the pupae – C.F.W.

I was all ready for the fray, the beetles did not oblige by putting in an appearance. Accordingly I did not use the new pattern, but a friend of mine, to whom I gave a copy, did, and scored one or two successes.

Since then, however, I have used this fly with great results on several lochs, and in time I discovered the reason for its power. The lure that was intended to imitate a green beetle, an accidental visitor to only a few lochs, is a much better imitation of the larva* of the Green Midge, an inhabitant of many lochs. I have caught the living larva itself, compared it with the artificial, and the result is an improvement on the pattern, the red hackle being replaced by one of blue dun. I believe that the deadliness of Teal and Green, which, by the way, seems to be peculiarly fascinating to big trout, is due to its resemblance to this same fly, and is in spite of its addition of teal wing. Some time ago I was interested to learn that a similar fly is used on Blagdon, made in imitation of the same insect, which fact takes away some of the satisfaction experienced.

That completes the list of flies which meantime seem to me to be sufficient and necessary for the loch fisher to know. Besides flies there are many other inhabitants of the loch which supply the trout with food. The most valuable of these, and, at the same time, that which lends itself most easily to imitation, is the freshwater shrimp. I have tried copies of it in various materials; the best the angler can look at is made from celluloid, but its density causes it to sink too vertically in the still waters of the loch; it is not possible to give it a lifelike action, and I have never found the trout taking it well. A Red Palmer or a March Brown Spider will give far more efficient service; in the water these suggest a shrimp for me, and I think that the trout takes these lures in mistake for shrimps.

5 ARTIFICIAL LOCH-FLIES

IN this discussion I propose to consider first those artificials which I intend to be, or take to be, copies of natural insects, and to follow that by an examination of other lures the efficiency of which justifies their existence, but whose powers of attraction

* More probably the pupa – C.F.W.

are due to some more elusive property than a resemblance to some form of food partaken of by loch-trout.

The tail-position of the cast is the most important of all and, therefore, deserves the greatest attention. The lure that occupies that place has the least amount of gut in its neighbourhood; it is comparatively free in its movements; with it, aim is generally taken when an opportunity of covering a rise is granted. Because it reaches a greater depth than any other fly on the cast, it should represent some subaqueous creature, a nymph, larva or shrimp; and, as its position confers many advantages upon it, the imitation should be as good as can be procured.

Making use of an old, well-known method employed in the imitation of various beetles which trout are in the habit of seeing and feeding upon, I had dressed for me a few patterns of nymphs in which the wing-cases of the living creatures were suggested by folding back and tying down part of the hackle. I experimented with these for the greater part of a season, but the results did not come up to my first expectations. I do not think they ever failed entirely, and on two or three very poor fishing days they brought me a few trout, when other lures did not score at all; they on no occasion did really well. Others who tried them express themselves highly satisfied; the lures were successful on reservoirs in the Isle of Man, and on Northern lochs and rivers some friends had exceptional sport with them. I was, however, disappointed with them, and, in an endeavour to find reasons for their indifferent reception, I examined their action and behaviour in the water; they are not buoyant enough, their passage through the water is laboured, not free and easy and suggestive of life. Consequently I have dispensed with the wing-cases altogether; that is to say, a relatively unimportant feature has been sacrificed in order to obtain a much more desirable property, an essential in every lure – viz, liveliness. In this I was partly influenced by the wonderful success of the Green Spider and have modelled all nymphs on that lure, which had now better be called the Green Nymph.

Three patterns are required, olive, black and green, and their dressings are as follows:

Olive Nymph – Body of swan herl dyed medium olive, ribbed with finest gold; hackle and tail of olive hen.

Green Nymph – Body of swan herl dyed apple-green, ribbed with finest gold; hackle and tail of blue hen.

Black Nymph – Body of black ostrich herl, ribbed with fine silver; hackle and tail of soft, dark-speckled guinea hen.

There are two other claimants for the tail position, viz what I take to be imitations of the shrimp, the March Brown Spider and Red Palmer.

If the cast carries four flies any one of the first four mentioned may be used for the first dropper as well as for the tail.

As for the method of using these lures, it must be evident that any virtues they possess cannot be displayed, unless to them is imparted the appropriate movement. Nymphs progress with an undulating motion, rising and falling; shrimps pass a great deal of their time under stones along the edge of the loch and among weeds, but they emerge sometimes, and then their movements are, or seem to be, erratic. These actions, therefore, have to be imitated.

Let us suppose now that rising fish are nowhere seen, a very common state of affairs. It does not seem sensible to persist with imitations of winged flies, when the trout are very obviously not feeding on flies. Someone may say that he has often had an excellent basket with winged flies under precisely the circumstances as are being considered. That is quite possible, and proves, if it proves anything, that the sport would have been very much superior, had the cast carried one or two professing nymphs instead of flies which, on being drawn through the water, had their wings pressed over the body, and so acquired a fair resemblance to nymphs. It would certainly be better to use imitations of what the trout may be feeding upon than copies of what they are evidently not taking. Even so there is still room on the cast for one or two ordinary loch patterns, if the angler feels he must have them.

There is still another case to consider, by far the most interesting of all. Now and then a trout may be seen making a fine boil on the surface, but if the angler will watch carefully for a time over a small area he may find not a single fly floating on it, and yet he may see the same welcome sight of a feeding fish again. The trout are following up ascending nymphs,* and sometimes seize them just as they are on the point of escaping

* Or pupae – C.F.W.

into the air. That seems to be a favourite moment for the event, but we are justified in concluding that, if a few are taken then and there, many victims fall beneath the surface without any swirl to mark their going. It is at such times that the nymph scores best.

The selection of pattern does not offer great difficulty; an examination of the surface, a stirring-up of the bushes along the shore, an inspection of the mouth of a lucky capture may, any one of them, disclose the secret. The Black Nymph may be the correct one to use from the very beginning of the season, the Olive from the end of April, and the Green from June onwards. The shrimps may be tried at any time; they seem nearly always able to attract a fish, but I think their best time is the earlier part of a summer evening.

The intermediate position or positions on the cast are those which the angler generally finds the most difficult to fill. Much depends on the individual and on his particular method of working the lures. He may fish his flies high in the water, or he may prefer to keep them low; in the latter case, and also if his cast carries four flies, he should, as suggested already, use one of the patterns described above. In other cases his choice, restricted meanwhile though it be to imitative lures, is fairly wide, consisting of Blae and Black, Corncrake Sedge, Cinnamon Sedge, Woodcock and Yellow, Blae and Yellow. As between the last two, especially after they have had a few journeys through the water, there cannot be any appreciable difference, he is left with four from which to make his selection, and it should not be difficult to arrive at a decision. The flies on the water, the period of the year and the time of day will influence and assist him. Generally the sedges or caddis-flies may be reserved for summer evenings, but should the natural flies appear during the day, the angler ought at once to accept the hint. The last of these five flies might, without much, if any, sacrifice, be discarded altogether.

We come now to discuss the bob-fly, only less in importance and luring power to the tail-fly; in fact on some days it is by far the most valuable on the cast. In the candidates for this position, it being understood, of course, that the bob-fly is to be used as such and not worked simply like one of the lower lures, there is one indispensable qualification; they must all be representations of fully developed flies. There is no doubt that the four patterns just given could be used for this purpose, but my experience is that a fly dressed with its wings spread and tied well back is infinitely superior to any other as a bob-fly. On this matter I have no doubts, having been convinced by the results of long-continued trials conducted both when trout were rising and when they were not. Of course Blae and Black and its rivals could be dressed in the same way, so imitating flies struggling to escape from the wave, in which case their wings would be extended, and I have not the slightest uncertainty as to the result of such an experiment, but I think that these patterns are already fully employed. The best bob-flies I can suggest are Greenwell's Glory, Medium Olive and Rough Olive, copies of the commonest duns.

Now the angler may be kind enough to say that what I have said sounds very reasonable, but he is almost certain to complain that some of his greatest favourites have received no mention. So it is with some of mine, and I intend to include them. I cannot account, with complete satisfaction to myself, for their undoubted acceptability, but, though the exact cause be withheld, it is something to be thankful for that the effects are known.

There is, for example, Peter Ross, which for various reasons is entitled to be taken first. I have not yet discovered a tail-fly which is more uniformly good; from the beginning of the season on to its end, any day that trout can be interested at all, that fly will kill fish for me. It has been suggested by some that it resembles a blood-worm, the larva of one of the midges, and by others a shrimp. If either of these is the reason for its deadliness, then there is no need for us to strive after imitations, and all respect for trout must immediately vanish. Now, I think that it is advisable for us to believe that trout are not so easily deceived, that they are entitled to great respect; if fishers do not believe that, they admit that they have little respect for themselves. A close imitation is necessary in some patterns; there are reasons why it should not be so essential in others.

Peter Ross occupies the best position on the cast. It rises and falls in the water; it darts and glides and hesitates; it suggests to a hungry or inquisitive trout nothing in particular perhaps, but something living – that is, something to be killed. And this reason alone is enough to make any feathered lure prove fatal now and then, provided that its size and brilliancy are not sufficient to make a trout flee in terror. There must, therefore, be some other reason for the greatness of Peter Ross. I am sure that the parti-coloured body of the fly is to a large extent responsible for its effectiveness; it will, as the lure moves along, changing its position relatively to the trout and to the light, alter its appearance, and from time to time emit the flash which arrests attention. That seems to me to be the chief explanation of the deadliness of this and of many another so-called fly.

If the suggested reason for the acceptability of this lure is the correct one, then it is not possible to place so much dependence on it as on another fly, which appears to the trout to be some familiar form of food, and which at the same time, be it noted, can be made to give forth attracting signals, though perhaps to a smaller degree, just as more fancy patterns do. The angler, therefore, while retaining Peter Ross for use on doubtful days, would be better served on occasions by one or other of the tail-flies described.

The Grouse and Claret, a favourite of many, should, if used at all, be the first dropper. It is not, so far as I have been able to discover, an imitative lure, and therefore its reception cannot be expected to be uniform. It actually glows in the water, and to this property no doubt its fascination for trout is at least partly due.

Teal and Green, an excellent tail-fly, does not quite belong to the same category as Peter Ross. I have before suggested that it owes its power to the similarity that exists between it and the larva of the green midge. As it may, however, rely on some other property still unknown to me, and as it is a proved killer from June onwards, I think it should be included in the stock of loch-flies.

That brings us to what is probably the most deadly loch-fly ever invented, viz, the Butcher. Dressed with split wings well laid back, used on the bob, and made to trip across the waves, it is an exceedingly reliable fly on every loch that I have fished. It does well among rising trout, provided there is a fair breeze; its powers seem to become greater under sunshine except, of course, on Loch Leven. Even when trout are not breaking the surface at all, it is able to bring them up, and I think that, on these occasions, the fish are eagerly watching for flies. For this conclusion I can give no adequate reason; perhaps the Butcher happens to be just sufficiently conspicuous to excite curiosity without arousing suspicion. In any case it is very deadly. If winged in the ordinary way it is quite a good tail-fly, and used by many in this position with considerable effect.

Besides these there are dozens of other patterns all very lovely to look upon, and all capable no doubt of exciting the predatory instincts of trout, but not, one would imagine, likely to arouse the desire to eat. They are really too numerous to mention. I have possessed them, used them when in despair, killed trout with them, but I think that their usefulness is not of the same pronounced type as their beauty. Perhaps some anglers find one or more of them generally effective; it may be that they can put them through the correct evolutions, or that they know the conditions which bring out their peculiar qualities. These are certainly possibilities, but I have never happened to hear anyone say very much in favour of these lures.

It must be apparent that no fly can be worked correctly at all stages of the draw; that is an argument in favour of using more than one fly on the cast. When the lures alight on the water, at that moment they will all appear to the trout as flies just arrived from the air, and for such may be taken. As soon as that moment passes, the lures begin to sink, for the angler generally pauses, and should pause, before proceeding to bring them towards the boat. He is not only preparing for the backward cast, he is also fishing his flies. He may draw them slowly or quickly, at a uniform pace or in a series of jerks, by raising the rod, or by pulling in line with the left hand, or by an application of both methods simultaneously. Supposing that there are four flies on the cast, the lower two will be behaving more or less after the manner of nymphs and shrimps, while the remaining two will appear as flies, for the trout is probably unable to tell whether a fly is on, above or just below the surface. After a time the bob-fly reaches the top, and it alone is then fished; it is to the trout a fly making efforts to escape from the water. Many of the rises to the bob are wild, or rather they only appear to be wild, the fish in their eagerness overshooting the mark or, troubled by reflections, making a mistake in aim. Soon the rod loses command of the fly and another delivery must be made.

I might try to give the angler some assistance in making up his cast of flies. It would offer no difficulty whatever to suggest a serviceable cast for any given period of the year, but to prescribe a really good one is only possible on the particular day and after being afloat for some time on the loch; even then the cast would almost certainly require some alteration during the day. Any cast he makes up should be looked upon as an experimental cast, subject to modification at the slightest hint from the water, from a capture, from even an offer. I must, therefore, content myself with an attempt to indicate the general principles on which he should go.

In the first place, he should not have a cast all fitted up for the day's work; instead in a damper he ought to have a few casts with dropper-points attached ready at once to take the lures that seem the best. It always surprises me, at Loch Leven for example, where it is easy to notice what is going on, to see anglers taking a cast of flies from the damper and attaching it to the line before they set sail. As they are rowed out to the drift they trail the flies behind or cast them out from the boat. When that is the procedure, where was the benefit of having the cast in a damper? It would pay them far better to examine the water as they go along, to keep a look-out for flies, or watch the surface for shucks of flies that have but lately hatched out. After a decision is reached, it should not take two minutes to fix on the flies. He should know exactly what they are and the positions they occupy; there may be one or more of which he is more doubtful than the rest.

He should then fish not only with a view to catching trout, but also for the purpose of finding out if his deductions are correct, and with the intention of changing whenever they seem to have been wrong. When the trout are coming with satisfactory freedom, he is generally loath to spend time in making changes; if he will take careful note of the flies that are making the captures, he is almost sure to discover that one is meeting with less acceptance than the others, while it may be entirely ignored. In such a case he should have no hesitation in replacing it by another. Of course I have seen a fly long-neglected coming into its own at last, so that I cannot always have followed my own advice; to one that knows a certain loch and its flies well such an occurrence is not entirely accidental, but in most cases it is not sensible to persist with a lure that is temporarily out of favour.

6 THE DRY-FLY ON THE LOCH

As a lure for the loch-trout the floating fly cannot compare in general usefulness with the wet-fly, but there are particular occasions on which it is infinitely superior, and these times are much less infrequent than is commonly supposed.

With the exception of only a few, which rejoice in an abundance of fly-life, in which strong hatches recur day after day over a long period of the year, our lochs offer at most times very slight inducement to the trout to feed on the surface. The fish, therefore, are compelled to find by far the greater portion of their food in the depths, and it is only when a sufficient hatch of flies occurs that they can be persuaded to cease for a time their attack on subaqueous forms. That being so, anglers should decide their methods by the behaviour of the trout, and should use the wet-fly when the fish are not showing themselves and the dry-fly when a rise is in progress. Since the nature of the food available varies, or, rather, since floating food is occasionally provided, it follows that methods may require to be changed, perhaps several times in the course of a day; and it is this necessity for changing that is principally accountable for the slow adoption of the dry-fly by the loch fisher.

When he sets sail on the loch, there usually lies before him the prospect of a fine, long, uninterrupted drift under a good breeze. The probability is that, at the start, few flies are on the water and few fish are showing, for that is the general state of affairs. A cast of wet-flies is therefore put up and used hopefully enough for a time, and perhaps quite successfully. During the course of the drift a trout may be seen to rise within casting distance, but it is not likely that he will at once change to the dry-fly. The opportunity of covering a clear mark may have been long delayed: another may not come for a long time, and therefore an attempt is made to lure the fish with the wet-flies. I certainly would not change in these circumstances, for there is not the slightest doubt that a wet-fly thrown at once over the rise is better than the daintiest fly cast after the lapse of a minute or two. A second invitation of the same kind, following soon afterwards, should be accepted in the same way. If these attempts succeed, the angler is doing very well; he is not tempted to change, and so he persists with the wet-fly. I think that he is making a mistake. He should conclude from these signs that the trout are willing to come to the surface, that the only thing preventing a hearty, general rise is a scarcity of flies. Some of my best days with the dry-fly have been had under exactly the conditions described – that is to say, when flies on the surface were few but were being freely taken.

On the other hand, flies may hatch strongly and the rise become very pronounced; the species occasioning the rise may be easily ascertained; a fine copy of it may rest in the fly box; but even then no change in method may be made. It is not difficult to appreciate the unwillingness of an angler to alter his tactics, even when the conditions clearly indicate that an alteration is highly advisable. Changes take time to effect, and to spend time otherwise than in fishing when fish are rising is none too easy. He does not know whether the rise is to last an hour or two, or only a few minutes; he should not trouble himself with such speculations, but instead, at the first appearance of a general rise, he should change to the floating fly with the minimum of delay, and he will enjoy for some time, long or short, as the case may be, sport such as the wet-fly could not yield under these conditions.

The prevailing impression is that the dry-fly is restricted in its use to the calm, unruffled loch. It is true that, when trout are rising in a calm, they are more readily taken by a floating fly than by any other means; but that is not the lure's only opportunity. It should be used whenever the trout are taking fully developed flies.

Fishing the floating fly on a loch, when the trout are not rising, is apt to be a monotonous way of spending time. There is so little for the angler to do; he casts, leaves the fly floating, and casts again; if the sequence is interrupted now and then by a kill or even a rise, of course there is no complaint. Still the variety of treatment that may be given to the wet-fly is absent. I have shed the dry-fly often in such circumstances, mainly after the other lure had proved to have absolutely no attractions, and sometimes in consequence I have obtained sport. The angler should put into practice the same methods as he adopts when confronted on the river with similar conditions – that is, when he is obliged to 'fish the stream'. Over known haunts of trout in a familiar loch, for instance, over shallows near the bank and far out from shore, along the edge of reed-beds, in the vicinity of weed-patches, across the mouths of tributaries, casting at a venture may often be attended with pleasing results, simply because a fly floating on the surface is quite an expected and common sight in such places. It looks like a natural fly, and if a breeze curls the water it may be promptly taken, more readily than a sunk fly might be. On a poor day, when hope is apt to dwindle away, the dry-fly is worth at least a short trial, if for no other reason than that it helps to renew the angler's interest and delays the wandering of his thoughts towards the miseries of trolling.

For dry-fly fishing on the loch the line must be well greased to make it float; if that is not done, the fly drags along the surface as the line sinks. If the water is calm, this preliminary treatment cannot be dispensed with, but, when trout are rising well in a breeze, it is not so necessary, though still advisable. The loch fisher brings forward an objection to preparing his line in this way, viz., that it becomes unsatisfactory for wet-fly fishing, for, when that method is tried, the lures must sometimes be allowed to sink well, and the floating line to some extent prevents that being effected. If the trout are coming high, the objection vanishes; in fact the line is an assistance, in that the slightest change in direction from one side to another or the faintest hesitation in its advance betrays an offering fish, while it also permits the strike to act very quickly. No doubt, the most satisfactory arrangement is to have two rods prepared and in readiness; that offers comparatively little difficulty when the angler is fishing from the bank or has the boat to himself, but otherwise the best plan he could adopt is to have his line prepared for dry-fly fishing, and to use it, with its advantages and its disadvantages, for the wet-fly, when circumstances appear to declare that the better lure.

Whenever he sees a rise, at no matter what part of the loch, he should try to determine whether the feeding trout is stationary or travelling, for according to his decision must his subsequent procedure be. The loch-trout is given to roaming in quest of food, but there are many which, having acquired some specially good post situated in a land of plenty, do their best to retain it against all comers. These fortunate creatures do not wander far from home. Sometimes it is easy to say whether a fish is on the trail or settled down; at other times it is difficult; but these things are already known to the wet-fly fisher who has had the same problem to solve many a time. The attempt at solution is always interesting, and when the floating fly, suddenly disappearing in a fine swirl, shows that the solution was correct, satisfaction is supreme.

The dry-fly season on the loch generally starts in average years about the end of April, when flies begin to hatch out freely. Of course before that the Blae and Black may be plentiful, should be, in fact; but, as I have already pointed out, these flies do not frequent the water so much as one would expect, though a few are usually to be seen riding the waves; their number, however, is infinitesimal as compared with the enormous masses of empty shucks that may be seen floating on the surface even in March. When the Dark Olives* appear, the trout never ignore them; it is fine to see these handsome flies on a breezy day sweeping across the water and watch the fish plunging after them, but the less wind the more sport for the rod. Even on cold days they may come; any day the dry-fly may be accorded a hearty welcome.

In May the Olive duns† arrive in strength, and thereafter may be confidently looked for in suitable weather down to the end of the season; in the earlier part temperature seems to determine their appearance, sunshine and warmth being apparently to their liking, but later they are quite to be expected on less cheerful days. They do not, of course, always hatch out in the same numbers, and often they, unfortunately, do not appear at all, but the possibility that they will be the sole cause of trout rising should never be overlooked. The best results to the floating Olive are obtained, I think, when the natural insects arrive in detachments, at intervals throughout the day and in various parts of the loch; sport is then intermittent in character, the quiet periods serving only to make the fruitful times the more enjoyable. By watching carefully the conduct of martins and swallows, as well as the less easily tolerated sea-gulls, one may discover where hatches are occurring in distant bays, and in this way more complete advantage may be taken of the opportunities.

When June comes, the necessity for the dry-fly becomes more pronounced. Any calm evening may find the loch covered with Pale Watery Spinners‡ when the floating fly will alone be the means of persuading a trout into the creel. A slight breeze at gloaming and a hatch of caddis-flies ensure a glorious hour; but,

Probably: * Pond Olives. † Lake Olives. ‡ *Caenis* spp – C.F.W.

let it be well remembered, even on the most inauspicious evening there is almost certain to be a brief period, perhaps lasting only a few minutes, when the angler will begin to take particular care in his casting. The feeling comes to him that something is about to happen, and in this he is seldom mistaken. It comes to everyone; some inexplicable intuition it may be, and yet there always seems to be some difference in the atmosphere, so subtle that he scarcely dares to mention it; still it comes, and with it comes the expected rise.

As the season approaches its close, good fishing days come but seldom, and the angler sometimes finds it difficult to lure a trout. Light airs and brilliant skies are common in August and September; on many days the wet-fly proves unable to deceive and the floating fly becomes more and more useful. Caddis-flies are plentiful even by day, and, in a fair breeze, their representations are at times well received. In calm weather duns take quickly to the air, and undergo their last great change; it is therefore generally spinners that induce the trout to rise, and then hackled artificials will be found more attractive than the fully winged types.

As for the dry-fly patterns, the angler should make sure that he has an abundant and varied stock of Olives, for greater detail is advisable in dry-flies than in those intended to be fished wet. It is very unlikely that a trout is able to distinguish differences in shade of wings of flies floating on the surface, but the angler can, and it gives him confidence when he sees that his artificial is a good copy in every particular of the natural insects with which it is competing. For this reason he should aim at obtaining the closest approximation possible to an exact imitation. I think those of Olives are required all three shades – dark, medium and light. The Rough Olive is also a splendid dry-fly pattern. Greenwell's Glory, while somewhat of a nondescript, is still worthy of retention on account of its general similarity to various dark duns, to imitate which exactly might not be practicable.

For evening fishing in summer, when the trout are cruising among the fallen hosts of Pale Watery Spinners,* the Blue Hen Spider is really excellent, or, perhaps more correctly, the best pattern that I have tried. Another very useful fly is the Badger Hackle; its turn comes when the tiny diptera, minute varieties of the Blae and Black, are thick on the water. These

*More probably *Caenis* spinners – C.F.W.

two flies are often present at the same time, for both select the same sort of conditions for their excursions, viz, calm, hot weather. For very gentle breezes, hackle-flies, light and buoyant, are to be preferred to the heavier winged patterns; they fall very softly on the water, hovering often in the air before they settle down; it is a pleasure to fish with them, they are so deadly and so dainty.

Caddis-flies will be sufficiently represented by the Corncrake Sedge and Cinnamon Sedge, exactly the same as those recommended for wet-fly fishing. There are, of course, very many members of this family, but those mentioned should, on all but rare occasions, prove to resemble closely enough any species present to meet with a good response.

The time has come when the floating fly is a requisite lure for the loch, and no angler should delay realizing the fact; the longer he postpones acquiring the few necessary additions to his equipment and undertaking the very slight practice demanded, the longer he will be in experiencing the joys that the loch is ready to provide.

7 TACTICS ON THE LOCH

THE time-honoured advice given to the loch fisher, 'Keep the flies on the water', is thoroughly sound, for there is no doubt that sheer hard work has put many a trout into the creel, and on certain days, or for certain periods of each day, will alone have that desired result. The more opportunities the fish have of seeing the lures, or, rather, the more fish that are given a view of them, the greater is the likelihood that some will succumb to their attractions. Continuous casting accompanied by undivided attention to the work in hand, must obtain its reward, not perhaps commensurate with the energy expended, yet greater than would accrue from less work performed in the same way.

A reward, however, which demands from the angler a complete detachment from his environment, is one involving a sacrifice far too great. A few – I think there must be very few – may be totally beyond the influence of the sights and sounds of the loch, may measure their enjoyment merely by the number of the slain, and may be quite indifferent as to methods of capture. We all like to catch trout, for that is the real purpose of fishing; but some of us refuse to be contented with a monotonous repetition of the old, tiresome system, cast after cast in endless succession to no point in particular and every one the exact counterpart of its predecessor; we want to know why one fly is taken and another refused, why a cast in a certain direction is preferred before all others, why one method of working the lures finds greater favour than another, why variations in acceptability occur from day to day. We may not yet know all these things, but we can think about them, put our conclusions to the test, and, whether they prove right or wrong, the interest of fishing is already materially increased. It must be admitted that on occasions one must consent either to indulge in casting in hope of an accident or to cease fishing altogether, but it is so long before one is called upon to make the choice that the uninteresting period is much reduced in length; it may even be eliminated sometimes as, before the experimental investigation is completed, the trout may have been aroused out of their lethargy and show clearly their desires.

It is time, however, to come to the subject, and in the first place let us consider good fishing days – that is to say, days on which all the anglers on the loch catch some trout. It is when the trout are in taking humour and the fishing conditions are difficult that anglers separate themselves according to their proficiency with the rod, their acquaintance with the loch, their knowledge of lures and methods and their powers of making and using conclusions from experience or observation. I consider that perhaps the most valuable power the loch fisher can possess is the ability to cover a rise neatly in calm and breeze alike, at whatever angle to the boat it occurs, not after studied deliberation, but without the slightest hesitation. This may require instant shortening or lengthening of the line, and demands an immediate decision and execution, the entire lack of preliminary trials or false casts such as the dry-fly fisher is recommended to indulge in; but before such an acquisition can be his, he must undertake some practice. On the river, it is sometimes necessary to give the rising fish time to regain its original position, but in the loch, so far as my experience goes, in the great majority of cases the artificial cannot be laid too quickly on the spot from which the natural insect has just been removed.

Being thoroughly convinced of the great efficacy of promptitude combined with the utmost accuracy and delicacy, I have spent many hours in practising casting over rises real and imaginary, not straight down wind, of course, but all round the boat, and the belief is continually being more firmly established that many fine trout would not have found their way into the basket when they did, had I been content with casts so simple that they need no training. Some anglers, who have been doing such things so often and for so many years that they have forgotten that there was a time when they were not accomplished in the art, may consider that the matter is not worth mentioning. Neither is it to the expert, but the beginner, who has his attention drawn to it, and takes the trouble, however slight or great he may find it, to acquire it, will find his sport and the interest of his sport largely augmented. A word of warning may be advisable: when the sudden break appears on the surface, the eager angler is very liable to throw his flies on the water, instead of which he should, of course, allow them to flutter delicately down over the critical spot.

As usual, an exception must be noted. In the case of travelling fish, cruising leisurely about in search of food or progressing at speed, obviously a cast over the mark will bring no answering rise, but the rule as to quickness still holds, the great difference being that the flies must be laid at the estimated distance across the course and not to a point. An error in judgement may not prove fatal as another guide may be furnished, and another cast, and sometimes more than one cast, may be possible before the opportunity is gone for ever. When the feeding fish occupies a definite post, however, the first cast is the only hopeful one, and, if neatly performed and in time, the result should doubly please the angler, for he feels, and is entitled to feel, that it has been brought about by his efforts, not by some stroke of fortune.

No opportunity of covering a rising trout should be neglected; even although the fish appears to be considerably beyond the angler's distance, he should make the attempt. With the help of a fair breeze an astonishing length of line can be cast and shed. I expect that many do not know how far the tail-fly reaches; until I realized it, I have on occasions found myself pulling off line and making haste to cover a rise only to learn suddenly that the fish was already hooked. It must not be forgotten that, as the boat drifts before the wind, the distance between the angler and the feeding trout is every moment being reduced; and it does take a few seconds to recover, extend and deliver the line. A loch-trout apparently can see a fly 2 or 3 ft away from it and, moreover, appears willing to come the distance; nevertheless an accurate shot, exactly on the target, is infinitely to be preferred. The angler certainly ought to try everything within his radius, in front of, and also even behind, the boat; he knows he is over a feeding fish, he is prepared for the rise and the answering strike, and consequently, if the offer is forthcoming, an acceptance in all probability follows.

Some anglers rejoice in the possession of a faculty which, though it may be fairly common, is certainly not universal: they are immediately aware of a rise, even a delicate, silent rise, to right or left of them. Many can see none but those rises which occur in close proximity to the line of their cast; several are able to see only those boiling eddies which are apparent even to the non-angler. Besides these obvious disturbances there are others, quiet rises made by good trout feeding in deadly, sober earnest; the fish raise themselves slowly and silently in the water beneath a fly, which they suck down almost without breaking the surface. I have noticed that many loch fishers cannot detect these slight marks, and in that they are very unfortunate, because a trout rising in that fashion is an easy conquest; to me there is no more welcome sight on the loch than such a mark distant from 10 to 15 yds away; it fills me with confidence, and in nearly every case the hook sinks home. Therefore must the angler not only acquire facility in covering a rise, but also train himself to detect the dainty, dimpling trout feeding quietly at the surface.

Sometimes a bay may be covered with flies of one species, eg Olive duns or Corncrake Sedges, and not a single trout may take notice of them. Yet the angler may put on his cast a wet-fly, a copy of the natural insect on the water and, as a consequence, obtain good sport. Such is quite a common experience on the loch. One is tempted to ask why it is that an artificial fly is preferred to the natural insect. The preference is most probably not real. Why are the trout not taking the fully-fledged flies and accepting their imitations? The reason is that the fish are playing havoc among the ascending larvae to which the artificial bears a fair resemblance in shape, coloration, size and, above all, in position. An accurately designed copy of the nymph in favour would do very much better, until the trout turned their attentions to the surface when, of course, the floating fly would become the correct, and by far the most profitable, lure.

Let us suppose that a rise has been observed, covered neatly, and that the fish has been induced to rise again. Sometimes it will miss the fly altogether; in fact that is a frequent occurrence on the loch, and it need occasion no surprise, for the play of light, the vagaries of the lure influenced by the wind and wave, and the length of the journey all tend to make it difficult for a trout to locate its prey unerringly. How will the loch fisher act in such circumstances ? In all probability he will at once place his cast again over the boil and in so doing he is guilty of a serious, or rather a fatal, error in tactics. He must note that while he has been casting, raising, striking and again casting, the boat has been moving forward on the drift, slowly or quickly as the strength of the wind determines, and in consequence the length of line that was sufficient before, is now too great.

There is no time to reel in line; therefore the angler must pull in line with his left hand, as much as he deems sufficient for the purpose, and present the bob-fly to the expectant trout. The disappointed fish, denied its prey just as the angler is, hovers around at the surface seeking for what has escaped it. This trick has gained me literally hundreds of trout from all sorts of lochs; the accomplishment of it is very pleasant; when it is successfully performed the angler feels that he has laid the fly into the trout's mouth, and that is the impression made on the boatman or other spectator. The only difficulty there is in carrying it out is to remember in the excitement of the moment to pull in line; the rest is very easy. In fact I do not mind a trout missing at its first rise; the second, if it comes at all, is a rise to kill. One factor likely to prevent it coming is a vigorous strike. Nor will it come if the first rise was of the spluttering order, for that generally shows that the miss was intentional.

Perhaps it is well that I should lay emphasis on the fact that it is the bob-fly with which aim should be made. The fly that occupies the highest position of my cast is invariably dressed with split wings in the well-known Clyde style; that is to say, the feather for the wing is tied on in a bunch and then divided, and at the same time pressed well back by means of the tying silk. It represents a fly struggling at the surface, where, in the circumstances described, the trout is eagerly cruising.

It may be objected that the trout of some lochs never make

a second attempt at a fly. Such lochs are unknown to me, for in none that I have fished has that trick failed, and there is none, I venture to assert, in which it will fail, provided that striking is done quietly though firmly; the strike that ploughs a furrow across the surface will, of course, scare away any self-respecting fish, however anxious or annoyed it may be.

On many days, and especially on good fishing days, I find, or perhaps it were better to say I am inclined to the belief, that the cast straight down wind is the least remunerative. There are exceptions, certainly, and very happy exceptions too, which must be noted. Sometimes the trout take the fly the moment it alights upon the water, when the cast in question is the best of all, because the line is tight and the strike almost certain. When such a blissful state of affairs obtains, rising fish may not be anywhere seen; generally that is the case. I have no doubt that the trout are poised near the surface, eagerly watching for what wave and wind may bring. The pattern of fly used is not very important, because the fish, having perceived the flies coming through the air, is already rushing to welcome them before any recognition is possible. That is why certain flies like the Teal family, which give of their best when well sunk, and the gorgeous, fanciful creations, which are capable of arousing the ire of quiescent trout, are on such occasions as keenly accepted as more reasonable patterns.

That is one exceptional case; there is another. As we all know only too well, trout are generally neither feeding at the surface nor roaming around there expectant; they are in the depths fasting or picking up the unresisting snails or pursuing elusive creatures of the lower waters. Consequently the lure has to be brought before their notice; in other words, it must be sunk deeply, and that can best be effected, if the angler is fishing from a boat, by a cast straight down wind. In this case the dressing of the pattern may be very important, but, as so much has to be guessed, the cast at first should carry a nymph, a shrimp and one or more of the brightly coloured varieties of loch-flies. An examination of the first accidental captive ought to furnish information which will make possible a more scientific form of fishing.

Apart from these occasions the cast across wind will be more effective than one down the wind. If the angler is alone in a drifting boat, he has a full semicircle of water before him in which to fish with comfort, but if, as is general, and also more agreeable, he is accompanied by another angler, the area of his activity is halved. If the other occupants of the boat are at all nervous, or he is not quite proficient in the art, he had better reduce his area still further. I find the cast across the wind, that is, one at an angle of about 45° to the line of the boat, the deadliest of all. The breeze plays upon the line and brings the flies at speed across the waves and very near the surface; highly attractive they are then, at times of course, to the trout of Loch Leven especially, but to those of other lochs as well. Owing to the great curve on the line, striking, as generally understood, is not possible; but neither is it necessary, for the sudden stoppage to the quickly moving flies is sufficient to drive in the hook. Many of the rises obtained are of the wild, spluttering order, which come to nothing, but others, again, are made with deadly intent.

When the trout show great interest in the flies worked after this fashion I put two split-winged flies at the top of the cast, and have often found the one quite as good as the other. Apparently flies crossing the waves, skipping the crests, exercise a great fascination over the trout, and some of my best days have been entirely due to the tactics mentioned. Should a trout be observed to rise to a natural fly not in the path of the boat, I think it is a mistake to attempt to cast across it, because the strength of the wind may not admit of that delicacy which should always be regarded as necessary. Instead I cast above and beyond the fish, and allow the wind to work upon the line and drift the flies across the mark. In most cases that procedure calls out the desired response.

There are many glorious opportunities of obtaining sport of the very highest class on the loch which are completely thrown away by those anglers who are not aware of the procedure correct in the circumstances, who adopt the same tactics, whenever they go and whatever the conditions. I know now how numerous have been the occasions on which I have had only mediocre results, when I might easily have taken excellent baskets, had I learned the lesson sooner.

There are, nevertheless, some thoroughly bad days on the loch, when the fish give only the most meagre encouragement or none at all. The weather conditions may even seem to be perfect, and yet there is no response to the angler's efforts. I believe, however, that these days will become fewer in number as we learn more about the habits of loch-trout, though it is too much to expect that we shall ever be able to convert every day into a good fishing day. Meanwhile for such occasions I fear the angler must simply work hard, trying all the various types of lures, and perhaps he may discover something that will produce the desired result.

8 PROBLEMS FOR THE LOCH FISHER

THERE are many questions put to the angler during his hours spent on the loch, and during the period of his enforced absence from the waters many an hour is passed in pondering over them. The effort expended in endeavours to elucidate these problems is not necessarily vain or unprofitable, for, to some of them at least, a sort of solution may be found, and success in fishing must largely depend on the ability of the individual to find it and test its correctness.

We know, everyone knows, that the trout in a river face the current. The general belief is that resting trout in a loch lie head to wind, and it is highly probable that that is their customary position. I am quite satisfied on the point, and regard as exceptional other positions which I have seen them occupy. Accordingly it must have occurred to many anglers compelled to fish from a drifting boat that to cast straight down wind is not advisable, because the trout fished for, or hoped for, is facing the approaching boat, the angler and his outstretched rod; in a strong breeze it remains in ignorance of these dangers, but in a gentle ripple, as the more meagre sport then obtained clearly shows, it sees them only too well. However, it is a simple matter to cast across the wind – none too safe in some cases, for the other occupants of the boat – and, if this is done, the flies cross the area under the trout's observation; while, in addition the presence of those factors which are liable to create distrust in the proposed victim remains unsuspected. The cast suggested, whatever it derives its efficacy from, is always deadly, and particularly so when the trout are feeding on or near the surface.

Some anglers are well aware that fishing from the lee-shore of a loch is very often productive of good results. They have learned, and found to have been worth learning, the art of casting into the teeth of the wind. The superior sport they enjoy is no doubt partly due to the fact that a large quantity of floating food is washed across the loch to that shore; but, very probably, results would not be so good if the trout did not face the wind, and so were unconscious of the angler's presence. An hour or so among the tossing waves is enough for most people, and it is a pleasant and comforting change to wander leisurely along the bank, which allows a clean cast straight out across the wind. Moreover, many fish fall to the flies, and I think the reason is again two-fold; under the influence of the wind on the line, the lures are very lively, full of life and action, but it is to be noted as well that they are brought across the trout's field of vision, for the evidence seems conclusive that the loch-trout heads the wind. Those who fish the loch always from a boat will be convinced, if they consider the large number of trout they raise when they continue casting out as they are being rowed up the wind preparatory to settling down to a fresh drift.

Loch-trout, however, are not always inclined to remain stationary; they may move from one area to another, and even after settling down in the chosen area, they may roam about it in search of food. They do so very freely at times, especially when the surface is well supplied with flies. When the loch is calm on a warm summer evening, and generally after a fall of Pale Watery Spinners,* they indulge in cruising around, and their behaviour is apt to be riotous. It can scarcely be entertained that they move according to some prearranged plan, though appearances would certainly often lead one to that belief, and I have caught many a good trout by laying a fly on the track which, it seemed to me, the fish had mapped out for itself. At other times they splash about in all directions, quite obviously without plan or object save that of acquisition, and then the surface may undergo violent upheavals which seem to tell of fierce conflicts in the depths. The habit is not confined entirely to calm weather; the trout may travel, rising repeatedly on the way, even in a good drifting breeze. I have never seen a fish moving directly against the wind; they may do so, but all travelling trout I have seen moved at an angle to the breeze and always from left to right. I do not suggest that this preference of direction is invariable; further experience may show that a route

* More probably *Caenis* spinners – C.F.W.

at right angles to that hitherto observed is as frequently selected. One of the problems, therefore, that the loch fisher meets, consists in the determination of the correct direction and length of his cast when such an interesting opportunity as a cruising trout is afforded him; the decision must be made at the moment, and the only preparatory training he can undertake is to teach himself to remember that these happy chances do come, and to recognize them when they come.

Though it may not be generally recognized, it is a fact that some anglers do exceedingly well with certain patterns of flies with which others obtain no sport whatever; the first favourite of one may well be, and often is, useless to another. Frequently on the loch, and generally on occasions when sport is moderately, rather than exceptionally good, an angler may find one of the flies on his cast attractive beyond all the rest; everyone fishing the loch at that particular time may have the same experience; but the trout do not all fall to the same pattern. The specially successful flies may be very numerous and quite dissimilar; to each angler one fly brings all the sport, but the most acceptable lure varies with the individual. One man may be using the deadly fly of another as well as his own, and yet find the former of little or no service.

I think that the reason for this common experience is simple. The explanation is, that in every particular case there is a variation in the style of fishing, large or slight as the case may be, which is suited to certain lures and not to others. It gives the correct, or a more correct movement to the fly, endowing it with a motion which simulates the behaviour of the natural insect it represents or, if the lure happens to resemble no living creature in appearance, imparting to it a certain lifelike liveliness or other property which interests the questing trout. When it is remembered that a cast of flies may be subjected to an immensely varied treatment, the explanation seems reasonable. The cast may be delivered at various angles to the wind, fished high or low in the water, brought towards the boat quickly or slowly, at a uniform pace or in spasmodic jerks; it may have principally a horizontal motion without much rise and fall, and it may, on the whole, move vertically with only a slight forward movement. One of these methods may bring out the full capabilities of one fly, while making another only an object to be suspected.

The fact that one's regular cast is longer than another's may in itself suffice to give a particular lure greater attractiveness. A change in the strength of the wind may conceivably cause a transfer of attention, because it will be almost necessarily accompanied by a change in the pace with which the line is recovered. At the same time such an alteration in the conditions will affect the rate and extent of the vertical motion of the flies: while one member of the cast thus loses, another may gain. Some are very good with a well-sunk fly; others excel when the trout are coming high; but all must have their lures and their methods suited one to the other, if the full benefits of their skill are to be reaped.

There are anglers who declare that they fish throughout the season with the same three or four flies, and are perfectly content to do so; they maintain that the sport they thus enjoy is always as good as the conditions permit and as that obtained by others. While contentment may be the object of all striving, it remains a state of mind beyond all possibility of attainment; and a supremely contented angler must be a rare phenomenon. However, if what they say is ever approximately correct, then I conclude that their mechanical dexterity with the rod is so superlatively great that their unvarying relatively good results are produced, not because of their limited number of flies, but in spite of them. I am sure that they would have a more interesting time and even better sport if they would change their flies according to seasons and conditions and, above all, to the trout's desires.

Although sometimes clearly demonstrated, these desires are more often discovered only by systematic experiment, and making the corresponding alteration in method demanded by each fly is a matter necessitating careful investigation. Surely for our own self-respect it is advisable to assume that the trout is possessed of some little intelligence.

If it were possible to know the correct method of working every type of artificial fly and to apply it, there would be very few, if any, blank days, and many more really fine days, than there are in the life of the loch fisher. The main thing the individual has to realize is, that to every fly there belongs not only a position on the cast which is better than any other, but also a method of manipulation which enables it to display its full allurements; whenever that is understood, the determination of the requirements should follow sooner or later. I have tried to indicate the various means that so far have seemed to prove most effective against the loch-trout in some, at least, of its varied moods and humours.

9 WIND ON THE LOCH

THE glories of the flat calm are not universally appreciated; at the best they are known to very few, who are, moreover, not always inclined to admit their existence. It is generally recognized that in the gloaming and in the dark a complete absence of wind is the condition which produces the best results, but under bright sunlight it is so exacting in its demands that no angler sets out for a day on the loch hoping to find not the faintest zephyr astir. If the value of results is to be assessed by the difficulty experienced in their attainment, and not by the relationship between them and those impressive but comparatively easy conquests of simple conditions, the smooth mirror of the loch grants the greatest of opportunities; but most of us would not object to more reward for an expenditure of less labour.

The tourist may become enthusiastic in his admiration of the sleeping loch; he passes it by in a short time; the angler has to spend monotonous hours casting over an inverted world, and he enjoys it little more than the yachtsman motionless on a glassy sea. We all like a breeze. It makes us more cheerful. The trout appear to be in better humour too, rising with a dash which is altogether more inspiring than the leisurely, or even lazy, advance of the calm. Of course there is no certainty of sport in calm or breeze; success and failure are alike possible under both conditions. That is understood by everyone, but, when trout are obdurate, the angler can contrive to wait for a change in their mood more patiently, and for a longer time, if there is some wind to help out the cast, than he can should all such assistance be withheld. The chief reason is that he is better pleased with his own performance, more readily convinced that the continued failure is due to the indifference of the trout and is not a consequence of his imperfections.

Seldom indeed are we favoured with a fine, steady breeze,

constant in strength and direction. For too often it is squally, brushing across the wave-tops in ugly, black patches, blowing the line about this way and that, imparting to the lures various erratic movements which are perhaps attractive and perhaps not. The boatman has not a highly agreeable task, not only for the reason that it is hard work rowing the boat between the drifts, but also because he has to exert much effort on the drift to keep it so placed relatively to the wind that both anglers will have equal comfort in casting. Also the labour involved in remaining on a stretch, which is producing frequent rises, is so great that generally this most advisable course of procedure is abandoned, and the chance of a good basket is in consequence lost. On an open bay or broad shallow the trouble is not so evident, but should the wind blow on to a prolific shore, a favourite hunting-ground, it is clear that only one angler can perform satisfactorily, and therefore there is in the boat one who is, for a time at least, somewhat neglected and rather unhappy.

A strong wind, that is also steady, is not open to the same objections, and there are some, I believe, who actually hope to be tossed about from wave to wave when they go in pursuit of the loch-trout. Certainly sport can be very fine on a day when there is no necessity to cast at all, when, instead, all that is required of the angler is to hold up the rod and then lower it; the wind does the rest; the beginner may vanquish the expert. On Loch Leven I have found the trout coming very well indeed under a gale which made it almost impossible for anyone to stand up in the boat and very difficult to manage a strong-running fish. It is under these conditions that the folly of allowing a trout to run far to windward, or of bringing it too soon behind the boat, is made most clear.

I expect that one great reason for the popularity of a high wind lies in the fact that ground is rapidly covered; there is a continual change of water, and hopefulness is revived at every new drift reached. This appeals to many an angler, but the boatman has a different opinion of it. On the smaller lochs the whole fishing area is searched, perhaps over and over again, and therefore, when the day is done, there are no regrets or disturbing thoughts that likely stretches were omitted. Often success on a large loch depends to a very great extent on the ground selected, but on a small one during a high wind the angler can try every little corner, and he feels sure that sooner or later, and somewhere or other, he will find the trout in the right humour.

One great objection to the strong wind is, that the boat drifts down on the flies so quickly that it is scarcely possible to communicate any movement to them or to work them in the most attractive fashion. That does not apply to the bob-fly, which, under precisely these conditions, can be made to perform its evolutions most effectively; the cast should be switched out from the boat, and the flies brought in across the waves, if the true deadliness of the bob-fly is to be demonstrated.

However fine the results in the stormy open, I should on no account neglect to have the boat steered into the lee of a wood on island or mainland; if, unfortunately, the loch has no such feature, I should look for a calm belt under some steep shore. On the line where the wind first strikes the water, and for some distance beyond it, trout lie in wait for flies blown off the trees or grass. A long cast lightly delivered may bring up a fish instantly, and a pleasant hour may be spent in comparative comfort. It is generally profitable too; in fact, there is no surer cast on a stormy day, and a search of all these areas available should be thoroughly and repeatedly carried out.

No matter how much the rolling wave or the crested breaker may appeal to some anglers, my first desire, when I am afloat on the loch, is to see the gentlest of breezes curling the water, just a faint ripple, enough to conceal imperfections in the lure, the cast and the casting. Generally accompanying that is an abundant hatch of flies, and there will be seen, almost without fail, here and there over the loch the slow, rolling rise of big trout and, more frequently, the eager, noisy splash of the smaller fry. If the day is dull under a well-clouded sky, there should be enough to keep the attention fixed on the water; even on these days the eyes will wander to the hills and the trees, but the temptation is more easily resisted than it often is. The boat may not drift at a pace satisfactory to those who like stirring conditions of wind and weather, and sometimes it is painfully slow, for instance, when a fine boil eddies itself out at a tantalizing distance away. Haste then seems necessary, for well it is known that the cast which reaches the mark on the instant is the deadliest of all for any but a roving trout, but to hurry in these circumstances is unwise; it is better to fish quietly up to the spot than to drive the boat at speed towards it. The best plan is to select a good, broad bay or a long shallow and to leave the boat to itself; the boatman had better be told to ship his oars.

It is true that such an opportunity of experiencing the joy of a gentle, warm breeze comes but seldom during the day, but with the first of the hopeful gloaming it quite often arrives, and then is the time to see the loch at its best and to learn what it is capable of giving. Only then do I want the boat to myself, no boatman to worry me with his restless oars, no other angler to consult or persuade as to choice of ground, nothing to interfere with the full enjoyment of the peace that descends at the gloaming. It would be selfish so to monopolize the boat, and if there were no other available, I should gladly give it up to any angler who desired it, and conduct the campaign from the bank instead.

10 IN A FLAT CALM

WHEN the surface of the loch is uniformly rippled over, it matters not how slightly, I look forward to a day full of possibilities; if the wind is strong, so long as it is not strong enough to forbid the launching of the boat, I can contrive to be very hopeful; if the loch is one long, flat, unbroken expanse, a lifeless calm, it is with no great haste or pleasant anticipation that I put up the rod and push off from the shore. I expect that all anglers experience much the same sensations.

Before much enjoyment can be extracted from the loch in such circumstances, two conditions appear to me to be absolutely necessary. In the first place the angler should be accompanied only by his boatman, and, secondly, the surface should be dotted with rings of rising trout. Given these two conditions, sport is assured to anyone who can throw a delicate fly; if the first is a-wanting, vexation is inevitable, and, in the absence of the second, weariness and failure are the most probable, though not the invariable, result. The presence of another angler in the boat converts what might prove a spell of intensely interesting and profitable sport into an aggravating sequence of opportunities presented only to be lost, and, drifting being impossible, the man at the oars has a hard task before him if he attempts to come within reach of feeding fish. It is a sad company, with the boatman probably the saddest of the three, that sighs for a rattling breeze and declares that fishing in a calm is the most tantalizing of all sports.

If the two anglers are so inseparable that neither can be persuaded to go ashore, they should at least consent to fish only one at a time; through such an arrangement both would certainly obtain more sport than can be possible when both rods are going simultaneously. The one whose turn it is to test his skill should be seated in the stern; the boatman should then back the boat slowly and cautiously down towards each rise as it appears. The best lure is a floating fly, a good imitation of the fly most abundant on the water. The boat should be stopped quietly at the angler's best casting distance, and kept there for a full minute to give the fish every chance of accepting the fly that has been laid upon the rise. The trout may come up the instant the fly alights or after all hope of response from it has passed; it very often rises just as the angler is about to lift preparatory to delivering the fly again, I suppose, because the hackles move to the action of the line and become seemingly endowed with life. In any case, before abandoning hope altogether, he should give a gentle twitch to the line, just sufficient to affect the lure, but he must make sure that that effect is obtained.

When trout are not showing at all, fishing in a calm may be very dreary work indeed, and many, no doubt, would be unwilling to suffer such an extreme trial of patience and endurance. They would rather sit idly on the bank, or return home at once, than undertake a task that to them seems hopeless. It is not hopeless, however, and those of us, who have long journeys to make before we reach the loch, are not to be prevented from fishing by reason of adverse conditions. A breeze may spring up at any moment to ruffle the surface of the loch; it is worth waiting for. The finest fishing ripple may settle down into a calm at any time of the day; the only sensible procedure is to learn the art of fishing in a calm and so become, as far as may be, independent of the wind. The period of calm need not be one of inactivity.

In every loch there are some places more hopeful than others, and on these attention should be concentrated. For example, where trees overhang the water, trout are always to be found, and they seem to be always inclined for food; a long delicate cast which lays the tail-fly neatly under the branches is quite capable of bringing up a good fish, although the surface is innocent of the faintest ripple, and all the trout in the loch appear to have retired to sleep. The fly I should use with greatest expectation in such a place is the Red Palmer. It resembles fairly well not only a shrimp, a probable inhabitant of any bit of water, but it also seems to suggest to a trout one or another of various caterpillars which may drop from the trees. In fact the deadly pattern was originally modelled on one of these creatures. The lure should be allowed to sink, and then recovered in a series of jerking movements by the left hand pulling on the line; it should be brought quite to the surface by a gradual simultaneous raising of the rod, before it is removed from the water. The coils of line must be shot out again by a number of false casts in the air. This treatment removes from the lure most of the water it has absorbed, and the next cast into some other likely spot is in consequence all the more delicate, all the more capable of enticing a fish to take.

If, as is quite probable, no trees throw their branches over the water, the angler must search for other spots which are favourite haunts of trout, the outer edge of a reed-bed or clear spaces among the tall, motionless stems. There is no need to fear the loss of a fly; if a reed is hooked, the fly can be easily recovered, the only misfortune being that the disturbed area is lost temporarily, but there are other promising places not far away. Should, on the other hand, a trout be hooked, the rod should be kept vertical and the trout held firmly. There is little likelihood of a breakage occurring, and, though such treatment of a fish does not permit of the usual stirring fight, it brings the angler some satisfaction – a trout killed under difficult conditions; every moment he expects disaster, but that seldom, if ever, comes.

If both trees and reeds are absent, the vicinity of sunken rocks, both near and off the shore, projecting points, and the mouths of tributary streams may be tried with some prospect of success. I think that the angler should not pay any attention whatever to large, open bays, or indeed any broad expanse of water, that is during a calm, when fish are not rising. The great secret is to confine operations entirely to certain restricted areas and neglect the main body of the loch. He must avoid the depressing effect of an apparently lifeless, broad stretch of water; that would make him feel helpless and hopeless, but if he selects some small part which, appearances inform him, holds plenty of trout, he will

128

find himself fishing it just as he would a pool on the river; that is, with every care and probably with result.

An offer brings much satisfaction, for its coming proves that casting has been skilfully executed. The water is so clear and calm that the fish may be seen leaving its hiding-place to go in pursuit of the fly. Then it is that the angler must restrain himself, to act as if unconscious that anything had taken, or was about to take place until the fish turns; then the hook should be fixed.

A calm at sundown in summer is never unwelcome. It can scarcely fail to be accompanied by a display of rising trout, and sport is likely to be good. As daylight fades away the rod will be kept busy as long as the calm continues, but should a breeze spring up it is generally the signal for all activity to cease. Delicate work is not so supremely essential as it is by day, and a tight line is the greatest necessity. I cannot say whether the floating-fly or the wet-fly is the better, both seem to do equally well, but the 'tug' to a sunk fly on a dark night is something really worth knowing, a sensation that is not beaten by anything in fishing.

The advent of a calm is not something to be deplored as if it were a sort of calamity; during the day it is an occasion for doubt perhaps, but no excuse for inaction or reason for despair; at evening it gives a promise of happiness which generally is fulfilled.

11 DAPPING (by Kenneth Mansfield)

DAPPING a fly on the surface of a lake with the assistance of a wind-blown line is a long-established branch of trout fishing which may have originated in Ireland – where it is still employed in the traditional manner, with immensely long rods and baits of live Mayflies or Daddy-long-legs according to the season. It was in general use there as early as the 1830s, and I dapped successfully on several Irish loughs in 1920 and '21, with self-tied bushy artificial flies, when I had no orthodox tackle by me and the political conditions made it impossible to buy any. Since then I have dapped for trout and other surface-feeding fish in other countries and on many types of water.

In 1935 some spectacular catches of sea trout on dapped artificial flies in Loch Maree, Wester Ross, aroused more general interest in the method, and it is now quite commonly employed on lakes, reservoirs and wide rivers when the conditions are right.

The requirements are a long rod, a floss line, a natural or artificial fly – and a wind sufficiently strong to stream out the line.

Rod
This should be light in weight with a stiffish action, preferably about 15 ft long and certainly not less than 12 ft.

Line
Floss silk lines are made for this purpose, but cotton floss, as used for embroidery work, is equally good and much cheaper. No 6 is a suitable size. The reason for using floss line is that it is light but thick and fluffy, so that the wind can get a grip on it. The working portion need be no more than 30 yds, but this must be backed up with one of the usual backings. A 2 to 3 ft monofilament cast joins fly to line.

Flies
In my experience the natural fly has no advantages over the artificial, especially as a natural Mayfly looks a sorry mess when impaled by an angler unversed in this delicate operation. The widened interest in dapping demands artificial lures, for it is used at all seasons and there are times when no natural species large enough to use are on the water. Pattern is not of great importance providing the fly be large, hackled and well treated with floatant. It adds to the interest, of course, if a selection of colours and sizes is available in order to experiment when sport is slow.

Method
Dapping is usually done from a boat, though it can be successful from the shore if the wind is behind the angler.

The rod is raised vertically, or with a forward tilt of not more than 25°, and the line fed out until some 15 to 20 yds are being blown about by the wind. The rod is slowly lowered until the fly alights on the water. By manipulating the rod-tip it can be made to skitter on the surface or to become airborne for a few moments.

Striking is the most difficult part of dapping. The fish is seen to rise, often in a boil of water, and it is difficult not to strike too soon. Wait for the fish to turn down, though if the pluck is *felt*, strike at once.

General

Critics of dapping claim that it is a boring way of fishing. I can think of nothing less true. There is constant expectancy as the fly lies on the water, and it is certainly more thrilling than making the fiftieth fruitless cast with a team of wet-flies when the fish are not interested.

There need not be a general rise: often when the fish are disinterested in any normally presented flies they will come up to the dapped one, and sometimes these are bigger than average fish from a fair depth. The liveliness of the lure and its considerable size may make the effort seem worth while to fish which would not rise to small naturals that happen to be emerging at the time.

Dapping is not a substitute for standard wet and dry lake fishing: it is an interesting change of method when wind conditions are right.

BOB CHURCH

Still-water Trout

RESERVOIRS like Blagdon have been fished since the beginning of the century. They were made before the war by damming a valley, allowing it to fill with stream water and stocking it with trout. By 1939 the sport had developed particular methods, tackle and flies which differed fundamentally from those used in rivers and in many respects from those used in trout fishing in natural lakes – mainly due to the different strains of trout and the very different food supply.

Since the war the number of reservoirs has increased enormously, and in addition to these there are hundreds of water-filled sand, gravel, clay or iron pits (known comprehensively as 'wet pits') which have been stocked with trout. The fishing rights on some of the smaller reservoirs and pits are held by syndicates, but most of them are owned by Councils or angling clubs who issue day or period tickets.

This great increase in the still-water trout fishing available to all has led to changes and improvements in angling methods, tackle and mental outlook. It is my aim here to discuss the modern techniques of the sport.

I am very lucky to live in Northampton, as it is close to most of the country's leading reservoirs. Within 30 miles of my doorstep are Grafham Water, Draycote Water and Eyebrook, and less than 8 miles away are Pitsford and Ravensthorpe. On occasions I motor down to Bristol to fish at those two other famous reservoirs, Chew Valley Lake and Blagdon.

In the near future – 1976 to be exact – we have another exciting prospect, the opening of Empingham reservoir. This giant sheet of water will be England's largest, covering 3,100 acres with a perimeter of 24 miles. The fishing at Empingham will, in my opinion, offer the best and biggest fish so far. A water of this size can cater for a lot of fly fishermen, and as this branch of our sport is growing in popularity very fast, it will fill a much-felt need.

Most reservoirs are stocked with both brown and rainbow trout. Much of the time, these two species have differing feeding habits, so methods of catching them also differ. There has been some experiment in recent years, notably at Ogston reservoir in Derbyshire, with the introduction of 'Supertrout' to the water. This is a crossbreed (rainbow brown) but early expectations of its meriting its tag were soon forgotten, as it in fact tended to become rather stunted. Another experiment, which took place at Llyn Alaw reservoir, Anglesey, was the introduction of landlocked sea trout. The late Cyril Inwood, who was an expert fly fisherman, fished there and caught a four-pounder. He reckoned the idea was a sound one and that the fish could eventually grow into double figures.

I will assume you have bought most of your tackle, but if your fly lines consist of a floater and a fast sinker only, you'd be well advised to buy two more – the now very popular sink-tip and slow-sinker. With these to choose from, you should be equipped to face any conditions, whether you're fishing from boat or bank.

The slow – and fast-sinking lines should take the form of shooting heads, ie 10 yds in length and No 9 in weight. The floater and sink-tip I use are the new long belly shape, which for a full fly line casts and presents flies perfectly. Two rods, one 10 ft with plenty of power for luring, the other longer and softer, for small fly fishing, will complete your tackle; permutations of these set-ups should enable you to cope with any fishing conditions you're likely to meet.

1 LURE FISHING

FOR the purposes of this chapter, I will call a normal trout fly a 'small fly' and anything tied on a No 8 long-shank hook or larger a 'lure'. The two most important colours in a lure's make-up are undoubtedly black and white. There are several patterns, all of them good fish-catchers; orange is another colour which really comes into its own during high summer, when the rainbows seem to go for it best.

At the start of each trout season, with the water temperatures still very low, most anglers fish with a single lure of some kind. If I am fishing from the bank, I set up a sink-tipped line and a three yard leader. My lure pattern will obviously be changed around until I find which the trout take best, but 99 times out of 100 my Black Chenille cannot be bettered (Tying, page 142).

After casting, the lure sinks slowly; it is very common to get takes the moment it touches the water. When it reaches bottom I retrieve very slowly, giving it a 'rise and fall' motion. I have found that trout will take more confidently with this style of fishing than when I use a full sinking line from the bank.

Depths of up to 20 ft can easily be fished with the sink-tip line. It is rare to find deeper water than this within casting distance of the bank except, perhaps, off a dam wall. My favourite conditions for this technique are a left-to-right cross wind; after casting out, the line can simply be allowed to drift round in a wide arc. This is an excellent method for both lure and small-fly fishing and takes are rarely missed, as the trout are usually hooked firmly in the scissors of the jaw. This technique has endless possibilities, and should come in handy from both bank and boat throughout the season.

When I am lure fishing from a boat, I frequently use a shooting-head slow-sinking line, particularly where there are both rainbows and browns present in good numbers. The line allows me to fish slowly through the upper water levels where the rainbows are likely to be in the summer months; if I fail to make contact I let the line sink well down to the bottom and have a shot at the 'brownies'.

Almost more important than my choice of fly line when I'm boat fishing is ensuring that the craft is drifting at the right speed and in the right place. A tall order, you may think, but it's not really as difficult as it sounds. My favourite and most successful method is to drift with a large drogue out astern, which allows the boat to run bows first down the wind. I select a spot 60 to 100 yds from the bank, and try to find depths from 15 to 20 ft; it is my experience that this is where the most fish are likely to be lying. The idea is for each angler to cast out from different sides of the boat; in this way a 60 yd strip of water (30 yds each) is covered, and as we are moving over fresh ground all the time, the maximum possible number of fish get a look at our lures.

Early in the season, when the water temperature is very low,

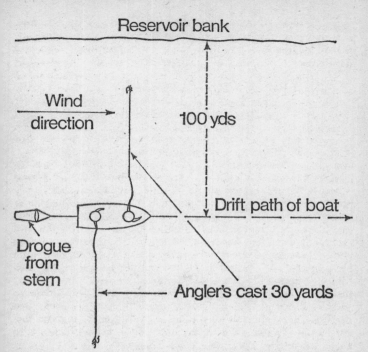

Reservoir bank

Wind direction

100 yds

Drift path of boat

Drogue from stern

Angler's cast 30 yards

FIG 16. A 60 yard strip of water is covered when this method is used.

it sometimes pays to anchor and fish very slowly. At such times a buoyant lure can be very useful. I designed an early model made with an underbody of dense cork, but since then, Dick Walker has come up with a much better material, Polyethylene. When he introduced this material he also launched a new pattern of lure to go with it, which he calls 'Rasputin'. It imitates a small fish.

My buoyant lure tackle consists of a fast-sinking shooting head and a 6 ft leader of 10 lb nylon, with an 18 in tip section of 7 lb nylon tied on with a blood knot. I pinch a small soft shot on to the line just above the knot to remove any possibility of its slipping.

After the cast, the whole tackle sinks quickly to the bottom as far as the shot. Beyond it is 18 in of 7 lb line which the buoyant lure carries vertically up from the bottom. When retrieving, an inch or two of line can be twitched in very slowly. Takes are usually good pulls with the lure taken well back into the mouth.

2 NYMPH FISHING

IT seems that many anglers are prepared to go to a reservoir, put on a black or white lure or flasher of some kind and stand in a favourite hotspot, chucking it out and pulling it back in basically the same fashion all day. I would be the first to admit that this can at certain times, be a very killing method, particularly if you click to what the trout fancy or if you find them preoccupied with sticklebacks or small fry of some kind. It's true that trout in the early months are usually looking for something fairly substantial to satisfy their appetite, and will often take a lure, particularly in new reservoirs. It's not always the case, though, and at times anglers are likely to go home fishless if they don't change to line nymph. The best bet at these times is a black, green or brown buzzer nymph or an imitation like the Pheasant Tail or Caddis. From the beginning of May through June/July, this kind of insect will often be high on the trout's diet. I catch many of my limit bags on small flies of this type tied on No 10 and No 12 hooks.

Nymphs are basically small creatures that live on and in the mud and weeds at the bottom of the reservoir. At certain times of the year they ascend to the top layers of the water where, provided that the water and air temperatures are right, they hatch into adult flies in great numbers. It is when they are moving towards the surface, and especially when they are struggling to change from nymph into fly, that the trout find them almost irresistible.

If you find this happening, try to pick a position where you will be able to cover the greatest possible number of fish – perhaps a headland with the wind blowing across it. Put on a team of buzzers, as they are the most prolific form of nymph food in the early part of the season. When you get the size and colour right, you will find it a constantly successful technique.

On many days, however, there are cool winds blowing and

the top layers of the water are quite cold. Any nymphs coming up from the bottom may reach this layer and go back down again instead of hatching. At times like this, you will find more trout rising and nymphs hatching in sheltered bays where the water surface is slightly warmer. This is an ideal situation, so approach with care, cast across the path of the rising fish, and very slowly tweak the nymphs along in the surface layer. This is usually done with a floating line and a 12 to 15 ft leader. To this tie three nymphs, one at the point and the other two on droppers. These nymphs are usually of the buzzer type, of fairly simple design, and a variety of colours (Tying, page 142); the hooks can vary in size between No 10 and No 14. The cast is greased to within 4 in of each nymph.

Many anglers are under the impression that if they cannot see trout rising they are not feeding. This is a fallacy. Trout feed on these insects throughout the day and can be caught on the imitation, but the taking depth may vary considerably. Remember that the nymphs are sometimes rising from water as much as 30 feet deep, which means that they may sometimes take hours to reach the surface. In this situation, you should obviously present the bait where the trout are feeding; you can find exactly where in a number of ways. The easiest method is to use a floating fly line with a long leader, say 15 feet of about 5 or 6 lb breaking strain. One nymph goes on the point and the other two droppers are 4 ft 6 in apart. The cast is not greased and the point nymph can be leaded to facilitate sinking. This is then cast across the wind, and retrieved when you feel that it has sunk to the desired depth. By varying the speed of your retrieve and the depth to which you let your tackle sink, you should discover exactly how and where the trout are taking.

This method is particularly good when there is not much wind and when the day is very bright, particularly in deep-water areas. If you do not get takes when you have tried a number of permutations, change the colour or size of the nymph and try again. It also means that if the fish start feeding nearer to the surface you will find out quickly by taking a fish or two on the top dropper. When this happens, simply take off the leaded nymph on the point, replace it with one that doesn't sink so quickly, and partially grease the cast to increase its buoyancy. If you grease the whole of the cast so the nymphs swim in the surface layers, there may be no need to move them at all, particularly if there is a slight breeze blowing; the wind will bring them round in a nice slow natural arc. When the fish takes, you should feel a good solid pull, even though the line is coming round in a big bend. You should find that this helps to hook the fish much more securely, as it gives him time to turn before you feel him. In this way you will be letting the waves do all the work while covering the maximum number of fish, without frightening them off by continuous casting. With the buzzers, the more slowly they are moved the more takes you will usually get.

If you have greased up and the fish go down again you can always clean the line with some washing-up liquid carried in a small bottle or, better still, a paste made up of fuller's earth and washing-up liquid. If you don't have this handy, soft mud rubbed along the line will serve the same purpose. This also takes the shine off the line, which may be a good thing to do on hot, bright days.

These methods can also be used in conjunction with a sink-tip fly line which will enable you to get the fly down even deeper. This is a much better way of nymphing really deep than lengthening the cast to more than 15 feet, as it is much easier to cast without getting in a tangle, and there are no complications when landing fish.

As I have said, it is by no means a bad thing to have a bow in the line, particularly when surface fishing. But if this happens when you are fishing the nymphs deep and the wind is quite strong, you will find that by the time you have felt the pull of the take, so will the fish. This can result in many missed or lightly hooked trout.

If this happens, you can try using the same team of nymphs and fishing them on a slow-sinking line. After casting, allow them to sink; always be ready for a bite on the drop. When they have sunk to the required depth, you can start your retrieve. You do, however, need to use this method in fairly deep water, or you are for ever getting snagged on the bottom. This is a more difficult technique to master than the other two, as the tendency is to start the retrieve too quickly, thus defeating the object of the exercise. It is, however, particularly useful from a boat on very bright and calm days, as at such times the fish have usually headed for the deeper cooler water.

If by using these methods you are fortunate enough to catch a trout, you can then 'spoon it out', with a marrow spoon. Once the fish has been dispatched you can stick the spoon down the throat into the stomach, give it a slight twist, withdraw the contents, and see exactly what the trout has been feeding on. Obviously, the food from the front of the stomach is the most recent the trout has eaten.

If you can't see the individual insects, put some water in a cup and tip the contents of the spoon into it. This will separate the nymphs and you will see their exact size and colour; you can be pretty sure that there will be other fish who share this one's taste. Leave on the nymph which tempted the trout, but on the other two droppers put a size and colour corresponding with what you found in its stomach. This should considerably improve your chances of taking fish.

Although the nymph can be deadly when fished from the bank, it can also be used in boat fishing, but you'd be well advised either to anchor or to fish with the boat drifting very slowly. I find that if you anchor the boat at both ends across the wind, you can fish in very much the same manner as from the bank. The boat gives you greater scope, though, as you can be sure of being over fish all day long. I usually look for a spot where the wind is pushing or funnelling the food life into a concentrated area like the corner of a bay. The ideal place, particularly if you're in a boat, is a 'wind lane', as these calm areas amongst the ripple are usually full of food. Whether you anchor or drift slowly down one, there is no doubt that you will be covering a number of fish.

These methods are very simple but effective and do not take long to master. If you are new to reservoir fishing you will find them less tiring than lure fishing and on many occasions you will have an equal share of fish. Remember one thing, though; on most occasions, the more slowly you retrieve, the more you will catch.

3 SMALL WET-FLY FISHING

WITH the same tackle and the same basic methods you can also fish many of the small wet-fly patterns like the Peter Ross, Dunkeld, Butcher, Mallard and Claret, and Greenwell's Glory. Although there are thousands of these small flies, they fall into two main categories: the natural imitations tied to represent the adult flies like the Olives and Sedges, and the 'flashers', which usually resemble nothing more than the flash of a small fish or one of the many aquatic insects. These small flies are, I think, best fished on a floating or sink-tip line, and always close to the surface of the lake. They should be fished in the same style as the nymphs but much faster, particularly in rough and choppy conditions, when they score very well indeed. When I'm fishing flashers I normally use a bright or light-coloured fly like the Dunkeld, Teal Blue and Silver, or Peter Ross on bright days, and on dull days a dark fly like the Butcher or Teal and Black. The Dunkeld is a very good rainbow fly and is always worth trying. It is a good idea to have a variety of sizes in your fly-box, as you may find that you are catching a few fish, say, on a No 12 Butcher, when the wind gets up, the light starts to fade and the takes decrease. If you then put on a larger size, it will frequently have the desired effect.

It is also worth fishing two traditional flies on a cast with a flasher either on the point or top dropper. Don't be afraid of skittering these small flies fast through the surface in the traditional manner, and don't be too hasty to whip them off the water as you finish your retrieve, as this can be the killing moment.

When fishing these flies from a boat drifting down the wind on a drogue, there is no need for long casting. Short casts and a skitter through the surface waves is enough, as you will be continuously drifting on to fresh fish. If you are using this method in a boat and happen to see a wind lane, do not hesitate to get the boat into it and drift down it. This style of boat fishing was one of the late Cyril Inwood's favourites, and in this way he took thousands of trout. He also used this method when it was very rough, but at such times he usually substituted a big bushy Palmer fly for the small flies on the top dropper and then fished them very fast in the waves. Properly used, this technique can be really lethal to big rainbows.

4 DRY-FLY FISHING

HERE, we try to imitate the adult fly resting on the surface or laying her eggs. Many dry flies succeed well on the reservoirs, particularly patterns like the Lake Olive, Drone-flies, Crane-flies

(Daddy-long-legs), and, probably most important of all, the Sedges.

Flies like the Drone or the Crane are worth having because at certain times, perhaps because of a fluke of nature like a heavy wind blowing them on to the water, they cause an exciting and hectic rise.

I remember one day arriving on the bank at Grafham in the early morning; as I walked across the fields, the damp grass seemed to part in front of me as the 'Daddies' lifted off and flew out of my way. I started fishing, but without much success until, at about 11 o'clock in the morning, the wind changed and started to blow them on to the water in their thousands. The trout moved in and started to gulp down the easy pickings. I was fortunate in having a couple of imitations in my fly wallet, and after changing over to one I took my limit. To do this I greased the 6 lb leader to within a few inches of the fly, which was then dressed with a silicone floatant. I then cast out and left it completely still. This is how I fish most dry-flies; the main thing to remember is not to strike as soon as the fish breaks surface, but to wait a few seconds for him to turn down. If you don't, you will inevitably pull the fly out of his mouth.

5 SEDGE-FLY FISHING

FROM mid-June to the end of August, Sedge are the commonest fly on our various reservoirs. They hatch every evening when conditions are right, and the trout love them, so there's almost always a rise. Reservoir anglers enjoy this time of the year most of all, for they have the chance to use many different styles of fishing. Not only do the trout feed on the hatching Sedge in the evenings, but for most of the day they mop up on the bottom where the caddis grubs (sedge larvae) are active.

These grubs creep slowly along the bottom complete with their little protective houses, but they are very easy prey for the trout, who are not fastidious about them; they eat them case and all.

On hard-fished reservoirs, bank anglers who have been finding the fishing difficult suddenly start catching again. One very successful method at this time is to fish with a 'Stick Fly' (Tying, page 142). If you're fishing from the bank use a floating fly line with as long a leader as you can manage. In areas of deeper water a sink-tip line would be a better choice, but the tactics are always the same; fish slow and deep.

Other good caddis imitations are the Worm fly, Black Lure variations and the smaller Red Tag. In the deeper water fished from a boat the same flies can be used but on a sinking line.

When evening approaches and the hatch begins, several methods are available. A team of three small wet-flies in sizes varying from No 12 to No 6 can be deadly. One of my favourite casts is a No 10 Invicta on the top dropper, a No 12 Cinnamon and Gold in the centre and a No 12 Amber Nymph on the point. If I am out in a boat I short-line, skittering the Invicta on or near the surface.

If fish are rising and easy to cover I find they will take any of these patterns as well as other favourites like Wickham's Fancy, Silver March Brown, Ginger Quill, Red Sedge, Silver Invicta, and Muddler Minnow.

When trout are seen to be taking the adult winged fly, I use a single dry-fly on a No 12 or No 10. I make up these dry-flies myself using cock hackles in ginger, brown, honey and buff. The wing can either be mottled brown mallard or light brown hen. As both types are common on the reservoirs it pays to have some of each tied up.

Fly and lure tyings

The 'Stick Fly': tie on a No 6 or 8 long-shanked hook. *Body* thick peacock herl ribbed with fuse wire. At the *throat*, one turn of yellow wool and a circular buff-coloured cock hackle to lie back along the body. Finish with black shiny *head*.

My Black Chenille lure: again, No 6 or 8 long-shanked hook. *Tail*, black cock hackle fibres. *Body*, black chenille spiralled with silver tinsel. *Hackle* of black cock fibres, tied as above. *Wing*, four selected black cock hackles.

Buzzer Nymphs: although the tying is the same, there are many body colour variations. Tie on a No 12 or 10 medium-shanked hook. Start tying the *body* right round the hook bend, select your colour using fine wool ribbed with fuse wire. At the *head*, build up a thorax with two strands of bronze peacock herl. Finally, add a small piece of white raffent to represent wing cases, and tie off.

W. T. SARGEAUNT

Rainbow Trout

1 DESCRIPTION AND HABITAT

Identification

THE chief identification mark of the rainbow is the stripe along the flanks from cheek to tail. This may vary from an iridescent red bar to a pink flush.

A rainbow has small black spots over the whole body in regularly distributed clusters. The tail fins are spotted and usually also the dorsal fin and the adipose fin. There are no dark spots on the cheeks or gill covers.

Brown trout, on the other hand, generally have some red spots, especially along the lateral line, and a red edge to the adipose fin. There are almost always spots on the cheek and gill covers. Usually the tail fins are not spotted, but large fish sometimes show a few faint dark spots, which cannot be mistaken for the thick clusters of small spots on the tail of the rainbow.

Distribution

The rainbow trout is a native of the Pacific shores of North America. It has been found as far north as the Bering Sea and its southern limits extend into Lower California. Over these vast distances and during the immense stretch of geological time, it has developed into many local races to which the nineteenth century delighted in giving specific names.

Nomenclature

The late Dr Hildebrand, of the US Fish and Wild Life Service, recorded fourteen specific names and said that his list was not complete. All these races interbreed and it is now generally accepted that they are one species.

A further difficulty arises, since it was long held that the seagoing Steelhead was a separate species. It is now accepted that it may be a Rainbow Steelhead or a Cut Throat Steelhead according to the particular species inhabiting the river from which it comes.

This need not worry British readers, since the rainbow introduced into British (or indeed other waters) that go down to the sea do not come back. It has relevance, however, to the scientific name. In 1836 Gairdner named one of the American Salmonidae *Salmo Gairdneri*. But the description does not fit the rainbow except possibly in its steelhead form. Hildebrand thought it may possibly have been based on a salmon.

The name *S irideus* was given by Gibbons in 1855 referring to the lateral rainbow stripe, the rainbow's freshwater uniform. This clearly differentiates it from the cut throat which has a red streak beneath the mandible, and no lateral stripe.

Shasta and Kamloops

The rainbow in Britain are, certainly in more recent years, preponderantly of one of the two varieties called Shasta and Kamloops.

S shasta comes from a lake of that name in California and is probably identical with *S stonei* from the neighbouring McCloud River and so named by Jordan in 1894. Its two advantages were that it was supposed to have outgrown its seagoing habits and it bred in the winter and not in the spring, as do most rainbow sub-varieties. The world demand for Shasta has been so great that it has been largely crossbred with other strains, and one can only now safely speak of 'a Shasta type'.

The Kamloops, described in 1892 by Jordan from a lake of that name in British Columbia, reaches a very large size and is an exceptional fighter. Our experience of them is that they are more stream-lined than the Shasta and the rainbow mark is less in evidence. But this may not be a general rule.

New Zealand strain

It is probable that, in some British waters, there is also a New Zealand strain. The Auckland Acclimatization Society Records show that the first successful stocking was in April 1883 from ova of a seagoing strain which came from the Russian River north of San Francisco. These were so successful that their progeny supplied all New Zealand and were widely exported.

Acclimatization in the British Isles

Early introductions

So far as can be ascertained, the first introduction of rainbow was in 1884, when 3,000 ova of Shasta strain were imported from the USA. The next year there were 1,500. From 1888 to 1905 there was an annual shipment of mixed stock from the USA. The next large importation was in 1931 of 50,000 Shasta type and further ones in 1938 and 1939. This was all of course fresh blood, to reinforce the hatcheries' own stock. The Kamloops importations, it appears, came later.

In rivers

The list of waters stocked must necessarily be incomplete, where innumerable owners possess relatively small fisheries. Of rivers known to hold a stock of rainbow in some stretches are the Malling Bourne in Kent, a tributary of the Medway; the Garrow in Herefordshire, a tributary of the Welsh Wye; and a short length of the Surrey Wey, another of the Whitewater.

The more important river fisheries fall into three groups: the Cam and Granta in Cambridgeshire, which have been stocked regularly for fifty years or more; some of the Chiltern streams; the Gade, Chess, Misbourne and Mimram, these mostly since the last war. In this river system there were stockings before the war in the Thorney Weir fishery on the Colne, but these have it seems not survived.

Since most modern fisheries are so heavily fished that periodic stocking is necessary, it is difficult to say in which of these waters rainbow breed sufficiently to justify a claim that they are established. There can be no doubt about it however in the Chess and the Misbourne, where over stretches the rainbow have ousted the brown.

The same is true of the Derbyshire Wye. The history of the rainbow in this stream is fairly well known. They were first introduced into a lake in Ashford Hall above Bakewell about

1909. Thence they escaped into a dam belonging to the DP Battery Company at Bakewell. (The Wye is dammed throughout its length, originally to work the cotton factories, and the pools so formed are called dams.) These formed a breeding stock, breeding upstream from the Battery Dam for some three miles to another dam at the Bobbin Mill (where the bobbins were made for the cotton factories).

The weir at this mill stopped the fish going up. They eventually escaped below the Battery Dam and colonized the river right down to its junction with the Derwent at Rowsley. Rainbow do not like the Derwent water and this more or less stops their further penetration.

In this stretch of the river the rainbow have completely ousted the brown, and below Bakewell they have bred so much that the stretch is probably overstocked. The original stock appears to have been of the autumn spawning strain, although they now spawn late owing to the coldness of the water. Consequently the fishing season does not open until 1 June. In the Battery Dam, they stock with 11- to 14-in fish of the Shasta type, and so overcome this disadvantage.

Remarks on river stocking

The history of acclimatization in Kenya and Australia seems to show that, for success, some barrier to free access to the sea is required, and the best barrier is water that the rainbow will not face either because it is too hot, too acid or too polluted.

It may well be that the only really successful stockings in the Wye, the Chess and the Misbourne are due to the fact that these streams run into other rivers, the Derwent and the Colne, which rainbow will not face.

Rainbow are only happy, as a general rule, in alkaline water of 8 pH and upwards (7 pH is neutral and below that acid).

Since brown trout are at their best in chalk and limestone streams it is probably superfluous to introduce rainbow into such waters.

Blagdon and similar large reservoirs

Types of water in which rainbow are at home and live happily

146

alongside brown trout are large lakes fed by tributary streams which the rainbow can ascend to breed.

In Britain the chief of these is Blagdon which was stocked in 1904 a few years after it was opened. There brown and rainbow continue to flourish alongside each other, and breed.

Eire

The acclimatization plan in Eire is still in the experimental stage. Shasta (autumn spawning) strain are used. Pallas lake near Tullamore, a small limestone lake of about 30 acres with an underground outlet, has been largely cleared of pike and stocked with brown and rainbow.

Kilbrean lake (Killarney) has been stocked with brown and rainbow since 1957.

Lake Labe (Ballymote), an alkaline mountain lake, has been stocked since 1951 with rainbow alone. From this lake fish of $2\frac{1}{2}$ lb have already been recorded. The chief difficulty at present is the scarcity of natural fly. The fish tend to feed in the bottom on crayfish and freshwater shrimps. Attempts are being made to introduce sedge-flies.

Small artificial waters

There is a great future for the rainbow in artificial waters of quite small extent, from two acres upwards. Disused gravel pits, cleared of coarse fish, come to mind, as do small reservoirs, and water artificially created by bulldozing. In Eire they are already using the last type of water. There is a chain of small artificial ponds in Hampshire which is producing trout of up to 7 lb.

At Aldershot two reservoirs fed by springs, one of two acres and the other of nine, have been stocked for sixty years or more. Various combinations have been tried, and the most successful has been found to be to use rainbow alone.

The reasons for this are that rainbow rise so much more freely, fight better, they are much better eating and in the 12-in size there is a saving of about £80 on a thousand fish.

Neither brown nor rainbow will breed much in these small waters, which is really one advantage, as all fish are takeable. It is easy to maintain the necessary alkalinity by adding slaked lime from time to time in waters of such limited extent.

2 FOOD

May differ from water to water

IT must be remembered that not only has the rainbow to acclimatize itself to the waters but also to the food available. Consequently 'the habits of the fish are likely to vary from water to water'.

There has been a considerable amount of information collected from New Zealand where the most successful acclimatization has taken place in the lakes of the North Island.

It has been found that the fish come on the feed at certain periods. They do not feed continuously, but they feed more frequently than brown trout, and have larger appetites. They tend to feed in shoals, and the feeding will usually be caused by the abundance at the time of some species of food. It may be a hatch of mayfly or march brown or sedge. (The Ephemeridae of New Zealand, although different species from the English ones, have been given English names. Thus the species most resembling a mayfly is called 'Mayfly' and so on.) Or it may be a fall of spinners. There is a Red Demoiselle dragon similar, except in colour, to our blue Demoiselle which is eagerly taken. At certain times of the year two sorts of land beetles, brown and green, blow on to the water in large quantities and cause a rise.

A small fish of the smelt type has been introduced on which the fish feed freely near the surface, when anglers take them with a silver-bodied fly fished with a greased line rather in the style of greased-line salmon fishing.

All this indicates that the rainbow is by nature a surface or mid-water feeder.

Information from Eire

The Irish information available tends to show that in Eire waters the trout feed largely on midge and gnat and on duns and spinners, and sedges when available. Only if surface food is lacking they tend to feed in the deeps on crayfish and shrimp. Thus it is said of Lake Labe; 'If adequate numbers of large insects, eg big sedges, were present the larger rainbows would probably feed on the surface, and means to increase the quantity

148

of big fly are being studied at present. Meanwhile the indications are that the big rainbows are feeding among the stones on crayfish which suggests that big flies fished really deep are more likely to be successful than wet-flies fished (as they usually are) only a foot or so beneath the surface.'

Examination of the stomach contents of fish up to about $1\frac{1}{2}$ lb were made and these indicated mostly surface feeding, consisting of land flies and ants, land beetles, water beetles and water boatmen (not unlike a beetle in appearance, there are many species) and quantities of gnat and midge both in their winged and pupa stages.

English rivers

As the rivers in which rainbow thrive are alkaline they may be expected to be rich in fly life, particularly the Ephemeroptera (Mayfly, duns and spinners) and the sedges (trichoptera). There are also on rivers and lakes many species of fly of the family Diptera. These have largely been neglected by writers on flies (except for the black gnat of which more anon) on the ground that they are mostly so small that they are difficult to imitate. But they form a substantial part of the food of rainbow in rivers, and more so in lakes, so we must do our best.

To turn to another group of animals, rainbow are particularly fond of crayfish, freshwater shrimp and freshwater louse. They also feed on a snail whose scientific name is *L stagnalis*. This is normally found in still water, but also in the River Cam, and rainbow from that stream may well be found with this snail in their stomachs. It has two peculiarities which probably make it suitable as food for the rainbow. It has a very fragile shell, particularly in the Cam, where the variety is known as *fragilis*. It has a habit also of frequently casting loose from its food plant and floating on the top of the water, where no doubt the trout take it.

Still water

Some of the Ephemeroptera live in both rivers and lakes, particularly the Mayflies. The olives of still water are different species from those of rivers but so alike that one species is called *simile*. Nearly two hundred species of sedges have been recorded and there are no doubt more waiting discovery. So the lake varieties may well have different scientific names but will look like those of rivers.

The midges will assume increased importance. The larvae of some species are unique in having haemoglobin in their blood which oxygenates it, and so they can live in water too deep for most flies in the underwater stage of their existence.

These blood-worms, as they are called, rise to the surface from time to time to renew their oxygen, when they are eagerly taken by the fish. They are also found in some rivers, for instance in a stretch called the Broadwater at Greywell where the Whitewater rises. This is stocked with rainbow, and the appearance of blood-worms there has been the subject of articles in the fishing papers. Other flies which hatch from the water in still waters are some species of crane-fly (Daddy-long-legs) and the small blue dragonfly called Demoiselle. These are both eagerly taken. But apparently the fish do not take the large type of dragonfly.

Land flies and beetles get blown upon most waters, but particularly on large sheets of water. Bees and wasps, blue-bottles and house-flies are all taken, but the insects most likely to cause a rise are ants during their mating flights and greenfly (aphis).

Snails, shrimp, louse and crayfish will also form a considerable part of the food, and probably most of it in the winter when flies are scarce. There is one snail about the size and colour of hemp seed called *Potamopyrgus jenkinsi* which up to 1893 lived only in brackish water. Since then it has invaded fresh water. It breeds so fast, that a friend of ours stocked his ponds from about 50 collected off a bunch of watercress. Where present, rainbow take it eagerly. Perhaps also the roach take hemp seed for this mollusc.

Summary

When one considers the immense amount and variety of creatures who live their lives, or part of them, in fresh water, the above list seems very restricted. But it will not surprise fishermen, who are familiar with the very specialized feeding habits of most fish. With the exception of crustaceans which seem everywhere particularly attractive to rainbow (eg in

Kenya, Australia, New Zealand), the main food seems to be insects more or less inert on the surface or some two or three feet below it. Creatures active on the surface, such as beetles and water boatmen, seem to be taken but rarely. Even blue dragon-flies, which they chase at times, are mostly taken hatching out on the surface, or flown on it and spent and those chased are probably ones they miss when hatching.

3 FEEDING HABITS

Rainbow differs from brown

THE Eire Inland Fisheries Trust, in a Report, says: 'A point which must be borne in mind – but which some anglers tend to overlook – is that the rainbow is a distinct species from the brown trout and so will not necessarily behave as the brown trout would. It may, consequently, take freely at times of the day – or of the year – when a brown trout wouldn't and vice-versa. In some waters rainbow may have to be fished for with different types of flies, and by fishing such flies at quite different depths and/or speeds.'

The window

Direct light can only penetrate through the surface to the eye of a trout in a cone of about 45° on each side of the eyes. This is called the 'window' and varies in size with the depth at which the fish feeds.

The brown trout when feeding on surface flies and hatching nymphs takes up a position close to the surface. Thus he has a small window. The rainbow feeds much deeper, he has consequently a much larger window (Fig 17). Now the brown trout will normally only take up his surface feeding position, will rise, as we say, when there is sufficient surface food to make it worth while. Otherwise he will be feeding down below, or lying dormant. The rainbow requires much more food than the brown, and he gets it by feeding in mid water, with an eye on the surface. So he will rise more freely than the brown. He will also be interested much more than the brown in such small stuff as midge larvae and the smaller types of gnat. He is also gregarious

151

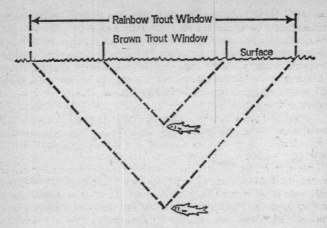

FIG 17. The Window.

and will cruise in shoals, whereas the brown cruises much more rarely, and then singly.

Rise forms

It is useful also to study the types of rise.

(a) There is first a swirl under the water. This means a fish taking a midge pupa or nymph. It will sometimes be followed by a splashing surface rise, or even by the fish leaping out of the water. You may fish the swirl with a sunk fly or nymph, being ready to change to a floating fly if the surface rise follows. This means that the fish is chasing active nymphs up to the surface or even leaping after them if they escape. This last rise form is very usual when the Mayfly is hatching.

(b) The second type of rise is a series of splashing commotions on the surface with every now and then a pronounced head and tail rise. This will probably be at sedge and if you watch you will see sedge hatching out and scurrying over the surface. There will be a similar rise to the Blue Demoiselle dragonfly of which the rainbow are very fond. They will often leap out of the water at them.

(c) The third type is the head and tail rise. This always fills one with excitement which one knows all along to be quite unjustified. For some reason the appearance of the tail half-submerged makes the fish look so much bigger than it is. None the less, to see a shoal rising over a quiet pool is a great sight. This rise usually means that the fish are taking floating duns.

(d) At a fall of spinners the rise is a very quiet one. The shoal will move about fairly high in the water. This rise may not inappropriately be described as 'sipping'. There is a similar rise to midge pupae. But the shoal moves more rapidly and it is interspersed with an occasional boil when the pupa hatches before being taken and sometimes a fish will leap out of the water at a midge that has hatched and escaped.

This rise puzzled the author before he got to understand it. In one part of our lake, a shallow bay, during the evenings there was a fall of mayfly spinners and this 'sipping' plus a boil used to happen. The fish ignored the artificial spent gnat, and it was only after two days that a fish taken later on a sedge was discovered to be full of Caenis, a little white fly which is actually one of the Ephemeroptera but behaves more like a midge. Its vernacular name is 'Fisherman's Curse' which well describes it. The fish were taking that and not the spent gnat at all.

It is always most important to observe the type of rise, as this gives one a clue to the pattern of fly to use and the best method of fishing it.

Feeding stations (rivers)

It is dangerous to generalize too much about the habits of any fish. One of the charms of fishing is the unexpected, and of course one river differs from another, and indeed, rivers differ very much in various stretches. But on the whole the rivers where rainbow will be found are likely to have fast, comparatively shallow water alternating with deep pools with a fair current flowing through the pools, causing backwaters. There will also be a proportion of flats with little current. If you are accustomed to chalk-stream fishing for brown trout you will perhaps ignore the rapids. It is a great mistake. Rainbow tend to move up from the pools into the rapids, particularly in the mornings where they may be fished for upstream wet, or dry with a well-hackled fly that floats well. If this fails (and both are hard methods of fishing as it is difficult to see the take, or to strike in time) a biggish wet-fly fished downstream is often deadly. Many of the rainbow with which Thorney Weir on the Colne was stocked before the war were caught this way on a large Invicta.

In the pools the shoals will rise in the current, but the smaller fish usually at the tail. The larger fish will be more often found in the backwaters, which are particularly difficult to fish unless you can find a position facing downstream, where you will, of course, be fishing the backwater up.

A difference between the feeding methods of the brown and the rainbow is particularly noticeable in the still pools. If you bungle a cast or show yourself or your rod, the brown trout will go down but the rainbow shoal will merely move up a yard or two. You are then faced with the decision whether to wait until they drop down again, to pursue them upstream or to go somewhere else. Unless these are the only feeding fish you have spotted, it is usually best to go somewhere else. They may not return for some time, and if you pursue them, they have become wary.

If you hook a fish and pull him down quickly, you can often take others out of the same shoal from the same spot.

Feeding stations (still water)

Where the surface area may vary from the vast stretch of Blagdon to a small artificial lake of say two acres, it is even more inadvisable to generalize than in the case of rivers. None the less, one general statement can be made. The fish will be found feeding where the food is. Yet even this generalization needs substantial qualifications.

You will be impatient to start fishing. But always have a look first at as much of the water as is possible in a short time. You will, of course, be immensely helped by knowledge of the water. Knowing where the fish are likely to be found under prevailing conditions, time of year, time of day, weather, wind, are some of the chief factors which will affect this.

Bottom feeding

There are times, particularly early in the season when surface food is scarce, and also when the water freshens up and cools after rain, when a large fly fished close to the bottom and well out will give results.

Rainbow are particularly susceptible to a big fly with a gold or silver body worked fairly fast, or else allowed to fall on the bottom and fished with a sink and draw motion. A stout cast is necessary, as on these occasions fish take with a bang.

4 ARTIFICIAL FLIES FOR RAINBOW IN RIVERS

(Note: Freshwater entomology is discussed in other sections of this book – Ed.)

Requirements in general

IT will be seen that the rainbow angler must have artificial flies which will attract fish either:
  on the surface;
  in the first foot or two under water, near the bottom.
The surface flies must represent

> Duns
> Spinners
> Sedges
> Gnats and midges
> Land insects blown on the water

The nymphs must represent nymphs, larvae and pupae of duns, sedges, gnats and midges, and the wet-flies must represent mainly crustaceans.

The first requirement of any fly is that it must be attractive to the fish. To do this it must look like food, and preferably like the food on which the rainbow is feeding at the time.

River ephemeridae

A rainbow feeding on duns is perhaps not so particular as a brown trout. As he feeds from deeper in the water he will make his meal of nymph and dun indiscriminately, which the brown trout rarely does. Also, of course, taking the long view of evolution, all British flies are strange to him. Therefore he is not so exacting as to patterns. One pattern however you must have. That is the Coachman. It is impossible to guess what the attraction of the Coachman is to the rainbow. In Kenya, they say they catch three-quarters of their rainbow on it. It may be it represents an ancestral memory of something on which they feed in their native rivers.

The other general fly is a Wickham's Fancy. This is a heavily hackled fly with a gold body and is particularly useful in fast waters where it floats well and can be seen. These two are obviously flies which look to the fish like food, but not the particular food on which they are feeding.

(The following list is a guide to the beginner, which he will doubtless modify after experience on various waters – Ed.)

List of artificials

	Name of Natural	Season	Artificial	Size of Hook
1	Blue Dun or Large Dark Olive	April, May and again Sept.	Blue Upright	o or 1
2	Iron Blue	,,	*Iron Blue	oo
3	Olive	From May	Hare's Ear	o
3a		onwards	*or Olive Quill	
4	Pale Watery	,,	*Ginger Quill	oo or ooo
5	Blue Winged Olive	Aug. & Sept. mostly in evenings	*Orange Quill	oo
6	Little Sky Blue	Aug. & Sept.	*Greenwell	oo
7	Spinners		Pheasant Tail	oo or o
8	General Flies		*Coachman	1 to oo
			*Wickham's Fancy	1

Those marked * are winged, others hackled.

Nymphs

You can buy from the tackle shop representations of all the nymphs. In the writer's opinion, you will do far better with some of the old hackle wet-flies as follows:

Name of Natural	Artificial	Size of Hook
1 Blue Dun	Partridge and Green	1
2 Iron Blue	Snipe and Purple	oo
3 Olive	Partridge and Yellow	o
4 Pale Watery	Partridge and Yellow	oo
5 Blue Winged Olive	Grouse and Orange	o
6 Little Sky Blue	Partridge and Green	oo

The partridge and yellow in suitable sizes will usually do for all the nymphs.

Mayflies

This fly will appear from Mid-May to Mid-June depending on the river and the season. There are innumerable patterns, a good selection of which will be found on pages 170 to 173.

Sedges

The Brown Sedges are perhaps the commonest.
    Pupa: Ogden's Invicta fished sunk size 3.
    Imago: Ogden fished dry, or Coachman.
Black Sedges
    Pupa: Black Palmer sunk size 2.
    Imago: Black Palmer fished dry or Alder.

Midges

The Fisherman's Curse (Caenis) is included under this heading though it is really one of the Ephemeridae. One peculiarity of this fly is that its dun stage is only a few minutes; it changes at once to a spinner, a tiny insect with transparent wings and a white body with a few dark rings. When it appears, usually on hot evenings, the fish ignore all else, including usually the fisherman's artificial, and set out to feed on Caenis, cruising around in shoals, apparently with mouths open sucking in the delicacy. The fisherman's best plan is to go home.

The tackle makers do sell representations. The best is perhaps a fly called Hackle Curse. The fish will occasionally take Halford's Pale Water Female. A ooo Coachman is sometimes effective.

The difficulty in copying the true midges is their minute size. This difficulty is best overcome by tying double flies with a hackle at each end, called Knitted Midges. These no doubt represent the male and female flies mating on the water.

There is a famous Derbyshire model called the Double Badger, body peacock herl between two badger hackles, hook size oo or ooo.

The Knitted Midge is usually tied with a black ostrich feather body between two black cock hackles. A very small Greenwell or Coachman will sometimes be taken. It is little use fishing the pupa since they don't hang about but rise to the surface in an air bubble and immediately hatch out.

Land flies

The chief of the land flies to be blown on the water is the black gnat which is neither black nor a gnat. It is a fly called *Bibio johannis*, being of a thirsty disposition and appearing round about St John's Day. Dunne's Black Gnat is undoubtedly the best representation.

Body: Dark olive artificial silk.
Hackle: Honey dun.
Wings: A bunch of mixed red and bottle-green hackles.

A small Greenwell ooo is also effective.

The alder is represented well enough by a Black Palmer, as is also the black ant but in a smaller size. A small Pheasant Tail will take when there is a fall of red ants.

Wet-flies

A fly called the Silver-bodied March Brown, (silver body and partridge hackle) size 1 is probably taken for the water louse.

Teal and Red (or Peter Ross which is said to be an improvement on the original tying) and a very lightly hackled Wickham size 3 will be found all that is needed for downstream wet-fly. They no doubt represent crustaceans.

Check list

Year in and year out most rainbows in rivers will be caught on one or other of the following flies:

- (*a*) Mayfly and Iron Blue needed in season for these flies only.
- (*b*) Greenwell in various sizes dry.
- (*c*) Coachman in various sizes dry.
- (*d*) Pheasant Tail in various sizes dry.
- (*e*) Wickham (well hackled)
  also Wickham, lightly hackled for wet-fly fishing.
- (*f*) Ginger Quill winged dry.
- (*g*) Red and Black Palmers.
- (*h*) Double Badger.
- (*j*) Partridge and yellow wet.
- (*k*) Teal and red wet.

5 ARTIFICIAL FLIES FOR RAINBOWS IN LAKES

THE Author's club fishes two small reservoirs stocked wholly with rainbows. There is a steady turnover of membership, and newcomers, especially those whose experience has been on rivers, usually spend some time fishing their favourite flies before they visit the water bailiff and examine his stock. There they find some standard flies, Mayflies, Coachman and so on, and others new to them, such as Blue Dragon flies, large sedges, heavily hackled Olives, all designed for two reasons, as good floaters and as visible at a distance among the ripples – or sometimes waves. Similarly many of the wet-flies will be much larger than he would use for river fishing, size 5, 6 or 7, and rather thinly hackled. Others, however, March Browns, Greenwells and so on, will be the normal river sizes, 1 to 3.

Local patterns

Those who tie their own flies may like to try three patterns which have proved very successful in our Club. They are illustrated in Fig 18. The main point is that they are all tied with plastic nylon tubing for body. This can be had by pulling out the wire of nylon-covered electric flex or may be bought from surgical suppliers, where it is known as Portex flexible nylon tubing. The fore and aft is usually tied with undyed body and a white hackle fore and a ginger aft. This is a floating fly.

Blondie: pale buff hackle and wing, and ribbed gold wire is the wet equivalent.

The detached body of the Blue Dragon should be dyed blue and painted with a few black markings with cellulose paint. The hackle is white in front of black. A few strands of fluorescent hackle may be included.

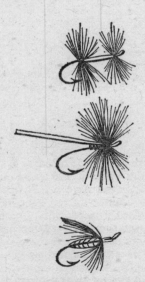

FIG 18. Fore and Aft: Blondie: Blue Dragon.

Check list

Floating Flies:
   Mayfly: included with Male and Female Spinner, size 6 and 7.
   Pond Olive: tied with a yellow-olive hackle, size 2 and 3.
   Lake Olive: Brown olive hackle, size 2 and 3.
   Coachman: Size 6.
   Alder: Size 4.
   Wickham (Dry): Size 4.
   Butcher (Dry): Size 4.
   Fore and Aft: Size 5.
   Dragonfly: Detached body, 4 or 5 hook.

Large Wet-Flies:
   Alexandra.
   Butcher: Size 6 and 7.
   Peter Ross.
   Ogden.
   Blagdon Bug.
   Blondie.

Small Wet-Flies:
   Greenwell: Size 2 and 3.
   March Brown: Silver body.
   Black Palmer.
   Butcher.

Midges:
   Black Palmer: Size oo.
   Ditto with white hackle: Size ooo.
   Ditto olive hackle.
   Black Gnat.
   Greenwell (Dry): Size o.
   Coachman.

C. F. WALKER

Trout Flies: Natural and Artificial

FOREWORD

THERE are now quite a number of books dealing with aquatic entomology available to the fisherman, but to the best of my belief only one of these, *The Dry-fly Fisherman's Entomology*, by M. E. Mosely, is small enough to be carried to the waterside in the angler's pocket. This is an obvious advantage in a book of this kind so, as more than forty years have passed since Mosely's work was first published, the time seems ripe for the appearance of a second book of a similar convenient size. In the present case, detailed descriptions of individual species of sedge-flies and stone-flies, which were included by Mosely, have been omitted as being unnecessary for practical angling purposes. On the other hand, a number of insects found only or primarily in lakes have been added to those described by him.

The descriptions of the natural flies have been taken verbatim from my own chapter on entomology in *The Complete Fly-Fisher*, published by Messrs Herbert Jenkins, Ltd. To render the book more useful to the angler, however, dressings of the artificial flies representing the insects described have been added to these. In some cases, such as that of the Mayfly, the patterns available are so numerous that they cannot all be included, so I have confined myself to one or two typical dressings. In other instances, either there are no standard commercial imitations or these are considered unsatisfactory, and where this is so I have given details of patterns of proved worth devised by amateur fly dressers, including some of my own. For the details of some of these dressings I am indebted to that wonderfully comprehensive book *A Dictionary of Trout Flies*, by A. Courtney Williams.

Lest the beginner should find himself appalled by the number of patterns given in this book, I should perhaps explain that it is not intended that he should carry all or even half of them in his fly-box. Rather, having first acquired a sufficient knowledge of entomology to be able to recognize the more important insects, he should then choose a selection of patterns most likely to prove of value in the waters where he is accustomed to fish.

C. F. WALKER

1 INTRODUCTION

WHETHER the fly fisher is deliberately using representations of natural insects or merely general flies with fancy names, I believe that the majority of trout which take his artificial do so because they mistake it, if not for the species of fly on which they are feeding, at all events for the type of food they are accustomed to see at that particular time of year. This, moreover, is equally true of both wet- and dry-fly, and of lakes as well as rivers, despite the fact that, to the human eye, some of the patterns sold as loch flies bear little resemblance to any known form of animal life. If this premise is accepted, it follows that some knowledge of the insects on which trout feed is essential to the angler who would make the most of his opportunities. This does not imply that he need become an entomologist in the scientific sense, but merely that he should learn enough about the appearance, behaviour and habitats of these insects to enable him to fish his artificials intelligently and with that degree of confidence which begets success.

The food of trout. At the outset it should be stressed that trout, being extremely catholic in their tastes, will at times be prepared to eat almost any kind of insects which chance or a puff of wind may blow on to the water, not excluding such apparently unpalatable objects as wasps and bees. Those who have read Leonard West's book, *The Natural Trout Fly and its Imitation,* may recall that it includes descriptions and illustrations of no less than 102 insects, a great many of which are land-bred species which the average angler would be unlikely to see on the water once in a lifetime. Such comprehensive treatment, however, defeats its own object by making the subject of entomology unnecessarily complicated, and for present purposes, with a few important exceptions, I am confining myself to the true aquatic species.

It must be realized that a substantial proportion of the trout's diet consists of creatures which, for one reason or another, it is virtually impossible to imitate in fur and feather. This includes such things as plankton crustacea (a very important source of food supply in lakes), snails, newts, tadpoles, larvae of many kinds and caddis in their cases. With the exception of the last-named, which form an essential link in the life-history of the sedge-flies, these are omitted from my descriptions, together with small fish and the larger crustaceans, which, although they are probably represented by certain loch patterns, do not truly come under the heading of entomology.

Nomenclature. Before we proceed to the descriptions it will be as well, for the benefit of the beginner, to explain the principle on which insects – and indeed the whole of the animal and vegetable kingdoms – are arranged and named by the scientists. They are divided into a number of different groups, known as orders, families, sub-families, genera and species, the insects within each group bearing a stronger resemblance to one another as we proceed down the scale, until we come to species, in which they are all virtually identical. The naming system, which is based on that introduced by the Swedish naturalist, Linnaeus, two hundred years ago, only takes account of the genera and species. These generic and specific names, usually of a descriptive character, may be likened respectively to our own surnames and Christian names, but they appear in the reverse order. It may be objected that the angler has no need to trouble himself with scientific names, and I agree that one does not want to hear Latin and Greek bandied about by the water-side. It is, nevertheless, essential to include these names with the written descriptions of insects, for several reasons. First, the classical languages are international; second, some British insects have no vernacular names; third, some vernacular names are applied to different flies in different parts of the country, while, conversely, some flies are known by more than one such name. With the scientific names these ambiguities can never occur.

Habitats of insects. The habitats are included in the descriptions of each insect, and it should be noted that although many species are found in both flowing and static water, others occur in only one or the other kind. Unfortunately it is not as easy as might be thought to draw a hard-and-fast line between the two, since some rivers contain almost stagnant pools, which so far as the insects are concerned possess all the characteristics of a lake, while on the other hand there are stream-fed lakes with a strong current extending for some distance beyond the point of inflow, where the conditions resemble those of a river. Furthermore, there are certain species which, although primarily adapted for life in rivers, can sometimes be found on the stony margins of large lakes where the wave action creates a sufficient degree of aeration for them to exist in the absence of a current. It is, of course, on the requirements of the nymph or larva that the choice of habitat depends, and all land-bred insects, which only reach the water fortuitously and in the winged stage, may be found either on lakes or rivers.

2 ORDER: EPHEMEROPTERA (DAY-FLIES)

THE day-flies are of the highest importance to the chalk-stream fisherman, of considerable importance to those who fish in rain-fed rivers, and by no means so unimportant on lakes as some writers on the subject would have us believe. The same species, however, do not in every case inhabit all three types of water.

This is the only order in which it is both necessary and practicable for the angler to learn to recognize the different species: necessary because hatches of each species frequently occur in sufficient numbers for the trout to feed on them exclusively, and practical because they are few enough to be easily memorized. There are, in fact, only forty-seven British species all told, of which no more than half are sufficiently common and well-liked by the trout to merit the angler's attention. The remainder are omitted from my descriptive list.

In the descriptions of the flies, the colour of the back, or upper side, is given for recognition purposes, but in every case the underside is paler; a point to be borne in mind when selecting materials for dry-flies. With the exception of Halford, who dealt only with the chalk-stream species, I do not know of any writer on entomology who gives the sizes of flies when describing them. Yet as the British day-flies vary in length from about three-sixteenths to three-quarters of an inch, it has always seemed to me that some acquaintance with their *relative* sizes would be of considerable help to the beginner who is learning to recognize them. I therefore mention the size of each species, employing relative terms for this purpose and taking as my standard the Medium Olive dun, which measures about 8 mm from the front of the head to the extremity of the abdomen. Species of this length are described as medium-sized, those measuring from 9 to 10 mm as large, from 6 to 7 mm as small, and the few which lie outside these limits as very large or very small. It should be borne in mind, however, that certain species vary considerably in size, and where this is so the fact is stated. In most cases the female is slightly larger than her mate, and the length of the fore wing slightly greater than that of the body.

The life-cycle consists of four stages: egg, nymph, dun and spinner, and it is of interest to note that the day-flies are the only insects which go through two winged stages. After a short period, varying with the species and temperature of the water, the minute nymph, or larva, as it is more usually known at this early stage, emerges from the egg and at once starts to feed, mainly on algal growths. As it increases in size it undergoes a series of moults, until at the end of a year (or in the case of the Mayfly probably two years) it attains maturity. Then, when the time is ripe, it either swims to the surface or, in some species, climbs up a weed stem, the skin splits down the back, and the subimago, or dun, bursts forth. The newly emerged fly, after drying its wings, then takes off and flies to the bank, where it hides itself among the foliage until the time arrives for the final metamorphosis, which may take place within a few minutes or not for a day or two, according to the species and atmospheric conditions.

Now the skin splits once more and the perfect insect, known as an imago or spinner, emerges, leaving its cast-off garment on the leaf or grass blade where the transformation took place. The wings of the insect are now clear and iridescent (those of the dun being semi-opaque and fringed with hairs), the body has changed colour, and the cerci, or tails, are considerably longer. If a female, it will now go into hiding once more: if a male, it will presently join others of its species and the whole assembly will begin the nuptial dance, rising and falling alternately above the banks, or sometimes in the shelter of bushes. This usually takes place in the evening, and has the effect of attracting the females, who in ones and twos approach the dancers, to be immediately seized by the nearest males and carried off for a brief aerial honeymoon.

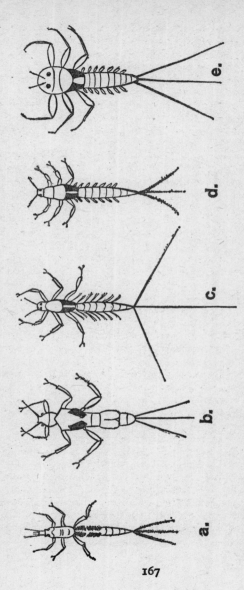

Fig 19. Types of Day-fly Nymphs. a, Burrowing. b, Crawling. c, Slow swimming. d, Fast swimming. e, Flat type living among stones. (For the sake of comparison of details all the nymphs have been drawn the same length. Actually, the Mayfly nymph (a) would be four or five times as long as the Broadwing nymph (b) the remainder being of intermediate lengths.)

As the last act in the little drama the now-fertilized females return to the water to deposit their eggs. For this purpose some species crawl down a weed stem, some dip repeatedly on to the surface, leaving a batch of eggs at each visit, while others drop the whole consignment from the air. But whichever method is adopted, the female, her duty done, ends by collapsing upon the water with outspread wings; the spent spinner of the fisherman. The males, on the other hand, have no need to revisit the water at all, and unless they are blown on to the surface accidentally they die inland.

From the foregoing account it will be evident that the trout have five separate opportunities of feeding on the day-flies: as immature nymphs on the bottom or among the weed-beds; as ripe nymphs either rising to the surface or in the act of hatching; as newly-hatched duns drying their wings before taking off; as

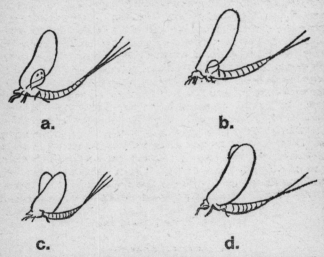

FIG 20. Day-flies: Wing and tail combinations. a, 4 wings and 3 tails (Mayflies, BWO, Sepia and Claret duns). b, 4 wings and 2 tails (Olives, Iron Blues, Pale Wateries, March Browns, August or Autumn dun and Yellow Upright). c, 2 wings and 3 tails (Broadwings). d, 2 wings and 2 tails (Pond and Lake Olives and Pale Evening dun). Only the commoner species are mentioned here, but all the British Ephemeroptera fall into one or another of these patterns.

female spinners in the act of depositing their eggs; and finally as spent spinners lying helpless on the surface of the water. The trout do not neglect these opportunities, though in the case of a few species, as we shall see in due course, the duns leave the water so quickly after emergence that the fish do not get a proper chance of taking them in this stage.

The day-fly nymphs fall into four categories: the burrowers, the crawlers, the swimmers (which may in turn be divided into fast and slow movers), and the flat nymphs which live under stones. It is not really necessary, and would in any case be difficult, for the angler to learn to recognize the individual species in their nymphal stage; so, as nymphs of the same genus are very much alike, a single description will suffice in each case. The duns require separate treatment according to species, though except in the case of the Blue-winged Olive, the sexes in this stage resemble each other closely enough to be dealt with together. (The males can be distinguished by the presence at the extremity of the abdomen of a pair of claspers for the purpose of holding the female during the mating process.) In the spinner stage, however, there is in nearly every case a very marked difference in body colour between the sexes, and although it is with the females that fish and fishermen are primarily concerned, the males are described as well to enable the reader to identify them during the nuptial dance; a useful clue to the species of females which may be expected on the water later in the evening.

Although all day-fly nymphs carry three tails, in the winged stages of certain genera these are reduced to two. Some genera, moreover, have two wings and others four, so that the combination of wings and tails helps to reduce the possibilities when deciding the genus of a dun or spinner seen at close quarters. A note of these characteristics will be found beneath each genus.

Family: EPHEMERIDAE

Genus: *Ephemera*

Characteristics: Four wings and three tails.

The nymphs are of the burrowing type, living in the silt at the bottom of a lake or river. They are long and comparatively slender, brown in colour and with plume-like gills which are folded over the back. Their tails are relatively short and fringed with short hairs. As they approach maturity wing-pads develop on the back; a feature common to all the day-fly nymphs which need not, therefore, be repeated in describing those of other genera. They spring from the middle thoracic segment and when fully grown extend over the first two segments of the abdomen.

GREEN MAYFLY, OR GREEN DRAKE

Ephemera danica

This is the common Mayfly of rivers and lakes, and has a preference for alkaline waters. It is a very large fly and hatches from the end of May to the beginning of June.

The dun* has broad, triangular fore wings and relatively large hind wings, their colour being greenish-yellow with dark brown veins and dark markings on the fore wings. The thorax is dark olive-brown and the abdomen pale straw-yellow with brown markings down the back which become more pronounced towards the tail end, those on the first five segments being either small or entirely absent. The legs are olive-brown and the tails almost black. The male is noticeably smaller than the female and of a darker shade throughout.

The male spinner, or Black Drake, has transparent wings strongly veined and marked with blackish-brown. The thorax is black and the abdomen ivory-white, marked down the back in the same way as the dun. The legs and tails are black.

The female spinner is sometimes known as the Grey Drake, and after oviposition by the rather ridiculous name of Spent Gnat. The wings are transparent with a blue-grey sheen and brown veins, the thorax brown and the abdomen similar to that of the male but with paler brown markings. The legs and tails are dark greyish-brown.

Artificials

Nymph. There is no standard dressing of the Mayfly nymph,

---

* The term dun is here used for the sake of uniformity, although, strictly speaking, it is not applicable to the larger *Ephemeroptera*, whose subimagos are not dun-coloured.

but I have had considerable success with the following dressing, which represents the nymph in the act of hatching:

> *Body:* Hare's ear.
> *Ribbing:* Gold tinsel.
> *Hackles:* Brown speckled partridge feather dyed in picric acid, followed by a similar feather undyed. One or two turns of each.
> *Whisks:* Three fibres from a cock pheasant's tail feather, short.
> *Hook:* Long Mayfly.

Dun. There are innumerable patterns on the market, of which the following are representative of the winged and hackled patterns respectively:

> *Halford's Green Mayfly, Female.*
> > *Body:* Undyed raffia.
> > *Ribbing:* Horsehair dyed medium cinnamon.
> > *Wings:* Mallard scapular feathers dyed pale grey-green and set on back-to-back.
> > *Head hackle:* Hen golden pheasant neck.
> > *Shoulder hackles:* Two pale cream hackles.
> > *Whisks:* Gallina dyed very dark chocolate-brown.
> > *Hook:* 2.*
> *French Partridge.*
> > *Body:* Cream floss silk.
> > *Ribbing:* Crimson silk and fine gold tinsel.
> > *Head hackle:* French partridge back feather.
> > *Shoulder hackles:* Two red cock hackles.
> > *Whisks:* Red cock hackle fibres.
> > *Hook:* 3.

Personally I prefer hackled to winged versions, as the stiff whole feathers used in most winged patterns tend to make them bad hookers.

Spinner. Here again there are plenty of patterns from which to choose, the following being typical examples of the two most common styles of dressing:

* Hook sizes refer to the new scale throughout.

Halford's Spent Gnat, Female.

    Body: Raffia dyed pale yellow ochre.

    Ribbing: Condor quill dyed dark chocolate-brown.

    Wings: Four medium Andalusian cock hackles set on horizontally.

    Hackles: Two pale Andalusian cock hackles.

    Whisks: Gallina dyed very dark chocolate-brown.

    Hook: 3, long-shanked.

The drawback to this style of dressing is that the wings have a tiresome habit of catching beneath the bend of the hook. The following pattern is free from this disadvantage:

Henderson's Spent Gnat.

    Body: Undyed raffia.

    Ribbing: Fine silver tinsel.

    Wings: A grey cock hackle divided into two horizontal bunches by figure-of-eight turns of the tying silk.

    Hackle: Grey partridge breast feather. (A badger body hackle is sometimes added.)

    Whisks: Three strands of cock pheasant tail.

    Hook: 5 to 7.

BROWN MAYFLY

Ephemera vulgata

Despite its name,* this species is much less common than the previous one, being chiefly confined to very sluggish rivers with a muddy bottom, such as those of the eastern counties. In view of this it is rather curious that this insect is seldom found in lakes, though I have seen it in some numbers on the Bourley lakes, near Aldershot. Its size and time of appearance are the same as for *E danica.*

The dun has brownish wings, more mottled with brown than those of *E danica,* while the colour of the abdomen is brownish-yellow, and the markings, which are roughly triangular in shape, are present on every segment. The legs and tails are dark brown.

The spinners, male and female, are virtually browner versions

* This can doubtless be accounted for by the fact that *E danica* was originally named *vulgata* by Pictet.

of the *danica* spinners, and can be distinguished from them by the markings on the back, described above.

A third British species, *E lineata*, resembles the foregoing, but is too rare to merit a separate description.

FIG 21. Mayfly Body Markings. A, The Brown Mayfly (*Ephemera vulgata.*) B, The Green Mayfly (*Ephemera danica*)

Artificials

Separate patterns representing the Brown Mayfly are seldom needed. If they are, slightly browner versions of the Green Mayfly dressings will suffice.

Family: LEPTOPHLEBIIDAE

Genus: *Leptophlebia*

Characteristics: Four wings and three tails.

The nymphs are of the swimming type, but are not very agile in their movements. They are torpedo-shaped and very dark brown in colour, which makes them hard to distinguish against a peaty bottom. From each side of the abdomen project seven pairs of gills resembling leaves with very long points. These gills are mobile, so that by moving them to and fro the nymphs can create a current along their bodies which enables them to live in still water. The tails are very long – at least as long as the body – and are held wide apart: a most distinctive feature of these nymphs, which is preserved in their winged stages.

SEPIA

Leptophlebia marginata

The vernacular name was suggested by me in a recent book, sepia being the predominating colour of the insect in all three stages. It hatches from mid-April to mid-May, and is found in lakes and slow streams. It is a large fly, somewhat local in distribution, but abundant where it occurs.

The dun has light sepia wings with a darker area near the tips of the fore wings, the two main veins being yellow and the remainder dark sepia, forming a strongly-marked criss-cross pattern. The thorax and abdomen are dark sepia, the legs warm sepia and the tails almost black. Unlike most of the day-flies, the males are slightly larger than the females.

The male spinner has transparent wings with a faint brownish tinge, veined and marked in the same way as the wings of the dun. The thorax is black and the abdomen dark sepia, becoming darker towards the tail. Legs and tails as in the dun.

The female spinner is similar to the male as to wings, thorax, legs and tails, but the sepia abdomen has an undertone of yellow, especially in the three terminal segments.

There are no standard patterns representing this species, but I have evolved the following dressings of my own:

Nymph.
    Abdomen: Dark brown seal's fur.
    Ribbing: Silver tinsel.
    Thorax and wing pads: Black seal's fur.
    Gills: A dark honey dun hen hackle wound at the junction of the thorax and abdomen and pressed backwards towards the tail.
    Whisks: Fibres from a black hen hackle as long as the body, splayed apart by the tying silk.
    Hook: 2 or 3.

Dun.
    Body: Grey-brown condor herl.

Wings: A bunch of fibres from a mallard scapular feather, set on with a slight rake towards the tail.

Hackle: A cock hackle dyed sepia.

Whisks: Fibres from a black cock's spade feather, splayed apart as in the nymph.

Hook: 2 to 3.

Spinner.

Body: Dark brown seal's fur mixed with a little ginger.

Ribbing: Gold tinsel.

Wings: Grey and ginger grizzled cock hackle.

Leg hackle: A cock hackle dyed sepia, or none.

Whisks: Fibres from a black cock's spade feather, splayed apart as before.

Hook: 2 to 3.

There are three ways of representing the wings of spinners, viz, two hackle points set on horizontally, two bunches of hackle fibres divided in the Henderson style, or an ordinary hackle. (In the last case no separate leg hackle is required.) To save repetition it should be understood that all my own spinner patterns may be dressed in any of these three ways.

CLARET

Leptophlebia vespertina

Both the vernacular and scientific names of this species are misleading, as it is not claret-coloured and the duns normally emerge at midday. Its size is medium to small and its habitats the same as those of the Sepia, with a preference for a peaty bottom, but it has a wider distribution. The main hatches take place from mid-May to mid-June.

The dun has dark grey fore wings, not unlike those of the Iron Blue dun, for which it is probably often mistaken, but it can be readily distinguished from the latter by its pale buff hind wings, which show up very clearly some distance away. The thorax is black and the abdomen variable in colour, being either dark brown or dark grey in the female and dark brown or glossy black in the male. The legs are dark brown and the tails grey-brown with faintly marked rings.

The male spinner has transparent wings, which are completely colourless except for two yellow veins near the fore margin. The thorax is black and the abdomen reddish-grey with dark brown terminal segments. The legs are brown and the tails pale grey-brown with pronounced dark rings.

The female spinner is virtually a smaller edition of *L marginata*, with the same yellow undertone showing through the abdominal segments.

Artificials

Nymph. As for the Sepia nymph, but dressed on a size o or oo hook.
Dun. As for the Sepia dun but dressed on a size o or oo hook and having wings of waterhen breast fibres in place of mallard.

Spinner.
>*Body:* Dark brown and ginger seal's fur.
>*Ribbing:* Gold tinsel.
>*Wings:* Pale blue or brassy dun cock hackle.
>*Leg hackle:* Dark furnace or none.
>*Whisks:* Brown mallard scapular fibres.
>*Hook:* o or oo.

Family: EPHEMERELLIDAE

Genus: *Ephemerella*

Characteristics: Four wings and three tails.

The nymphs are of the crawling type and live on the bottom among weeds and stones. They are relatively broader than any of the nymphs previously described and dark brown in colour. The plate-like gills are situated on the back, and do not project beyond the sides of the body. There are five pairs of these, of which the fifth pair is very small and hidden beneath the fourth. The tails are short and fringed with short scattered bristles.

BLUE-WINGED OLIVE

Ephemerella ignita

The BWO, as it is commonly known to fishermen, has a very

wide distribution and is found in rivers of all types, though it does not occur in lakes. On the Hampshire chalk-streams it seldom appears before mid-June, but on many other rivers it starts to hatch in April or May and continues throughout the season. It possesses several unusual characteristics, of which the following deserve mention. Firstly, it often appears to have considerable difficulty in withdrawing its body and tails from the nymphal skin, with the result that the hatching dun is an easy prey for the trout. Secondly, although it is commonly associated with the evening rise, when it is taken with avidity and a distinctive kidney-shaped boil on the surface, it sometimes emerges in broad daylight, and the trout's reactions to it are then more uncertain. On the Driffield Beck, in Yorkshire, for example, I have seen it taken eagerly all day long, whereas on the Test it usually seems to be ignored before sunset. Thirdly, the female spinners deposit their eggs in a very distinctive manner. Instead of returning singly to the water, they usually congregate in large swarms, often numbering many thousands, and fly upstream in procession, each spinner carrying a greenish ball of eggs at the extremity of the abdomen, which is curled forward underneath the body. On reaching a suitable place, sometimes where a bridge or mill forms an obstruction across the river, the eggs are dropped from the air, after which the spinners fall spent upon the water, and the trout frequently assemble at such places at dusk to await the large meal thus provided for them. The normal type of BWO is a medium-sized fly, but has relatively long wings, which make it appear larger than the Medium Olive. Occasionally, however, a much smaller form is to be seen, which has led many anglers to suppose, mistakenly, that the vernacular name covers two distinct species.

The male dun has medium smoky-blue wings, an olive-brown thorax, and a brown abdomen with an orange undertone (which no doubt accounts for the success of the Orange Quill when these flies are on the water). The legs are olive-grey and the tails, which often become twisted and crumpled in the difficult process of emergence, are grey with dark rings.

The female dun differs from the male in the colour of the body, the thorax being olive and the abdomen a variable shade of olive or yellow-green.

The male spinner has transparent wings with brown veins, a dark brown thorax and dark red-brown abdomen. The legs are yellowish and the tails amber with dark rings near the base, becoming grey towards their tips.

The female spinner, commonly known as the Sherry spinner, undergoes a considerable colour-change during her short existence. On transposition her body is yellowish-green, but after laying her eggs it turns to red, often a very brilliant shade. 'Red as any lobster' is how J. W. Dunne described it, but at all events it is not the colour of any reputable brand of sherry, despite the popular name.

Artificials

Nymph. The following is G. E. M. Skues's dressing, no XVIII:

> *Tying silk:* Hot orange.
> *Body:* Cow hair the colour of dried blood, dressed fat.
> *Hackle:* Two turns of woolly dark blue hen.
> *Whisks:* Three strands of dark hen hackle, short.
> *Hook:* 1 or 2, down-eyed round bend.

Dun. The most effective pattern for taking trout feeding on BWO duns in the evening is generally acknowledged to be the Orange Quill, which is dressed as under:

> *Body:* Condor quill dyed hot orange.
> *Wings:* Strips from a starling primary feather.
> *Hackle:* Bright ginger cock (sometimes dyed orange).
> *Whisks:* Bright ginger cock.
> *Hook:* 1.

The Orange Quill is less effective, and indeed sometimes useless, in daylight hours, when I have found the following dressing effective. It represents the female dun.

> *Body:* Blue-grey condor quill dyed in picric acid.
> *Ribbing:* Very fine gold tinsel.
> *Wings:* A medium blue cock hackle, or a bunch of medium blue waterhen breast fibres, set upright.
> *Hackles:* Yellow-olive cock.
> *Whisks:* Fibres from a speckled brown partridge feather.
> *Hook:* 1.

Spinner. There are various dressings of the Sherry spinner, most of which are too dull in colour. Lunn's pattern is one of the most effective and is dressed as follows:

Tying silk: Pale orange.
Body: Orange artificial silk.
Ribbing: Gold wire.
Wings: Two buff cock hackle points set on flat (or light blue dun hen for late evening).
Hackle: Bright Rhode Island cock.
Whisks: Pale ginger.
Hook: 1.

Family: CAENIDAE

Genus: *Caenis*

Characteristics: Two wings and three tails.

The nymphs are of the burrowing type, living in the surface of the silt, which adheres in small particles to their bodies and forms a very effective form of camouflage, as they are much the same colour as mud. They are short and relatively broad, with a pronounced 'waist' between the wing-pads and the second pair of gills, which take the form of large flaps lying on the back of the nymph. These totally obscure the remaining gills, except the first pair, which are no more than minute filaments scarcely visible to the naked eye. The tails are about two-thirds of the length of the body and are fringed with short bristles.

DUSKY BROADWING

Caenis robusta

Although sometimes referred to collectively as the Angler's Curse – a name applied indiscriminately to many small aquatic insects – the Caenidae have not hitherto possessed any vernacular names of their own. I have therefore suggested elsewhere that they should be known as Broadwings, from their most striking characteristic, with appropriate prefixes to distinguish the species. The Dusky Broadwing, first found in the nymphal stage by Dr T. T. Macan on the Norfolk Broads in 1951, has since been reported from three further English stations: two Lakes, near Romsey, Hampshire (where I found the duns, spinners and nymphs in 1958), a pond near Reading, Berkshire, and a canal in Shropshire. But in view of the widely differing conditions in these four places, coupled with the fact that it has recently been reported from all over Europe, it is probably much more common in England than this meagre record suggests, and as it becomes better known will no doubt turn up in many other parts of the country. It will be noted that it has so far only been found in still water (at all events in England), but there seems no reason why it should not exist in rivers, and this may prove to be the case when further reports come to hand. The angler has a unique opportunity of increasing our knowledge of this species by forwarding specimens answering to this description to the Entomological section of the Natural History Museum for identification. *C robusta* is a small fly, though as its Latin name suggests, the largest of the Broadwings. It hatches in the late evening from the end of May to early August.

The dun has very broad opaque wings of a watery-grey colour, marked with prominent brown veins near their fore margins. The thorax is dark brown and the abdomen pale creamy grey with variable dusky markings all the way down the back. (This is the only one of the Broadwings in which such markings appear on every segment.) The legs and tails are off-white. The duns of this and all other species of the genus change to spinners within a very short time – sometimes only a matter of minutes – of emergence.

The spinners of both sexes resemble the duns, except that their tails become longer. This is especially noticeable in the male, whose tails are some three times as long as its short, stumpy body. The method of oviposition, which is I believe unique, merits a brief description. After alighting on the water, the gravid female spinner extrudes her eggs in a single stream, held together by a gelatinous membrane and spreading out in the shape of a fan, the whole mass eventually falling off and sinking to the bottom. When thus engaged, she presents a sitting target to the trout.

Artificials

It is not worth while imitating the duns of the Broadwings, as they are more often taken in the nymph and spinner stages.

There are no standard patterns, the following being my own dressings:

Nymph.
   Abdomen: A few turns of medium brown condor herl.
   Ribbing: Silver tinsel.
   Gills, thorax and wing pads: Dark hare's ear in two sections, with a pronounced 'waist' between them.
   Hackle: Medium ginger grizzled hen.
   Whisks: Speckled partridge fibres.
   Hook: oo.

Spinner.
   Body: White seal's fur.
   Ribbing: Silver tinsel.
   Wings: Palest blue dun hen hackle.
   Leg hackle: Short white cock, or none.
   Whisks: Fibres from a white cock's spade hackle, very long.
   Hook: oo.

YELLOW BROADWING

Caenis horaria

This is quite a common species, occurring both in lakes and rivers, especially where there is silt on the bottom. It is a very small fly, and the duns emerge in late evening from June to August.

The dun is virtually a smaller edition of the foregoing species, except that in this case the abdomen is pale yellow and the greyish markings appear only on the first five or six segments.

The spinners are similar, but with much longer tails than in the dun stage.

There are three other species of this genus, but as two of them hatch in the early mornings, before most anglers are astir, and the third is too small to imitate, they do not merit detailed description here.

Artificials

Nymph. As for the Dusky Broadwing but dressed on a size ooo hook.

Spinner. As for the Dusky Broadwing but dressed on a size ooo hook and having a body of natural yellow silkworm silk in place of the white seal's fur.

Family: BAËTIDAE

Genus: *Baëtis*

Characteristics: Four wings, of which the hinder pair are very small, and two tails. Marginal intercalary veins double.

The nymphs are of the swimming type, with long torpedo-shaped bodies corresponding in colour to their respective duns. Seven leaf-shaped gills project from each side of the abdomen, and as these are not adapted for life in still water all species of this genus are found only in rivers. The centre tail is shorter than the outer pair, all three being fringed with hairs as an aid to swimming.

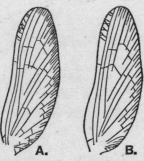

FIG 22. Fore wings of Baëtidae. In the genus *Baëtis* the small marginal intercalary veins are paired, as shown in A. In the rest of the family (*Centroptilum, Cloëon* and *Procloëon*) these veins are single, as in B.

PALE WATERY

Baëtis bioculatus

The vernacular name, which was employed by Halford to cover four different insects, is now most commonly applied to this species. It is a small fly, common in rivers and streams, with a slight preference for alkaline water. It appears from May to September, but as the dun is very quick off the water it is less often taken in this stage than as a nymph or spinner.

The dun has pale watery-grey wings, a light brown-olive thorax, and pale green-olive abdomen, becoming yellower towards the tail. The legs are pale olive-grey and the tails pale grey.

The male spinner has transparent wings with colourless veins, a dark brown thorax and pale yellowish-white abdomen, terminating in three dark brown segments. The legs and tails are greenish-white, and it can be distinguished from other small spinners of a similar type by the colour of the eyes, which are lemon-yellow.

The female spinner differs from the male in the colour of the body, which is golden-brown throughout.

Artificials

Nymph. Skues gave several dressings, of which I have selected the first, no XI.

> *Tying silk:* Primrose, waxed with colourless wax.
> *Body:* Blue fur from an English squirrel, steeply tapered.
> *Ribbing:* Yellow silk.
> *Hackle:* One turn of very small darkish-blue dun cockerel.
> *Whisks:* Strands from the pale unfreckled neck feather of a cock guinea fowl, short.
> *Hook:* oo Pennell sneck.

Dun. There are several patterns, of which a Ginger Quill is as good as any.

> *Body:* Peacock quill, bleached.
> *Wings:* Palest starling primary.
> *Hackle:* Pale ginger cock.
> *Whisks:* Fibres from a pale ginger cock's spade feather.
> *Hook:* oo.

Spinner. A Tup's Indispensable is a useful pattern to suggest the spinner of the Pale Watery. Here is Mr R. S. Austin's original dressing, as modified by Skues:

Tying silk: Yellow.

Body: Wool from the underparts of a ram mixed with a little cream and crimson seal's fur and lemon spaniel's fur, leaving a few turns of tying silk exposed at the tail end.

Hackle: Pale brassy blue dun cock.

Whisks: Fibres from a pale honey or blue dun spade feather.

Hook: oo.

SMALL DARK OLIVE

Baëtis scambus

This is another of Halford's Pale Watery duns, though as will be seen from the description, it certainly does not merit this name. Skues called it the July dun, but although it may be seen in this month I have found it in the greatest numbers in April and September. I therefore prefer Harris's name of Small Dark Olive, which aptly describes its appearance. It is a small species, common in the faster rivers, both alkaline and acid.

The dun has dark grey wings, not quite so dark or so blue as those of the Iron Blue, for which, however, it could be mistaken at a little distance. The thorax is brown-olive and the abdomen medium green-olive, becoming more yellow towards the tail. The legs are pale yellowish and the tails pale grey.

The male spinner is a slightly darker version of *bioculatus*, from which it can be readily distinguished by its red-brown eyes.

The female spinner differs from her *bioculatus* counterpart in the colour of the body, which is dark brown and tinged with olive in the early stages.

Artificials

Nymph. Skues's no IX represents this species.

Tying silk: Pale orange waxed with colourless wax.

Abdomen: Medium blue fox fur dyed in picric acid.

Ribbing: Fine gold wire.

Thorax: Dark brownish-olive seal's fur.

Hackle: 1 turn of rusty dun cock, very short in the fibre.

Whisks: Strands from a cock guinea-fowl's neck feather dyed in picric acid, very short.

Hook: oo Pennell sneck.

Dun. There is no standard pattern, but a small Greenwell's Glory serves very well.

> *Tying silk:* Yellow, waxed with cobbler's wax to darken it.
> *Body:* The tying silk.
> *Wings:* Hen blackbird, tied in upright, bunched and split.
> *Hackle:* Coch-y-bondhu.
> *Hook:* 00.

This is the original version, which was dressed as a wet-fly. For the floating pattern it is desirable to add whisks, which may be fibres from a blue dun cock's spade feather.

Spinner. A Pheasant Tail may be used to suggest this and other *Baëtis* spinners.

> *Body:* Herl from a cock pheasant's tail feather, choosing one with a marked ruddy tint.
> *Ribbing:* Gold tinsel.
> *Hackle:* Honey dun.
> *Whisks:* Fibres from a honey dun cock's spade feather.
> *Hook:* 00.

MEDIUM OLIVE

Baëtis vernus

Baëtis tenax

These two species are so alike that some authorities now doubt whether they are in fact, distinct. (A third species, *B buceratus*, is too rare to be included.) The Medium Olive is very common in rivers and streams of all kinds and is widely distributed throughout this country. It is of medium size and hatches all through the fishing season.

The dun has medium grey wings, often tinged with yellow, which was doubtless responsible for its old name, Yellow dun. The thorax is olive-brown and the abdomen yellowish-brown, in which the olive tint from which the modern name is derived is often hard to detect. The legs are olive shading to dark grey, and the tails pale grey.

The male spinner has transparent wings, the two main veins being brownish. The thorax is black, the first six segments of the abdomen olive-grey and the terminal segments brown. The legs are olive-grey and the tails off-white.

The female spinner has a yellowish-brown body, which changes to red-brown when spent.

Artificials

Nymph. Skues gives several dressings, of which I have chosen his no V.

> *Tying silk:* Purple or grey-brown, waxed with dark wax.
> *Abdomen:* Brown peacock quill.
> *Ribbing:* Silver wire (optional).
> *Thorax:* Dark hare's ear.
> *Hackle:* Dark blue dun hen or cockerel.
> *Whisks:* Strands from a dark neck feather from a cock guinea-fowl, very short.
> *Hook:* 0.

A Gold-ribbed Hare's ear is frequently successful during a hatch of Medium Olives and is believed to represent the nymph in the act of hatching. The original dressing, which has neither wings, hackle nor tails, is as follows:

> *Tying silk:* Yellow.
> *Body:* Dark fur from a hare's ear.
> *Ribbing:* Narrow flat gold tinsel.
> *Legs:* The body material picked out with a dubbing needle.
> *Hook:* 0.

Dun. Medium Olive dun and Medium Olive Quill are the standard patterns.

> *Body:* Seal's fur or peacock quill dyed medium olive.
> *Wings:* Starling primary feather.
> *Hackle:* Cock hackle dyed medium olive.
> *Whisks:* Fibres from a cock hackle dyed medium olive.
> *Hook:* 0.

Spinner. A Pheasant Tail or Lunn's Particular (see below), tied on a size 0 hook.

Baëtis rhodani

This is the Blue dun of our forebears, a very common species of
rivers and streams. Unlike other duns, it is a winter fly, hatching
from October until the end of April, and is therefore only seen
by the trout fisherman as its season is drawing to a close. It is a
large fly, and a very popular one with the trout. (*B atrebatinus*
is similar in appearance but relatively scarce.)

The dun has dark grey wings, much the same tone as those of
the BWO but of a less blue shade. The thorax is dark grey
tinged with olive, and the abdomen dark olive. The legs are
olive shading to grey, and the tails grey with faint rings near the
base.

The male spinner has transparent wings with dark brown main
veins, a black thorax and olive-grey abdomen with brown
terminal segments. The legs shade from olive to grey and the
tails are pale grey with reddish rings.

The female spinner is a larger and darker version of that of the
Medium Olive, becoming dark mahogany-brown when spent.

Artificials

Nymph. Skues's nymph, no I, is dressed as follows:

> *Tying silk:* Yellow, waxed with brown wax.
> *Body:* Darkest green-olive seal's fur, thickened at the shoul-
> der to represent the thorax.
> *Ribbing:* Fine gold wire.
> *Hackle:* Dark blue dun hen or cockerel with a woolly centre.
> *Whisks:* Strands from a dark guinea-fowl's neck feather
> dyed dark greenish.
> *Hook:* I or 2, down-eyed round bend.

Dun. Rough Olive, Greenwell's Glory, Dark Olive dun and
Quill, Blue dun and Blue Upright all represent the subimago of
this species. The first-named, which is a very successful pattern,
is dressed as under:

> *Body:* Heron's herl dyed in picric acid.
> *Ribbing:* Fine gold tinsel.
> *Wings:* Darkest starling primary feather.

Hackle: Cock hackle dyed brown-olive.
Whisks: Fibres from a cock's spade feather dyed brown-olive.
Hook: 1.

Spinner. Lunn's Particular was specifically designed to represent the female imago of this species.

Tying silk: Crimson.
Body: The undyed stalk of a Rhode Island cock's hackle.
Wings: Two medium blue dun cock hackle points, set on flat.
Hackle: Medium Rhode Island cock.
Whisks: Fibres from a large Rhode Island cock's hackle.
Hook: 1.

IRON BLUE

Baëtis pumilus

Baëtis niger

For practical purposes the two species may be treated as identical, the differences between them being too minute to be discerned with the naked eye. The Iron Blue is common and widespread in rivers and streams of all kinds, and despite its small size is often taken by the trout in preference to any other species which may be on the water at the same time. The main hatches occur in May, especially on cold, windy days, and there is a second brood in September.

The dun has very dark grey wings and thorax, the abdomen of the male being the same colour and that of the female a very dark olive-brown. The legs are dark olive to dark grey, and the tails dark grey.

The male spinner, known to our forebears as the Jenny spinner, is a beautiful little fly with transparent wings, black thorax and dark brown terminal segments, the intermediate segments being white and translucent. The legs and tails are almost white, and the eyes dark red-brown.

The female spinner is sometimes known as the Claret spinner, but as this causes confusion with the spinner of the Claret dun, the name is best avoided. She has colourless wings, a black thorax, dark red-brown abdomen, olive-brown legs and pale grey tails.

Artificials

Nymph. Skues's no X has proved a very successful pattern.

> *Tying silk:* Crimson, waxed with colourless wax.
> *Body:* Mole's fur spun thinly and tapered, leaving two turns of tying silk exposed at the tail end.
> *Hackle:* Cock jackdaw throat, one or two turns, very short.
> *Whisks:* Three strands of white hen hackle, quite short.
> *Hook:* oo Pennell sneck.

Dun. The standard pattern of Iron Blue dun is dressed as follows:

> *Tying silk:* Crimson.
> *Body:* Mole's fur, leaving a few turns of tying silk exposed at the tail end.
> *Wings:* Tom-tit's tail feather.
> *Hackle:* Blue dun cock.
> *Whisks:* Fibres from the spade feather of a blue dun cock.
> *Hook:* oo.

Spinner: Lunn's Houghton Ruby is one of the best imitations of the female Iron Blue spinner yet produced.

> *Tying silk:* Crimson.
> *Body:* Rhode Island hackle stalk dyed in red and crimson.
> *Wings:* Two light blue dun hen tips from the breast or back, set on flat.
> *Hackle:* Bright Rhode Island cock.
> *Whisks:* Three fibres from a white cock's hackle.
> *Hook:* oo.

Family: BAËTIDAE

Genus: *Centroptilum*

Characteristics: Four wings, the hinder pair being much narrower than those of the preceding genus, and two tails. Marginal intercalary veins single.

The nymphs are of the swimming type and resemble those of the genus *Baëtis*, except that the gills are more pointed and the three tails of equal length.

LITTLE SKY BLUE

Centroptilum luteolum

This was the third fly classed by Halford as a Pale Watery dun, and it is still sometimes known by this name. Later, D. H. Turing called it the Lesser Spurwing, the generic name being derived from the Greek κεντρωξ (spur) and πτιλου (wing), but as the spurs on the hind wings are too small to be seen with the naked eye and are in any case not confined to this genus, I prefer Harris's name, Little Sky Blue. It is a small fly, common in rivers and streams, and may also be found in lakes under the conditions described on page 164. It hatches from May onwards.

The dun bears a superficial resemblance to *Baëtis bioculatus*, but the colour of the wings is slightly paler, the hind wings are narrower and end in a sharp point, and the body is more honey-coloured than olive.

The male spinner may be distinguished from *BB bioculatus* and *scambus* by the shape of the hind wings and colour of the eyes, which are bright Indian red.

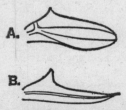

FIG 23. Hind Wings. A, Pale Watery dun (*Baëtis bioculatus*). B. Little Sky Blue, or Lesser Spurwing (*Centroptilum luteolum*).

The female spinner, called by Harris the Little Amber spinner, has a yellowish-brown body which becomes amber when spent. It can be distinguished from the *B bioculatus* spinner by the shape of the hind wings and the venation of the fore wings (Figs 22 and 23).

Artificials

The same patterns as those given under the heading of Pale Watery will serve for this species.

The other member of this genus, *C pennulatum*, is not of general importance, being very local in distribution and uncertain in its appearance even in its known habitats. It is a good deal larger than *luteolum* and has smoky-blue wings and a greyish body in the dun stage. This was the fourth of Halford's Pale Watery duns, but is now known either as the Blue-winged Pale Watery or the Greater Spurwing. It has not been recorded from lakes.

The only pattern of Blue-winged Pale Watery I know of is that devised by Skues in 1921. It represents the dun stage.

> *Tying silk:* Pale orange, waxed with colourless wax.
> *Body:* White lamb's wool.
> *Hackle (representing wings):* Dark blue dun hen.
> *Whisks:* Not mentioned, but should be grey to match the tails of the natural insect.
> *Hook:* 1.

Family: BAËTIDAE

Genus: *Cloëon*

Characteristics: Two wings and two tails.
Marginal intercalary veins single.

The nymphs are of the swimming type and of much the same shape as others of the family already described. Their colour is very variable, some being mottled in different shades of dull brown, others a warm chestnut-brown all over, and others again strongly marked with emerald green. They have seven pairs of gills, of which the first six are double and mobile, which enables them to live in still water, the last pair being single and fixed, probably acting as baffle-plates. The tails, which show a characteristic downwards curve towards their tips, are of equal length and fringed with hairs. They are remarkably agile swimmers.

POND OLIVE

Cloëon dipterum

The vernacular name was suggested by Harris on account of

its more frequent appearance in ponds than in large lakes, though it is a high summer temperature, rather than the actual area of water, which governs its choice of habitat. It is also found occasionally in the sluggish pools of rivers. The first hatches appear in May, after which it continues throughout the fishing season, the flies of successive broods gradually diminishing in size from large or medium to small as the summer advances. Both species of *Cloëon* become airborne almost instantaneously on emergence, and are consequently not very often taken as duns.

The dun varies in colour as well as size. The wings, which are broad at the base to compensate for the absence of hind wings, are medium grey, slightly darker in the male than in the female. The thorax is brown-olive, the abdomen of the male grey with brown terminal segments and of the female brown-olive with yellow terminal segments and red streaks. I have, however, found female specimens in which the yellow colour was much more pronounced throughout, and even a few with bodies the same colour as in the spinner (qv). The legs are pale yellow-olive and grey, and the tails pale grey or buff with reddish rings.

The male spinner has transparent wings with colourless veins, dark brown thorax and reddish-grey abdomen becoming red-brown towards the tail. The legs are pale watery grey and the tails pale grey with dark red rings.

The female spinner is a most beautiful fly, with yellow veins and a broad yellow band along the fore margin of the wings, yellow ochre thorax and abdomen the colour of a ripe apricot, streaked with red. The legs are pale yellow and the tails pale buff ringed with red.

Artificials

There are no standard patterns representing this family, so I give my own dressings for both species.

Nymph.
> *Abdomen:* Brown and ginger seal's fur mixed.
> *Ribbing:* Silver tinsel.
> *Thorax and wing pads:* Dark brown seal's fur.
> *Gills:* Pale yellow-brown condor herl following the turns of ribbing tinsel.
> *Leg hackle:* Medium honey dun hen.

Whisks: Fibres from a speckled brown partridge feather, short.

Hook: 1.

Dun.

Body: Grey condor herl lightly stained in picric acid.

Ribbing: Gold tinsel.

Wings: A bunch of fibres from a medium grey waterhen or coot body feather, tied upright.

Leg hackle: Pale honey dun or yellow-olive cock.

Whisks: Grey-brown mallard scapular fibres.

Hook: 2 to 0, decreasing as the season advances.

Spinner.

Body: Seal's fur dyed Naples yellow, mixed with a little amber and red.

Ribbing: Gold tinsel.

Wings: Golden dun or ginger cock, tied in any of the three ways previously described.

Leg hackle: Pale honey dun or ginger cock, or none.

Whisks: Grey-brown mallard scapular fibres.

Hook: 2 to 0, decreasing as above.

LAKE OLIVE

Cloëon simile

This species can stand lower temperatures than the Pond Olive, and therefore tends to prefer the larger lakes, though the two are often found together in the same water. Like the other, it begins to hatch in May, but then seems to peter out until September, when a second brood appears. In size it is medium to large, but although Harris states that flies of the autumn brood are smaller than those of spring, I have not observed this myself.

The dun has medium-grey wings suffused with brown or olive, a brown-olive thorax and grey-brown to olive-brown abdomen. The legs are pale olive shading to grey, and the tails dark grey without rings. The general effect is of a dingier-looking fly than the Pond Olive, but in cases of doubt it can be distinguished from the other by the number of small cross-veins in what is known as the pterostigmatic area, on the fore margins of the wings towards their tips. The Lake Olive has from nine to eleven of these small veins, and the Pond Olive only from three to five (Fig 24).

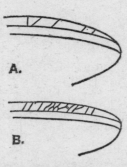

FIG 24. Outer Sections of Fore Wings. A, The Pond Olive (*Cloëon dipterum*) has from three to five pterostigmatic veins. B, The Lake Olive (*Cloëon simile*) has from nine to eleven of these veins.

The male spinner has transparent wings faintly stained with yellow-brown and brownish veins. The thorax is dark brown, almost black, the abdomen warm brown becoming red towards the tail end, legs grey and tails grey-brown with dark rings near the base.

The female spinner is similar but with a dark red-brown abdomen and brown legs.

Artificials

Nymph. As for the Pond Olive.

Dun.

    Body: Grey-brown condor herl.
    Ribbing: Silver tinsel.
    Wings: A bunch of fibres from a pale coot body feather with a brownish tinge.
    Leg hackle: Pale brassy-blue dun cock.
    Whisks: Fibres from a dark blue dun cock's spade feather.
    Hook: 2 to 0, decreasing as before.

Spinner.

> *Body:* Dark red seal's fur.
> *Ribbing:* Gold tinsel.
> *Wings:* Pale brassy dun cock hackle, tied in any of the three ways previously described.
> *Leg hackle:* Pale brownish or honey dun cock, or none.
> *Whisks:* Fibres from a medium blue dun cock's spade hackle.
> *Hook:* 2 to 0, decreasing as before.

Family: BAËTIDAE

Genus: *Procloëon*

Characteristics: Two wings and two tails.
Marginal intercalary veins single.

The nymph is a swimmer and of the same general appearance as the *Cloëon* nymphs, except that all the gills are single and the tails are more heavily fringed with hairs and held closer together.

PALE EVENING

Procloëon pseudorufulum

This is the only member of the genus, which stands very close to *Cloëon*, in which this species was formerly placed. Although I have found the spinners on a lake it is very doubtful whether they were bred there, and its true habitat seems to be the slow-flowing type of river. It is a small fly and may occur throughout the summer months, the main hatches being from June to August. The duns emerge in the late evenings, often so late that they are probably either overlooked by the angler or mistaken in the semi-darkness for one of the small Pale Watery duns.

The dun has pale greyish-white wings, often tinged with green near the base, a pale honey-coloured thorax and abdomen with reddish markings, pale yellow legs and watery grey tails.

The male spinner has transparent wings with colourless veins, a brown thorax, and translucent white abdomen with red-brown terminal segments. The legs are pale olive and grey, and the tails white. The eyes are lemon-yellow like those of *Baëtis bioculatus*, but it can be distinguished from that species by its two wings.

The female spinner has a pale yellow ochre thorax and abdomen becoming amber towards the tail, with amber markings down the back and fine dark lines on each side of the middle segments. The legs and tails are pale watery grey.

Artificials

There are no standard patterns and the only dressing I know of is Major Oliver Kite's, representing the dun.

> *Tying silk:* White.
> *Body:* Grey goose herl.
> *Hackle:* Cream cock.
> *Whisks:* Fibres from a cream cock's hackle.
> *Hook:* 0 to 00.

Family: ECDYONURIDAE

Genus: *Rhithrogena*

Characteristics: Four wings and two tails.

The nymphs are of the flat type, living among stones on the bottom over which they can move at high speed. Their bodies, particularly the head and thorax, together with the upper joints of the legs, are flattened and very broad in proportion to their length. Their colour is dark brown mottled with yellowish-brown. The gills are prominent features and consist of plates and bunches of filaments, the first pair being very large and meeting beneath the body. These help to keep the nymph attached to the surface of the stones in a fast current. The tails are relatively long, devoid of hair, and held wide apart.

YELLOW UPRIGHT

Rhithrogena semicolorata

The vernacular name is not very descriptive of this species, which is neither yellow nor more upright than any others of its kind. Nevertheless, it seems preferable to retain the name by which it has for long been widely known, rather than introduce a new one, such as Olive Upright, which was proposed by Harris. It is common in fast stony rivers and streams and is of great importance on the Usk and Welsh Dee, but although I have taken a single specimen on the Itchen and have heard of others, it cannot be classed as a chalk-stream fly. It is a large species whose main hatches occur from late May to July.

The dun has medium-grey fore wings and paler hind wings, a grey-green thorax and olive abdomen. The legs are pale olive and the tails grey. At a little distance it might be mistaken for a large Olive dun, but a certain means of identification is the presence of a dark streak on the femoral, or upper, joint of each leg in both the dun and spinner stages.

The male spinner has transparent wings with brown veins and a yellow-brown stain near the base. (Courtney Williams states that it is this yellowish stain, coupled with the spinner's habit of ascending in a vertical position during the nuptial flight, which gives the species its vernacular name.) The thorax and abdomen are dark olive-brown, and the legs and tails brown.

The female spinner has a medium reddish-brown body and pale amber legs and tails.

Artificials

There are no standard patterns, but the following dressing devised by the late Major J. D. D. Evans to represent the dun has proved very effective:

Body: Fur from a hedgehog's belly, mixed with a little rusty-yellow seal's fur.
Ribbing: Fine gold thread.
Hackle (representing wings and legs): Honey dun cock.
Whisks: Fibres from a pale brassy-blue dun cock's spade feather.
Hook: 1.

MARCH BROWN

Rhithrogena haarupi

For many years the March Brown was identified as *Ecdyurus* (now known as *Ecdyonurus*) *venosus*, but in 1931 it was discovered that there were, in fact, two species very similar in appearance but hatching at different times of the year and belonging to different genera. *R haarupi* was henceforth recognized as the true March Brown, emerging from late March to early May, while *E venosus* does not appear until the other's season has ended. It is a very large fly and a common one on rapid, stony rivers, but is unknown on the chalk-streams. A distinctive feature is its sudden appearance in large numbers at intervals throughout a spring day, but the trout feed more often on the ascending nymphs than on the duns.

The dun has light yellowish-brown wings and prominent brown veins, the cross-veins, which have dark borders, being absent from two areas in the centre of the fore wings, producing the effect of two pale blotches. The thorax and abdomen are dark brown, darker in the male than the female, the legs olive-brown and the tails grey-brown.

The male and female spinners resemble the duns, except that the wings are transparent and only tinged with brown towards the base.

Artificials

Nymph. The following is Skues's dressing:

> *Abdomen:* Herl from a cock pheasant's tail feather.
> *Ribbing:* Fine gold wire.
> *Thorax:* Hare's ear.
> *Leg hackle:* Light brown speckled partridge feather.
> *Whisks:* Fibres from a cock pheasant's tail feather, short.
> *Hook:* 2.

Dun. The March Brown dun is usually dressed as a wet pattern, and in Skues's words, 'It is quite a poor imitation of the March Brown and quite a passable one of almost anything else.' The standard tie is:

> *Body:* Hare's ear.
> *Ribbing:* Yellow silk.
> *Wings:* Hen pheasant secondary feather.
> *Hackle:* Grey-brown speckled partridge.
> *Whisks:* Fibres from a grey-brown speckled partridge feather.
> *Hook:* 3.

Spinner. There is no standard dressing of the March Brown spinner, but a Pheasant Tail should serve the purpose.

Family: ECDYONURIDAE

Genus: *Ecdyonurus*

Characteristics: Four wings and two tails.

The nymphs are of the flat type and similar to the preceding ones in general shape, but the first pair of gills are small and do not meet beneath the body. The most distinctive feature of this genus, however, is the front segment of the thorax, known as the pronotum, which ends on each side in a point projecting backwards over the second segment.

LATE OR FALSE MARCH BROWN

Ecdyonurus venosus

This is the species referred to as being formerly identified as the March Brown, and is common in the same types of rivers as those in which *R haarupi* is found, though it does not hatch in such profusion. It is a very large fly, appearing from May onwards.

The dun resembles *R haarupi* except that there are no pale areas in the centre of the fore wings.

The male and female spinners, known as Great Red spinners, can be distinguished from those of *R haarupi* by the colour of their bodies, in this case a bright red-brown.

Artificials

So far as I am aware, no separate patterns have been evolved to represent *E venosus*.

AUGUST OR AUTUMN DUN

Ecdyonurus dispar

The habitats of this species are the same as for the foregoing, but it is also sometimes found on the shores of large lakes under the conditions described on pages 164–5. This is another very large fly, though slightly smaller than *venosus*. It may be found from June to October, the main hatches being in July and August.

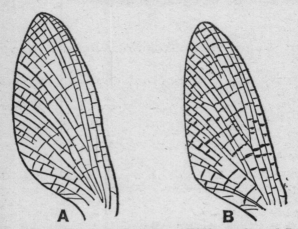

FIG 25. Fore Wings. A, the March Brown (*Rhithrogena haarupi*). B, the False March Brown (*Ecdyonurus venosus*). Note the pale areas in A due to the absence of cross veins near the centre of the wings.

The dun is very similar to *E venosus*, but the cross veins lack the dark borders, and consequently do not appear so prominent.

The male and female spinners are scarcely distinguishable from those of *E venosus* except in the matter of size.

Artificials

There are no standard patterns and I do not know of any dressing representing the nymph of this species.

Dun. H. H. Edmonds and N. N. Lee gave the following pattern in their book, *Brook and River Trouting*, published in 1916:

> *Tying silk:* Yellow.
> *Body:* Yellow-olive wool.
> *Ribbing:* Orange silk sparingly dubbed with fur from the nape of a rabbit's neck lightly dyed red.

Wings: From a mallard's breast feather, lightly tinged with brown.

Leg hackle: Medium olive hen.

Whisks: Two strands from a cock's hackle dyed medium olive.

Hook: 2.

Spinner. Skues evolved the following dressing on a visit to the Coquet in 1888:

Body: Tawsy gut flattened, dyed bright orange and wound over the bare hook shank.

Wings: The speckled part near the root of the red-brown tail feather of a partridge.

Leg hackle: Red cockerel.

Whisks: Fibres from a honey dun cock's hackle.

Hook: 1 or 2.

This disposes of all the commoner species except two: the Turkey Brown (*Paraleptophlebia submarginata*), which is very similar in appearance to the Sepia, and the Yellow May (*Heptagenia sulphurea*), a larger pale yellow fly except for the spinner, which is dark brown. Both these species have long been known to anglers, but the fact is that they are seldom taken by trout – possibly because they do not hatch in such large numbers as other day-flies.

The following less common flies have now been given names by Harris:

YELLOW EVENING (DUN) (*Ephemerella notata*), a close relative of the BWO but resembling the Yellow May dun in appearance.

PURPLE (DUN) (*Paraleptophlebia cincta*), somewhat resembling a large Iron Blue, but with three tails.

SUMMER MAYFLIES (three species of *Siphlonurus*), very large flies known to me as Large Summer duns and found chiefly in lakes.

BROWN MAY (DUN) (*Heptagenia fuscogrisea*), a very large fly bearing a general resemblance to the March Brown.

DARK (DUN) (*Heptagenia lateralis*), a dark dun-coloured relative of the foregoing.

LARGE GREEN (DUN) (*Ecdyonurus insignis*), a greenish-grey relative of the late March Brown and August dun.

3 ORDER: TRICHOPTERA
(SEDGE- OR CADDIS-FLIES)

ALTHOUGH they are of considerable importance, both on rivers and lakes, the sedge-flies, with a few exceptions, do not hatch simultaneously in such large numbers as the day-flies, wherefore the angler has no need to learn to recognize the individual species. This, perhaps, is just as well, since 189 species of British Trichoptera have been recorded.

The life-cycle consists of four stages: egg, larva, pupa and imago, or adult. The egg-laying habits vary with the species, some depositing their eggs on weeds or stones, others in the open water. On emerging from the eggs the majority of caddis larvae then proceed to build cases for themselves, in which the whole of their underwater existence is passed. These cases are made from many different kinds of material, such as sand, gravel, small stones, weed or bits of stick, each species having its own special method of construction. There are, however, a few kinds of caddis larvae which do not make cases, but live instead in silken tunnels attached to weeds or stones, from which they sometimes emerge in search of food. It is, incidentally, incorrect to refer to caddis larvae as nymphs, as some anglers do. Strictly speaking, the term nymph should only be applied to those larvae which bear a recognizable resemblance to their respective adults, such as those of the day-flies, dragon-flies, stone-flies and water-boatmen. All others should be called larvae, and should not be confused with pupae.

On reaching maturity the caddis larva pupates in a similar manner to a butterfly or moth, the case-making species spinning cocoons inside their cases and the others in shelters specially constructed for the purpose. When fully developed the pupa bites its way out of its home and either swims or climbs up a weed stem to the surface, whereupon the winged-fly emerges and struggles across the water to the bank, where mating takes place. The trout feed on the larvae (case and all), pupae, newly-emerged adults and egg-laying females. Those which escape the attentions of the fish and other predators live a good deal longer than the day-flies, probably for more than a week, while specimens bred in captivity and artificially fed have been known to exist for a matter of months.

As the sedge-flies vary greatly in size and appearance, according to their species, they can only be described in general terms, which will suffice to enable the reader to recognize them as members of the order Trichoptera. References to a few specific flies will be found at the end of the general description.

The larvae of the non-case-making species somewhat resemble caterpillars, but with longer legs and, in some cases, abdominal gills. The case-making species are generally fatter and more grub-like in appearance, but this is of no more than academic interest to the angler, who cannot well imitate a hard caddis case in fur and feather. Both types have short caudal appendages ending in hooks, by means of which they can maintain a grip on the shelters in which they live.

The pupae have fat, juicy-looking bodies and a rather hump-backed appearance. The antennae, springing from the head, and the legs, from the thorax, lie beneath the body, while the four wing-pads slope downwards from the thorax towards the underside of the abdomen. The centre pair of legs are longer than the others and fringed with hairs to assist the pupa in swimming to the surface.

The adults are not unlike moths in appearance, except that their wings are covered with hairs instead of scales. The fore wings are slightly longer than the hind wings and hide them when the insect is at rest with both pairs folded back over the body in the form of a ridge tent. The antennae and legs are long in proportion to the body, and there are no tails. The wings of most species are some shade of brown or grey, either plain or patterned, and the bodies brown, grey or green. The size varies according to species from a quarter of an inch or less up to an inch in length.

GRANNOM

Brachycentrus subnubilus

This is the only sedge-fly which the angler need learn to identify, as it is the only species favoured by the trout to hatch in any quantity. It is confined to running water and I have seen heavy hatches on the Don and lower Test, but it seems to be less common, especially on the chalk-streams, than it used to be. Where it does occur, however, it provides a sight worth seeing, and an opportunity which no angler can afford to miss. So sudden are the hatches that at one moment the river will appear lifeless, and in the next the whole surface will be covered with these little flies and boiling with the rises of trout, who go almost mad in their eagerness to make the most of what they probably know is but a fleeting chance of a good meal. Their usual procedure is to chase the ascending pupae towards the surface and to take them either just before or in the act of hatching.

The Grannom is one of the smaller sedge-flies,* with a greyish body less than half an inch long and grey wings with buff patches. The body of the pupa is a bluish green colour, which is no doubt the true reason for the success of green-bodied artificials, though these are generally supposed to represent the female imago carrying her ball of green eggs. The hatches take place in April and May.

Artificials

There are various patterns of Grannom on the market, of which the following may be taken as typical:

> *Tying silk:* Bright green.
> *Body:* Grey-brown hare's ear, with green wool at the tail end.
> *Wings:* Hen pheasant or partridge secondary.
> *Hackle:* Short ginger-grizzled cock.
> *Hook:* 1 to 2.

The following hackle pattern, which probably represents the insect in the act of hatching, was evolved by the Rev E. Powell and is extremely successful, as I can vouch from my own experience:

> *Tying silk:* Green.
> *Body:* Mole's fur dyed in picric acid.
> *Hackles:* Two greyish-brown speckled partridge feathers.
> *Hook:* 1.

The only other sedge-flies likely to be seen in large numbers

* The measurements used to denote the sizes of day-flies do not apply to the Trichoptera or other orders here described, where the sizes mentioned are purely arbitrary and relative.

are the Silverhorns, a name covering several very small species belonging to the genera *Mystacides* and *Leptocerus*. These are well-known to every angler on account of their habit of gyrating above the water in large swarms, but although an occasional immature fish will be seen jumping after them in the air, the fact is that they seldom figure on the trout's menu. One or other species will usually be found, both in still and running water, throughout the summer months, but they are not worth the angler's serious consideration.

The majority of sedge-flies emerge in the late evening, the Grannom and the Caperer (*Sericostoma personatum*) being the most notable exceptions. The latter is a medium-sized sedge-fly with mahogany-brown wings, which is of some importance on the chalk streams in May and June. It is, incidentally, a good example of the confusion which may arise through the use of vernacular names. Halford called it the Welshman's Button, a name properly belonging to a beetle, but it is now more often known as the Caperer, which to add to the muddle is also applied by some to *Halesus radiatus*, a quite different species emerging in the evening in late summer.

The following English names are also in use:

CINNAMON SEDGE (*Limnephilus lunatus*, Halford).
GREY FLAG (*Hydropsyche* species, Irish).
GREY SEDGE (*Odontocerum albicorne*, Mosely).
MEDIUM SEDGE (*Goëra pilosa* female, Halford).
SMALL DARK SEDGE (*Goëra pilosa* male, Halford).
SILVER SEDGE (*Lepidostoma hirtum*, Harris).

Some of these names are more often used to denote the artificial flies than their natural prototypes, and there are besides these several similarly-named artificials, which do not seem to have been copied from any specific insects. This probably applies to the Little Red Sedge, one of Skues's favourite patterns, and to the Orange and Kimbridge Sedges formerly in vogue on the chalk-streams.

Artificials

Pupa. There are no standard patterns of caddis pupae, but a number of amateur fly dressers have tried their hands at representing them. I give a dressing of my own below, in which the colours may be varied to suggest different species.

Body: Front half brown, rear half green seal's fur, spun on thickly in the centre and tapering towards either end.
Ribbing: Gold tinsel.
Legs, wing-cases and antennae: A furnace or coch-y-bondhu hackle with the fibres above the body removed and those below it stroked backwards towards the tail and thus secured.
Hook: 1 to 4.

Adult sedge. There are many patterns on the market, but it is quite unnecessary to carry more than a couple for all occasions. The following dressings may be taken as typical:

Halford's Cinnamon sedge.
Body: Condor quill dyed dull yellow-green.
Ribbing hackle: Ginger cock.
Wings: Mottled brown hen.
Shoulder hackles: Two ginger cock hackles.
Hook: 3.

Skues's Little Red sedge.
Tying silk: Hot orange.
Body: Darkest hare's ear.
Ribbing: Fine gold wire.
Wings: Landrail bunched and rolled, tied sloping over the body.
Body hackle: Deep red cock.
Shoulder hackle: Deep red cock, longer in the fibre than the body hackle. Four or five turns in front of the wings.
Hook: 1.

Lunn's Hackle Caperer.
Tying silk: Crimson.
Body: Four or five strands from a turkey's tail feather with a ring of swan's herl dyed yellow in the centre.
Hackles (at the shoulder only): Black cock followed by Rhode Island.
Hook: 1 to 3.

4 ORDER: PLECOPTERA (STONE-FLIES)

IT seems to be the custom to place the stone-flies immediately after the sedge-flies in angling entomologies, though in fact they are of less importance to the fly fisherman than some of the insects we shall meet later in this chapter. True, the stone-flies are taken by the trout in certain stages of their existence, but so far as the angler is concerned their chief function is to provide bait, in the shape of the nymphs of the larger species, for the 'creeper' fisherman of the North, and I agree with Courtney Williams that artificial stone-flies seldom justify their existence.

Nevertheless, the Plecoptera are true aquatic insects, and as fly fishermen have imitated, or attempted to imitate, them for several centuries, they deserve some mention here. The angler should at all events be able to recognize a stone-fly as such when he sees one, though he need not trouble himself overmuch with the individual species. Of these thirty-four have been recorded in Britain, mostly from stony streams and rivers. Only nine species occur in lakes.

The life-cycle consists of only three stages: egg, nymph and adult. There is no pupal stage. The eggs are laid on the surface of the water in much the same way as those of the day-flies, the precise method varying in the different genera. On emergence the nymphs live among the stones on the bottom, or in a few cases in water moss. As they attain their full growth – usually after one year as nymphs but in some genera up to three years – they crawl ashore, often at night, and take shelter among the stones and vegetation on the bank, where the adults emerge. Mating then takes place on the ground. Trout take the nymphs while they are crawling about on the bottom, but as it would be difficult to make an artificial behave in the same way, they are of little account to the fly fisherman at this stage. Owing to their habit of emerging on the bank, the newly-hatched adults are not seen by the fish, whose only opportunity of taking the winged-flies, therefore, is when the females return to the water to deposit their eggs.

The nymphs are not unlike day-fly nymphs in their general shape, but they have much longer antennae, stouter legs, often fringed with hairs, and only two tails, while the gills are either absent or spring from the thorax or the points of junction of the legs or tails with the body, instead of from the abdomen. As they approach maturity two pairs of wing-pads develop on the back, springing from the second and third thoracic segments respectively. The general coloration of the nymphs varies with the species. They are poor swimmers, and usually progress by crawling, in which they are assisted by the presence of a stout claw at the extremity of each leg.

The adults have four wings of nearly equal length, which are folded flat along the back when at rest. In the males of some species, however, the wings are so attenuated that the insects are unable to fly. The antennae are long, though not so long as those of the sedge-flies, and the tails variable in length, in some cases being no more than short stumps. The colour of the stone-flies is usually some shade of brown or yellow, and their size varies from about three-sixteenths up to more than an inch in length, the females being larger than the males.

The following English names are employed by anglers:

EARLY BROWNS (*Nemouridae* species, esp. *Protonemura meyeri*).
FEBRUARY RED (*Taeniopteryx nebulosa* female).
NEEDLE BROWNS, or NEEDLE FLIES (*Leuctra* species).
LARGE STONE-FLIES or MAYFLIES (*Perlidae* species and the larger species of *Perlodidae*).
WILLOW FLY (*Leuctra geniculata*).
YELLOW SALLY (*Isoperla grammatica*).

Artificials

As I have already suggested, artificial stone-flies seldom meet with much success, but they are worth a trial when the natural insects are on the water laying their eggs. There are a number of different patterns on the market of which the following may be taken as typical. The dressings vary, of course, with different firms.

February Red.
    Tying silk: Claret.
    Body: Orange mohair, or hare's ear with claret wool at the tail.

Wings: Hen pheasant or partridge (mottled).
Hackle: Claret.
Hook: 1.

Yellow Sally.
 Tying silk: Primrose.
 Body: Light yellow-green wool.
 Hackle: White cock dyed pale greenish-yellow.
(Yellow wings are added in some versions of this pattern.)

Willow Fly.
 Tying silk: Orange.
 Body: Mole's fur.
 Ribbing: Yellow silk.
 Hackle: Medium blue dun hen.
 Whisks: Medium blue dun hackle fibres.
 Hook: 1 to 2.

5 ORDER: DIPTERA (TWO-WINGED FLIES)

THERE are something like 3,000 species of this order, which includes the common house-flies, the crane-flies, gnats, midges and mosquitoes. Most of them only figure on the trout's menu in the shape of accidental windfalls, but there are some truly aquatic families and others which, although land-bred, fall on to the water in sufficient numbers to bring about a general rise. It is with these two classes that we are concerned here.

Family: CHIRONOMIDAE (*Midges or Buzzers*)

There are some 400 British species of this aquatic family, some of which are to be found throughout the season in every area of static water from the smallest pond to the largest lake, and as they form one of the principal articles of insect diet of the trout of such waters they are of great importance to the lake angler. They also occur in the sluggish pools and reaches of some rivers, but generally speaking are not of much account to the river fisherman. The majority of Chironomids are too small to imitate, but the genus *Chironomus* includes a number of relatively large species which are well worth the angler's attention.

The life-cycle consists of four stages: egg, larva, pupa and adult. The eggs are laid on the surface of the water, and the larvae live either among the water weeds or in small tubes composed of mud, but they can and do swim about. When fully grown they pupate, and in due course the pupae swim up to the surface, where the adult flies emerge. The trout take the larvae, pupae, newly-hatched flies and finally the egg-laying females, but they are most often taken in the pupal stage, when they hang suspended vertically just beneath the surface for a short time before hatching, thereby presenting the fish with an easy prey. The larvae, as will be realized from the accompanying description, are virtually impossible to imitate successfully, but the lake angler who carries one or two good patterns representing the pupa and adult – more especially the former – is assured of some good sport.

The larvae resemble very small worms, a resemblance which is heightened in many species whose blood contains haemo-globin, which gives them a red colour and incidentally enables them to live in deep water. The remainder are usually coloured pale olive.

The pupae begin to resemble their respective adults in colour and shape, except that the legs and embryo wings are tucked away beneath the body. The abdomen is slender and tapering, and the thorax, which occupies about a third of the length of the body, is very bulky in proportion. From the head arises a tuft of filaments which act as breathing tubes.

The adults have semi-transparent wings, which are held horizontally in the form of a V when the insects are at rest. The legs are very long and widely spread, and the male carries a prominent pair of antennae resembling small feathers. The swarms of Chironomids which are often to be seen among the bushes on the shores of lakes are the males awaiting the arrival of their mates.

The larger Chironomids are from a quarter to half an inch in length and they are of many different colours, the most common being golden-olive, bright green, brown and black.

The following English names have been identified with specific insects, but colour alone is not a sufficient guide to species because there are several of each colour, while individual species may vary considerably in this respect:

GOLDEN DUN MIDGE (*Chironomus plumosus*).
GREEN MIDGE (*Chironomus viridis*).
OLIVE MIDGE or BLAGDON BUZZER (*Chironomus tentans*).

Artificials

There are no standard patterns representing the Chironomids. The following are my own dressings, of which the pupa has proved particularly successful.

Pupa.

    Body: Gut or nylon stained to any desired colour and wound over the bare hook shank. It should be taken a short way round the bend of the hook to suggest the wriggling body of the pupa.

    Thorax: Ostrich, condor or peacock herl, occupying about one-third of the hook shank.

    Wing cases and legs: A short hen hackle with the topmost fibres removed and the remainder pressed close to the body.

    Hook: oo to 3, downturned eye.

Adult midge.

    Body: As for the pupa, but stopping short of the bend.

    Thorax: A knob of tying silk formed by figure-of-eight turns, well varnished.

    Wings: Not necessary, but hackle points or fibres can be added if desired.

    Leg hackle: Long grizzled cock divided by the thorax into four bunches, of which two slant forward and two backwards.

    Hook: oo to 3.

Family: CULICIDAE

Sub-family: CHAOBORINAE (*Phantom midges*)

The Phantom midges belong to the mosquito family, but bear a strong resemblance to the Chironomids and have the same life-cycle. There are only four British species.

The larvae, from which the family takes its English name, are completely transparent, although this does not save them from the keen-eyed trout, who frequently take them in large numbers.

The pupae are similar in general appearance to those of the

Chironomids, but are relatively shorter and fatter, and the breathing filaments are replaced by a pair of ear-like appendages.

The adults could easily be mistaken for Chironomids without a lens, which reveals the presence of a fringe of fine hairs round the wings. The only one of the four species I have found myself is *C crystallinus*, a rather spectacular insect nearly half an inch long with a pale blue-green body striped with black on the thorax.

Artificials
The Phantom midges can be imitated in the same manner as the Chironomids.

Family: BIBIONIDAE

Genus: *Bibio*

There are two species of this genus which, although terrestrial, are of some importance to both the lake and river fisherman on account of their predilection for tumbling into the water during or after mating. In general appearance they bear a superficial resemblance to house-flies.

Life-cycle: Egg, larva, pupa and adult. The larvae live and pupate in the earth or in the roots of plants, often in the vicinity of water, which seems to have a strange and frequently fatal attraction for the adults, once they are on the wing. The trout, of course, can only take them in the winged stage, when chance or some mysterious compulsion causes them to end their short existence on the surface of a lake or stream.

BLACK GNAT

Bibio johannis

Although the Black Gnat has for many years been identified with *Bibio johannis*, it has recently been pointed out that there are several other insects of different genera to which the English name could be equally well applied. They are a familiar sight to every angler as they gyrate over the water, often in huge swarms, in a similar manner to the Silverhorns. Sometimes these swarms disperse inland and not a single fly is seen on the water: at other times every single one seems to come down until the whole surface is strewn with them for several hours at a stretch. On such occasions sport is apt to be magnificent, for not only do these flies attract the biggest trout, but the fish seem to know they have plenty of time and instead of rushing madly about as they do after Grannom, they remain in their chosen places, taking a fly here and there with a deliberate and purposeful rise. In view of the competition which confronts the artificial fly, however, accurate casting, a good pattern and considerable patience are required if the angler is to make the most of his opportunity. The name *johannis* refers to the fact that this species is most prevalent around Midsummer (St John's) Day, though the heaviest hatches I have seen – which may well have included other species – have been in Mayfly-time and again in August.

It is, of course, unnecessary to describe the larva and pupa, which the fish never see, and to avoid multiplying scientific names I am taking *B johannis* as the type.

The adult has iridescent wings which are carried flat over the back when at rest but are often outspread when the fly lies spent upon the water. The body of the male is slender and cylindrical, that of the female fatter and egg-shaped. It is an old quip that the black gnat is neither black nor a gnat, but while it is true that the body is really dark olive, it looks black enough at a little distance to justify the first part of the name. The length of the female is about a quarter of an inch, the male being slightly longer.

Artificials

The commercial patterns of black gnat are commonly dressed with their wings in the vertical plane and bear little resemblance to the natural insect. I have found the following modification of J. W. Dunne's pattern extremely effective during a fall of Black Gnats:

> *Body:* A strand of herl from the bronze part of a turkey's tail feather.
> *Wings:* A mixed bunch of cock hackle fibres dyed green and magenta to give the effect of iridescence. They are tied in flat over the body and clipped off just beyond the bend of the hook.
> *Leg hackle:* As many turns as possible of black cock, the fibres of which are clipped quite short after winding.
> *Hook:* oo.

Bibio marci

This species takes its Latin name from the alleged date of its first appearance, namely St Mark's Day (5 April), but in this case the English name is more accurate, as it usually arrives with the hawthorn blossom. For the same reason it is yet another claimant to the name of Mayfly in some parts of the country. As in the case of the black gnat, it seems probable that anglers have confused two or more similar species, which might account for the apparent discrepancy in dates, but for practical purposes we will consider them as one.

I am inclined to think that the Hawthorn is a more local insect than the black gnat, and it certainly does not appear in anything like the same profusion, nor does it seem quite so fond of taking a bath. Consequently, although each individual fly represents a larger mouthful, and may tempt the trout on this account, it is seldom the cause of a general rise of fish. Indeed, the only really big hatch of Hawthorns I have ever witnessed was completely ignored by the trout, but from the experience of others it is evident that at certain times and places it is of some importance as an angling fly.

The adult resembles a black gnat but on a larger scale and with a blacker body. A distinctive feature, faithfully copied by most fly-dressers, is a pair of long, hairy hind legs, which it trails astern when in flight. It is nearly half an inch in length.

Artificials

The following is a useful pattern devised by Roger Woolley:

> *Body:* Two strands from the black part of a turkey's tail feather, showing the bright part of the quill.
> *Wings:* Strips from a pale grey jay wing feather.
> *Hackle:* Black cock.
> *Hind legs:* The surplus ends of the strands forming the body, secured so as to point backwards.
> *Hook:* 2.

This completes the tale of the more important Dipterans, but there are a few others which merit brief mention.

REED SMUTS, which belong to the family Simulidae, are true aquatic insects and sometimes hatch in such large numbers as to occupy the trout's exclusive attention. They are, however, really too small to imitate satisfactorily, and although a minute hackle pattern may score an occasional success, the angler is likely to experience an unhappy, not to say exasperating, time when the fish are engaged in 'smutting'. They occur in rivers throughout the summer months, and resemble miniature black gnats in appearance, but with relatively thicker bodies and shorter wings.

Artificials

The only imitations of the Reed Smut known to me are the five patterns devised by the late Dr J. C. Mottram, of which the following is one:

> *Abdomen:* Black ostrich herl.
> *Thorax:* Black wool.
> *Hackle:* White.
> *Hook:* Not mentioned, but presumably ooo or even smaller.

CRANE-FLIES of the Tipulidae family, popularly known as Daddy- or Harry-long-legs, often fall on to the water in late summer, when they receive a warm reception from the trout. Several ingenious patterns have been devised with legs represented by knotted strands of herl, but the majority of trout which succumb to the 'Daddy', especially on the Irish loughs, are victims of the natural fly used as a dap. There are several different species, varying in size, but they are too well-known to require description.

Artificials

The following is J. T. Hanna's dressing:

> *Body:* A strip of brown rubber wound between the legs from the shoulder to the bend of the hook and back again.
> *Wings:* Two brownish hackle tips tied in the spent position.
> *Hackle:* Red cock.
> *Legs:* Six strands from a cock pheasant's tail feather knotted in the middle to represent the joints. Four of these should point forward and two backwards.
> *Hook:* 3 to 5.

The GRAVEL BED (*Anisomera burmeisteri*) has long been known to fishermen and although of rather local distribution can be productive of fine sport where it occurs. I once witnessed a splendid rise to this fly on the Don, but mistakenly diagnosed Grannom, which had been hatching freely on the previous day. On discovering my mistake (thanks to a friendly angler on the opposite bank who was busily filling his basket) I rushed back to my hotel and dressed a couple of patterns, but by the time I returned it was all over. Those who fish the rivers of the north and west, therefore, would do well to be prepared for hatches of the gravel bed during the month of May. As its name suggests, it hatches out in the gravel beds by the riverside, and it is not unlike a Chironomid in appearance, with greyish wings, a dark lead-coloured body three-sixteenths of an inch in length, and long, almost black legs.

Artificials

The following is a useful hackle pattern devised by that well-known amateur fly dresser, Dr T. E. Pryce-Tannatt:

Body: Ash-coloured wool lightly varnished with diluted Durofix.

Hackles: Two turns of black cock with fibres twice the length of the hook, and a grey-brown partridge back feather in front.

Hook: 2 to 3.

6 SUB-ORDER: MEGALOPTERA

Family: SIALIDAE

Genus: *Sialis*

ALDER

Sialis lutaria. Sialis fuliginosa

THESE two species, of which *lutaria* is the commoner, are sufficiently alike to be treated as one. The Alder, or Orl-fly, as it was formerly known, is such a familiar sight by the water-side in May and June that it has been known to and imitated by anglers for centuries. Yet the fact is that it is not a wholly aquatic insect and in its winged state does not come on to the water except by accident, when it is very seldom taken by the trout. The undoubted success of the artificial Alder, therefore, is presumably due to its resemblance to some other insect – possibly a caddis pupa ascending to hatch, since most fishermen are agreed that it does best as a sunk fly. The larva, on the other hand, though unknown to the majority of fishermen, forms quite an important article of the trout's diet at certain times of the year, but to understand the true position of the Alder in the angling scene it is necessary to know something of the fly's rather unusual life-history.

The life-cycle consists of egg, larva, pupa, and adult, of which only the second stage is passed in the water. The eggs are laid on vegetation close to the water-side, and as soon as the small larvae emerge they make their way at once to the lake or river, as the case may be, there to live in the mud or silt for the best part of a year, feeding on other small larvae and nymphs. In the following March or April they crawl or swim ashore and proceed to pupate in holes in the bank. There the adults finally emerge, and as both mating and oviposition take place on shore, it will be appreciated that the trout only see the Alder in its larval stage, unless the winged-fly is unlucky enough to fall into the water, when in my experience it is invariably ignored. The larvae, however, are eaten in some numbers during their shoreward migration in the spring, and sometimes again towards the end of the season, when the new generation have attained a worthwhile size.

The larva is an uncouth-looking beast, mottled in shades of brown and full yellow and shaped rather like a carrot. It carries a pair of claw-like mandibles, and the abdomen is fringed with seven pairs of pointed tracheal gills. It is quite a fair swimmer and has a curious habit of rearing up the front half of its body when closely approached, doubtless for the purpose of intimidating potential enemies.

The pupa sheds the gills and tapering tail of the larva, and develops two pairs of wing-pads and a pair of antennae, which together with the legs are stowed away beneath the abdomen as in the sedge pupa. But as the trout never see the Alder in the pupal stage, this is of no more than academic interest to the angler.

The adult might be mistaken for a sedge-fly by the uninitiated, but the wings are rather more rounded in outline and are devoid of hairs. The body and legs are almost black, and the wings sepia brown with prominent dark veins. The length of the body is about half an inch, the wings being slightly longer.

Artificials

Larva. I do not know of any pattern except my own, which is therefore, given below:

> *Head and thorax:* Hare's ear.
> *Abdomen:* A mixture of brown and ginger seal's fur, tapering steeply from shoulder to tail.
> *Ribbing:* Gold tinsel.
> *Gills:* A pale ginger hen hackle following the turns of ribbing. The fibres above and below the hook are removed and those on either side stroked backwards towards the tail during the winding process.
> *Leg hackle:* Brown speckled partridge.
> *Hook:* Long Mayfly, 10 to 12, loaded with wire to make it sink.

Adult. The following is the standard dressing, though as I have previously suggested, it is probably not taken for an Alder by the trout.

> *Tying silk:* Crimson.
> *Body:* Peacock herl dyed magenta.
> *Wings:* Strips from a dark mottled hen's secondary feather, tied sloping over the body.
> *Hackle:* Black cock.
> *Hook:* 1 to 3.

7 ORDER: HEMIPTERA-HETEROPTERA (WATER BUGS)

THIS order includes a wide variety of aquatic insects differing considerably in appearance and habits, such as the water cricket, water measurer, water scorpions, pond skaters and water boat-men. Considering the boundless opportunities they provide, it is a surprising fact that the great majority of them are very seldom eaten by trout, virtually the only exceptions to this being the Lesser water boatmen of the family Corixidae. The remainder can therefore be safely ignored.

Family: CORIXIDAE (*Lesser Water boatmen*)

This family contains twenty-six British species and one variety of the genus *Corixa*, together with three species of allied genera. Except to the scientist, who is concerned with minute anatomical details, they are all very much alike except in the matter of size, which ranges from about one-eighth to half an inch, measured lengthways. Although they occur in some rivers, they are of more importance to the lake fisherman, the trout of different lakes seeming to vary in their partiality for them, regardless of the numbers available. Blagdon is the most notable example of a lake in which the Corixids form a significant proportion of the trouts' food throughout the summer, while records from many other waters show that they are taken chiefly in April, May, June and September. They can be distinguished from the rather similar water boatmen of the *Notonectidae* family (which the fish seldom take) by the fact that the *Notonectids* always swim on their backs.

The life-cycle consists of egg, nymph and adult, the nymphs in this case being no more than immature specimens of their respective adults. They normally live on the bed of the lake, but have to swim to the surface at intervals to renew their air sup-plies, and it is when thus engaged, no doubt, that they attract the trout's attention. Although they live underwater they are able to fly, and sometimes shift their quarters by this means from one lake to another during the summer months.

The adults bear a superficial resemblance to beetles, to which, however, they are unrelated. Seen from above they are boat-shaped, with large yellowish heads and a pattern of alternate light and dark brown stripes running across the body and wing cases, or hemielytra, which are folded across the back. Their undersides are flat and a dirty cream colour. The front legs are short and stout, the second pair long and thin and the hindmost pair, which are used as paddles, are fringed with hairs and held nearly at right angles to the body when the insect is at rest. The air is stored between the wing-cases and abdomen, giving the appearance of a silver halo as the Corixid turns downwards from the surface after renewing its supplies.

Artificials

I do not know of any standard pattern representing a Corixid, but give my own dressing below.

> *Head:* Yellowish-brown condor herl.
> *Body:* Opossum or any other buff-coloured fur.
> *Ribbing:* Narrow flat silver tinsel.
> *Back and wing cases:* The tip of a small wing covert from a cock capercailzie, lying flat over the body in the horizontal plane.
> *Paddles:* A grey-brown partridge feather wound in the centre of the body. The fibres above and below the body are then removed and those on either side secured so that they point slightly forward.
> *Leg hackle:* Pale ginger hen, or none.
> *Hook:* 3 to 4, lightly loaded with wire.

8 ORDER: ODONATA

Sub-orders: ANISOPTERA (*Dragon-flies*)
ZYGOPTERA (*Damsel-flies*)

THESE beautiful creatures are to be found in almost every lake and pond, as well as in some rivers, during the summer months, but although the trout sometimes eat them in surprising numbers they are too large to imitate satisfactorily except as immature nymphs, of which a good pattern often proves quite successful. There are twenty-seven British species of Anisoptera and seventeen of Zygoptera.

The life-cycle consists of egg, nymph and adult. The eggs are laid either on the surface of the water or an emergent weed, the different species, as always, differing in their methods. The nymphs, or naiads as they are sometimes called, live at the bottom or among weeds and are mostly carnivorous. On reaching maturity the nymph crawls up the stem of a water plant to a position well clear of the surface, where the adult emerges; a process which may take over an hour to complete. The trout take both nymphs and winged-flies – the latter probably in the shape of females in the act of laying their eggs, though immature fish may sometimes be seen making abortive attempts to seize them in the air as they hover over the water.

The nymphs of the true dragon-flies are squat, ungainly-looking creatures, varying in size and shape according to their species. They are fitted with a primitive form of jet-propulsion, which enables them to move at considerable speed over short distances. Damsel-fly nymphs are quite different in appearance and easier to imitate, being more like the nymphs of day-flies but with longer legs and three tracheal gills at the tail end. They usually proceed at a slow crawl, but can swim after a fashion with an undulating movement of the body. Both possess a curious piece of apparatus known as a mask, which is a kind of retractable grab used for the purpose of seizing their prey.

The adults need no description, being a familiar sight to every child who has dabbled in a pond. It may be noted, however, that the damsel-flies can be distinguished not only by their more slender build, but also by their habit of folding their wings over their backs when at rest, whereas the dragon-flies hold them spread apart in the flying position.

Artificials

The adults of both types are too large and the nymphs of dragon-flies too awkward in shape to be imitated satisfactorily, but damsel-fly nymphs can be copied with a reasonable degree of accuracy and are worth a trial in lakes.

Damsel-fly nymph. The following is my own attempt to represent an immature nymph, the colour of which may be dull green, yellow or brown.

> *Head:* Peacock herl.
> *Body:* Seal's fur, tapering slightly at the tail end.
> *Ribbing:* Gold tinsel.
> *Leg hackle:* A pale waterhen's feather.

Gills: The tips of three hackles tied in like a tail in the vertical plane and slightly separated by turns of tying silk.

Hook: Long Mayfly, 10–13, wire-loaded.

9 ORDER: COLEOPTERA (BEETLES)

THERE are no less than 3,700 British beetles, of which several hundred species are either aquatic or amphibious in their habits. It might be thought from this – and has indeed been stated by not a few writers – that beetles form an important source of trout food, but generally speaking this is not the case. At certain times and places, it is true, some of the terrestrial species are taken in large numbers, but for some strange reason trout do not appear to relish the water beetles, which are seldom found in autopsies. It may be that the fish only become interested in the Coleoptera when they are present in some quantities, and that this condition is only fulfilled when some of the land-bred species are hatching in the vicinity of rivers or lakes. This seems to happen more frequently in Wales than elsewhere, especially in the cases of the Coch-y-bondhu beetle, which Courtney Williams has identified as *Phyllopertha horticola*, and the Cockchafer or May-bug (*Melolontha melolontha*). The former hatches in June and July and the latter in May and June, and both sometimes fall on to the water in very large numbers. I have never witnessed this myself, but I remember seeing the streets of Brecon so covered with Cockchafers that it was impossible to walk without treading on them, and I was told that anglers on the nearby Talybont reservoir enjoy excellent sport on such occasions. When visiting waters where beetles are to be expected, therefore, the fisherman would do well to provide himself with an appropriate pattern, though as a general 'fly' I feel that the value of the artificial beetle has been somewhat overrated.

The life-cycle consists of egg, larva, pupa and adult, but the trout do not, of course, have an opportunity of taking the larvae and pupae of the terrestrial species. Even the aquatic beetles usually pupate out of their reach, either in the bank or on emergent vegetation, while their larvae are very rarely found in autopsies, possibly because they are equipped with prehensile claws which enable them to cling so tightly to the weeds that they

222

are difficult to dislodge. It is therefore unnecessary to describe the Coleoptera in these stages.

The adults vary greatly in shape and size, the aforementioned Coch-y-bondhu being an oval-shaped beetle about half an inch long and coloured reddish brown and black, with blackish legs. The Cockchafer is too well-known to need description. Most of the water beetles are more or less boat-shaped, and may be distinguished from the land-bred species by their flatter legs, fringed with hairs, which enable them to swim. They have to surface for air at intervals like the Corixids, which makes it all the more surprising that they are so seldom eaten by trout.

Artificials

I do not know any pattern representing the Cockchafer, though I remember seeing a most life-like imitation tied by a member of the Flyfishers' Club in which the wing cases were represented by a reddish-brown feather with a double black pattern taken from a cock pheasant. The Coch-y-bondhu is, of course, a standard pattern and is dressed as under.

> *Body:* Two or three strands of peacock herl.
> *Tag:* Flat gold tinsel.
> *Hackle:* Coch-y-bondhu.
> *Hook:* 1 to 3.

10 ORDER: HYMENOPTERA

THIS order includes the ants, of which there are several coloured, red, brown or black. They are, of course, land-bred, but when a swarm flies across a lake or river during the late summer months many of them fall into the water, and the trout seem to be inordinately fond of them. It has been said that an artificial ant is very seldom required but that when it *is* wanted it is wanted very badly, which no doubt is true, though in thirty years of fly fishing I never had occasion to use one myself. The ants, of course, require no description from me, and their life-history is too complex to be included here. Those who may be interested, however, will find a detailed description of the ants' remarkable story in Courtney Williams's excellent work, *A Dictionary of Trout Flies.*

Artificials

Commercial patterns of ants suffer from the same defects as those of black gnats. I therefore give two of William Lunn's dressings, which are much more like the real thing.

Red Ant.

> *Tying silk:* Deep orange.
> *Body:* The tying silk wound so as to form a fat blob at the tail end, followed by a few single turns to represent the 'waist'.
> *Wings:* Fibres from a white cock's hackle tied on slanting over the body and trimmed with scissors to the required length.
> *Hackle:* Light bright red cock.
> *Hook:* ooo to o.

Dark Ant.

> *Tying silk:* Crimson.
> *Body:* The tying silk wound as in the foregoing pattern.
> *Wings:* Fibres from a blue dun cock's hackle trimmed as above.
> *Hackle:* Very dark red cock.
> *Hook:* ooo to oo.

L. BAVERSTOCK

Bait Fishing

1 WORM FISHING

In general

WORM fishing demands great delicacy of technique in all conditions except coloured water or flood. There are, inevitably, differences of opinion as to the varying merits of bait and fly fishing and the purists of both methods sometimes get hot under the collar about each other. This is a great pity because worm fishing is an excellent way of taking trout when they will look at almost nothing else, especially on hot summer days with low water. I like to think of worm and fly fishing as complementary to one another and in no way in conflict. While there are times when the worm is the best way of taking trout there are also times when a fly will 'wipe its eye'.

The worm is an extremely versatile bait and can be fished successfully under every conceivable water condition. This is so true that, were you so inclined, you could use it throughout the year to the exclusion of everything else and finish up with an impressive number of fish. I do not think that that is the best way to use it, for several reasons. I dislike purism in any form and think that the better angler is the one who is prepared to vary his methods according to what is most likely to succeed at any given time. Apart from this a little variety makes fishing much more interesting. The use of the worm on brooks is a very wide subject and to avoid confusion I propose to divide it into Method 1 and Method 2. We will deal with high-water worming later.

Much has been written about the merits of different kinds of worms and if you take the trouble to study the variety of opinions on the subject you will most likely get thoroughly confused. Long ago, before I knew about the different ideas, I just used to go into the garden and dig 'worms', in the ground, manure or wherever they were to be found. As long as they were a reasonable size, well coloured and nice and lively I was satisfied. I see no reason to change that idea today. As long as you choose a size of worm which matches the size hook you intend using you will not go far wrong.

I firmly believe that it is a mistake to toughen worms for long periods before use. When they have undergone prolonged toughening they are like pieces of leather and prevent easy

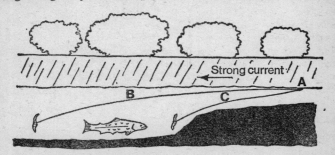

FIG 26. A, Point of entry. B, Worm only. Stays in rough surface water too long. C, Worm and shot gets down to fish quickly.

hooking of fish by masking the barb and stopping the hook from going in easily. A few hours in dryish moss is sufficient to remove surplus moisture and firm them up nicely. Only the roughest of casting would damage such a bait and if that happens it is the casting which should be attended to, not the bait. I think that fresh worms are more attractive than 'groomed' specimens and use them whenever possible.

A tin of assorted shot should be carried for use when necessary, such as in heavy water or to assist casting in rough weather. It is always best to use as little lead as possible. Admittedly, casting is much easier with the assistance of shot but they make quite a disturbance when entering the water and, just as important, they prevent the bait's natural movement downstream. To attract trout the worm should tumble naturally downstream, carried by the current, a thing it cannot do if held down by lead. Again, shot frequently get caught in the bottom and in this respect they make fishing more difficult.

When the current is strong, however, the worm should not be allowed to come to the surface otherwise it will be whipped away over waiting fish before they see it. In such cases a shot or two will have to be used and the bait must be got into the water some distance above the place where fish are likely to be lying so that it has a chance to get near the bottom in time.

Because of the rapidly changing character of the water there will have to be frequent alterations to the amount of lead. To do this easily it is essential that the shot are not pinched tightly on the cast. A good way is to put a tiny dust shot on as a stop about 8 in above the worm. This shot should be tightened just enough to stop it slipping. Any further shot needed can be pinched very loosely above the stop so that they can be easily removed when not required. Take great care when adding shot to a cast otherwise the fine nylon may get pinched and dangerously weaken the cast.

Method 1

I consider this to be the best way of fishing the worm and it is the method I like best. It is certainly the most sporting and least likely to damage undersize fish. My favourite hook is a round bend, about size 12. It must be razor sharp and mounted to very fine nylon. The worm is mounted by simply putting the hook through it at about its middle. This way the point of the hook shows but I have never found that this makes the slightest difference. If you prefer, the worm can be threaded on to the hook a little but don't overdo it otherwise the worm will be killed and lose most of its attractiveness. The success of this method depends, to a large extent, on presenting the fish with a lively, natural moving bait. Multiple hook tackles cannot achieve this very necessary requirement because, by their very nature, they hold the worm much more rigidly. In doing so they make fish more suspicious and prone to snatch at loose ends, the very thing they are intended to overcome. There is also no doubt that a single hook steers its way much more easily among the obstructions and stones on the bottom and so gets caught up less frequently.

The best places to fish are where there is a good deal of movement in the water, especially in the streams and runs. In such places the trout has little time to examine the worm before it is washed past and must make up his mind very quickly whether or not he wants it. The result is often a sharp snatch or knock and the instant this is felt the rod is quickly raised to hook the fish.

To do this successfully you must keep in touch with the bait as it moves downstream by lifting the rod point and pulling in line by hand. Every movement should be smooth and controlled so that although you avoid slack line, by raising the rod and pulling in line, you do not jerk the worm downstream. Everything depends on the fish thinking that the worm has somehow fallen into the water and is being helplessly washed straight into his larder.

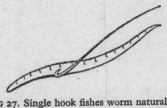

FIG 27. Single hook fishes worm naturally.

When you strike, don't forget that there are probably trees and bushes all around you waiting eagerly to trap your cast in some inaccessible height. Try and tighten away from them. It is better to avoid a directly upwards strike because, at the start, there will be a tendency for the cast to go sailing skywards. Experience alone will overcome this fault and it is most unlikely that anything in these pages, or anywhere else, will teach the beginner to overcome the natural reaction to the first few pulls from trout. Moderation is a necessity and after a few good tangles the lesson is quickly learned. There is one thing I must mention, however. Too hard a strike will break the fine cast and may lose for you the fish of the day. Always carry plenty of spare nylon and hooks so that any damage can be repaired at once.

If you cast too far, or the wind takes your line and dumps it on the far bank or on a rock, don't think that everything is ruined. It is quite likely that this misfortune can be turned to advantage. Take up any slack line very carefully then lift and pull, gently and evenly. In most cases the worm will move free of whatever was holding it and drop gently into the water, a deadly moment for taking a good trout. The worm enters the water in a most natural manner and any nearby fish is almost certain to grab it.

When using this method it is more than ever necessary that the bait should be lively and active and it should be frequently examined to ensure this. A limp worm or one which has been damaged should be replaced at once.

Casting

From what has already been said it will be realized that the worm should always enter the water as gently and as naturally as possible. In addition, considerable accuracy is required if each cast is to fish every tiny, awkward place. Trout are very shy and although you keep out of sight and get into a beautiful casting position it will do you no good if your cast is really bad. Bang the worm on to the water right on top of a fish and see what happens. A wild flurry, a tinge of mud and the trout has gone.

Except in the roughest of water try to fish as far away from the pool or run as you can comfortably cast. Where conditions permit I try to fish a pool or run in the manner I am going to describe. The trouble is that no two pools are alike and they all require different tactics. Anything resembling a fixed system is to be deplored but it is possible to give a few general hints which should be of assistance.

Let us imagine that we have come to a typical pool. A fast stream runs in between two rocks at the head and opens out into a modestly flowing middle section, broken here and there by large stones. The banks are fairly well covered with bushes and undergrowth.

I should start at the tail of this pool so my fishing would begin when I was standing well below the tail and a considerable distance from that attractive-looking stream at the head. A shortish cast straight up near my own bank first, then slightly longer casts at an increasing angle across stream until the brook had been covered right across. Move forward a little then, quietly, and repeat the process. We are getting into the main body of the pool now and particular care should be paid to the casts made close to the large stones. The inside edge of the stream, right next to that quiet water immediately behind the stone, is the place to aim for. Let the worm trickle around the stone.

We are stuck for the moment. We can go no farther along the bank because of thick bushes and wading would not be advisable owing to the disturbance it would make. Note how far we have fished by that branch sticking out of the water before we make a short detour. Some distance up the bank we come to a tiny gap in the bushes. It is slightly above the branch we marked so it will be an ideal place from which to fish. Ordinary casting will be out of the question because we are hemmed in on all sides and above by thick greenery. The only way is to bend double and move as close to the water as we safely can before starting to fish. We must now wind in the line until it is barely the length of the rod. By holding the cast firmly, just above the worm, we can pull down the top of the rod so that it will act as a catapult to spring the bait forward. This type of cast is probably the nearest we shall get to a flick and this is all to the good because sudden movement often damages the worm. The aim should be to achieve a smooth swing but, as we have seen, there are times when this is not possible and we just have to be as careful as we can.

Having made several short casts through the little gap and carefully retrieved the bait we can now tackle the fishy-looking headstream. A problem here straight away. Once we have left the last gap in the bushes the bank is covered with solid greenery until we get right to the very head of the pool where there is a good clear space. Let us move up to the last bush and begin operations there. Stopping well back in the protection of the bush we make a short cast, not far out from our own bank. As the worm enters the water we pull a yard or two of line from the reel and gently feed it through the rings as the bait disappears under the bush. This is one of the worst positions for hooking fish and for this reason we will not strike at once unless we get a good solid pull. Once a fish has been hooked we must hold him hard and give him no slack otherwise he may very well throw the hook and get away. Several casts can be made from this position, increasing the distance each time until the pool has been covered.

Although this chapter is intended principally to describe one way of fishing the worm, I have deliberately varied it in the above description because it is quite impossible, except in theory, to adhere strictly to any one method. The complications which I have added to the job of simple upstream fishing are constant companions to the brook fisherman and success under such conditions is all the sweeter.

Method 2

Much as I prefer fishing the worm so that I can strike at the first sign of a fish I am well aware that this is not always the best way. This is especially true when fishing downstream or in slowly moving brooks. I have watched trout cruising around a worm as it trundled slowly down through a pool, examining it and obviously trying to decide what to do about it. To strike at the first little pluck or stoppage when this is happening will result in very few fish being caught and an alternative method has to be used.

I still prefer the single hook, although it is a much larger size, a 6 or 7. The worm is also correspondingly larger so that it matches the hook. It is not usually possible to see exactly what is going on near the worm so you have to rely even more on what you feel and sense. The main difference between this method and the preceding one is that instantaneous striking is avoided. A hungry trout is thus given an opportunity to gorge the bait, something we try to avoid by using the larger hook.

Cast exactly as described in Method 1 but when you see the line stop or feel a tap, do not strike. Move the rod point towards the bait and give a little slack line. If the fish means business and you avoid scaring it by keeping plenty of slack line available, the tap, tap will come again. Only experience can really teach you when to tighten and the quickest way to learn is to make a mental note of the way each fish tackles the worm. As soon as a fish is landed see how it has been hooked. By comparing the way several fish take the worm with the way they are hooked you will very soon have a workmanlike system for hooking. Two or three seconds will be quite sufficient for some fish while others may require eight or ten seconds to make up their minds. If you keep catching fish which are hooked in the back of the throat then you are obviously giving too much time before striking and should remedy the fault at once. If you are bothered by sharp little plucks which never turn into a real 'run' you are almost certainly being bothered by very small fish and would do well to move on.

I have only mentioned the single-hook worm tackles so far because I prefer them and very seldom use anything else. Many anglers, however, use the two-hook Pennell or three-hook Stewart tackles and the beginner might well like to give these tackles a try before finally deciding which way he prefers fishing the worm. Whichever tackle he uses, the instructions I have given should help him to use them successfully.

Covering the ground

It must be realized that when fishing these small waters in summer conditions it does not pay to stop too long in one place. The essence of the sport is movement, finding a likely spot,

FIG 28. Pennell worm tackle.

having a few throws, then pushing on. Most brook pools can be covered with quite a small number of casts and it is simply wasting time to keep on trying a place, however fishy it may look, when it is obvious that everything there has already seen the bait or been scared.

The speed and amount of movement is governed by the particular fishing. If you are on a good long stretch it might well pay to ignore unlikely spots altogether and concentrate on covering a lot of ground and fishing only the best places. If the stretch is only a short one then you must take great care in approaching each pool or run and thoroughly search every possible place.

Closely allied to the business of covering the ground is the question of which method to use and how often it should be changed. Freedom of movement is restricted and fishing time lost if tackle or flies are changed at every other pool. For all-round efficiency the best way is to choose a method suitable to the day and time of year and stick to it. The first dozen or so casts will probably tell you if you have chosen a suitable method and as long as you do not try and fish dry-fly in a flood or worm in low water with 8 lb nylon, there are considerable margins for error and personal preference. If you are worm fishing and come to a place where a few trout are rising they can often be tempted by carefully casting a little above the rings and allowing the bait to come gently down. When casting to these marked fish

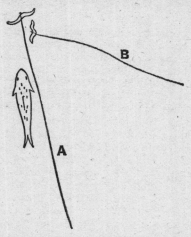

FIG 29. A, Try to avoid this. B, A good cast.

I try and avoid putting any line directly over them and do my best to arrange things so that the first thing they see is the worm.

There is no doubt that, under low-water conditions, it pays to keep on the move and the weight of the bag at the end of the day will frequently prove this point. Anything which can be done to limit the amount of time spent at the water-side fiddling rather than fishing is worth doing.

2 HIGH-WATER WORMING

ONE of the great advantages of brook fishing is that the water is seldom out of order for more than a few hours at a time. The short, often steep, courses quickly discharge the flood water into the larger rivers so that by the time the rivers are beginning to feel the cumulative effect of this water the brooks have already run out and are coming into perfect order. Even so there will be occasions when the angler arrives at the brook side to find it a swollen mass of swiftly moving colour. A casual glance would pronounce it unfishable but there is hope, even in these extreme conditions.

High-water worming, although not the most artistic way of catching trout is certainly not a 'chuck and chance it' method, especially on a brook. The narrow course confines the water and makes it all the more difficult to find the sheltered bays and back eddies which are so necessary for this kind of fishing. When a flood comes, fish seek shelter where they can lie and feed without being in a raging torrent and while the water is really high these are the only places worth fishing. The centre stream bores along the fastest so this should be ignored and attention focused mainly within a few inches of the banks. It is, at first, an unreal sensation to stand on the bank and use a short line to fish places which were dry stones an hour or so before but this is what you often do. Every boulder has its little pool of calmer water behind, which will hold fish and constant watch must be kept for these temporary sanctuaries. A place which normally holds a single fish may hold three or four when there is a flood.

Because of the coloured water it is not so vital to worry about being seen by the fish but it is very necessary to cover each likely place thoroughly before moving on. Flood conditions sometimes make it necessary to vary the low-water technique of moving quickly and covering a large amount of water. Fish are much less likely to be disturbed in coloured water and it has been my experience that it pays to spend a little more time exploring the possibilities of a place before moving on. Because of the murky water, fish cannot see a bait so easily and it frequently has to pass quite close to them before they will make a definite move. Apart from the colour, the increased volume of water will frequently whip a worm away over a fish before it has had a chance to sample it. These points were very forcibly demonstrated to me on a favourite brook.

The water was a rich brown and very high when I came to this particular pool. It held fish, even under normal conditions

I had counted seven good trout lying down the middle. It wasn't the centre of the pool that interested me at present though. At the head, on the left bank, was a half-fallen tree which jutted into the water and forced the main stream into a narrow race through the centre of the pool. Below the tree was a perfect slow-moving back eddy, just what I had been looking for. I made about half a dozen careful casts, without success, and was beginning to think I had been wrong about the prospects of the place when luck came to my assistance. A despairing cast went a few inches farther than my previous efforts and the worm plopped into the water right under an overhanging branch. A second or two later the line trembled and stopped and I was into a good trout. I landed the fish then cast to the same spot again, with the same result. This happened once more so that I ended up with three more fish than I thought I should get. The fact that I had caught them all in virtually the same spot was not lost on me and I never fail now to cover every likely-looking place as thoroughly as possible before moving on. Heavy flood water demands accurate casting so that the worm has time to dawdle around in the slack areas and get right down to the fish before being whipped away by the current. This all-important aim is best achieved by the addition of a little more lead to the cast, a sound move under such conditions. Although the surface of the water may appear to be quite placid there could quite easily be odd currents and whirls below the surface which would prevent a light bait being passed close to the fish. Extra lead also slows the downstream movement of the bait so that it fishes more slowly, an important factor in these tiny pools. Trout may well take a worm which hovers and trundles its way slowly by but they will rarely venture out into the main stream in pursuit of a bait which is already being borne away downstream.

Tackle

The most important thing required for high-water worming is a realization that low-water techniques must be varied. The tackle itself can be the same and my own preference is for the large single hook, of fine wire and round bend, to which I whip a small loop of nylon. Make up half a dozen or so of these hooks at a time so that you have plenty of replacements ready when required.

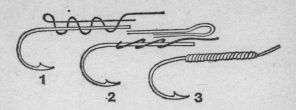

FIG 30. 1, A few wide turns of double tying silk as a base. 2, Lay the loop on the shank. 3, Wind tightly down and back. Finish with half hitches and varnish.

A warning

If you are used to fishing chalk-stream brooks or some of the quieter country streams, do not underestimate the possible danger if you tackle some of the mountain brooks when they are in flood. Many of these brooks can turn, in an hour, from gin-clear trickles to roaring torrents and you would be very unwise to treat them too lightly. Wading is unnecessary and should be avoided unless it is essential to cross the brook, when great care should be taken to ensure a suitable place and adequate footholds.

3 OTHER BAITS

Caddis fishing

THIS is an interesting and effective way of catching trout and provides a useful alternative to worm fishing. The supply of caddis varies considerably from one part of the country to another. It is usually possible to find sufficient caddis for a day's fishing without much trouble. The places favoured are the shallow stickles and edges of runs with pebbly bottoms. It is underneath the pebbles and stones that the caddis will be found. Dirty or muddy bottoms are not likely to yield many baits. They should be kept in wet moss in a draw-string worm bag or tin with air holes punched in the lid. To 'shell' the caddis, hold it between the forefingers and thumbs of both hands and carefully bend the case until it snaps in the middle. The caddis itself is very soft and pliable and in nine cases out of ten is quite un-damaged by this apparently fatal treatment. When the case has been snapped it will pull off the caddis quite easily and the caddis is then ready for baiting.

Method

In the main, caddis fishing is similar to clear-water worming although I think the technique is a little more difficult because of the fragile nature of the bait and its very light weight. When casting the caddis it is absolutely vital that all movements should be smooth and unhurried and because force cannot be used it is only possible to fish a very moderate length of line. Anything like a flick will probably leave only a bare hook, or a bait so badly damaged that it is of no further use. I like to use two caddis, or if they are not very big, as many as three. Put the hook through the tail end or nip them through the skin of the back.

All the places which would be fished with a worm can be tried with the caddis but for my own part I like to concentrate on water which is slower flowing than the best worming water. Caddis makes an excellent dapping bait but more of that later. To help casting as much as possible I carefully pinch a couple of small shot about 8 in above the bait. This also helps to sink it and keep it well down in the water where it is most likely to attract fish. To my mind, caddis is essentially a low-water bait and it will succeed when even a perfectly presented worm has been ignored. I would never use caddis at a time of high-water, when, apart from the difficulty of finding them, they are much less effective than a worm.

Creeper fishing

Around May comes what many fishermen think is the cream of trout fishing and there is some justification for this. Trout caught on the creeper always seem to be just that bit lustier and better conditioned than those caught by other means and there is no doubt that the very best fish are taken with it.

The creeper (Larva of the stone-fly) is not the most beautiful of creatures, and as a small boy I used to treat them as though they were charged with electricity. However, even a small boy quickly overcomes his qualms on learning that his dragons are one of the best trout baits.

They are to be found under stones in shallow runs, in fact they frequent very similar haunts to the caddis but are very much more difficult to catch and a certain amount of know-how is required to do the job properly. The stones should be turned up gently and slowly, against the current, so that no mud is disturbed to cloud the water and cover the creeper's escape. If the stones are turned up too quickly they cause a whirl in the

FIG 31. The Creeper.

water which lifts anything light, including the creeper, from the bottom and allows the current to whip it away. If the stones are turned carefully you will probably see a slight movement as a creeper disappears under a convenient pebble. Keep the large stone upright in the water so that it acts as a current break and allows you a clear view. Creepers in the open, can, of course, be picked up at once. The large ones are best, over an inch long and they can be kept in a tin of wet moss with a perforated lid. I like to use them as soon as possible after they have been caught because there is no doubt that the fish prefer a lively bait.

Tackle

Fly rod and 3 ft of fine nylon will do very nicely. For most creeper fishing we will need a little more lead than would be used for caddis or grasshopper fishing. I like a single hook, about a No 10. It should not be too small otherwise the relatively hard body of the creeper may prevent it from getting a good hold. Two-hook enthusiasts will find the method of making up tackles (shown in Fig 32) simple and effective and all shapes and sizes of mounts can be made up.

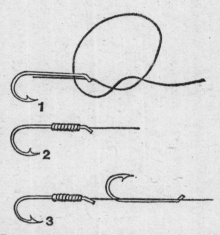

FIG 32. 1, Pass nylon through eye then throw seven or eight half hitches. 2, Pass nylon back through eye again. 3, Repeat 1 and 2 on second hook.

Method

The streams are the best places to use the creeper and brooks usually abound in suitable water. Sometimes, when the light is right and the day is calm, you can see the creeper swimming down through the water, then watch for the way the trout rush at it with gaping mouths. They know what they like and creeper is very high up on their menu. The real season for them is only a matter of a week or two and trout usually make the most of their precious opportunity. The only thing which can really spoil this fishing is high water, and if the weather should be consistently bad and accompanied by a cold wind there may be no creeper fishing that year. Because the period during which it is worth fishing creeper is so short it is necessary to keep an eye on them after early April to see how they are progressing. All one has to do is to turn over a few stones and when this discloses numerous large creepers it is time to begin. The period during which their use is most effective can vary by several weeks from year to year, warm dry weather often producing an early season.

The creeper is the ideal bait for conditions of low clear water and it is usually fished upstream into all the little streams and pieces of rough water. The bait is invariably taken boldly and a firm tightening is all that is required to securely hook the fish.

Grasshopper fishing

Later on in the season, around August, the grasshopper comes into its own as a trout bait and a very deadly one it is. It is certainly one of the most exciting baits to use and I always feel a tingle of expectation as I see it floating towards me, kicking away on the surface of the water. On a really good hot day, grasshoppers appear in force and they can be collected in a narrow-necked bottle which has air-holes in the cork. It is important to use a narrow-necked bottle so that the grasshoppers can be removed one at a time.

Method

The single hook should be passed carefully through the back of the grasshopper, not much below the skin, which is quite hard. Essentially a low-water method, grasshopper fishing offers all the excitement of fly, where rises are seen, coupled with the undoubted extra attraction of life and movement in the bait itself. This ensures that once a fish has made up its mind to take the bait it does so in a determined manner. A savage lunge or slash is often the result and it is at this moment that most fish are lost. The immediate reaction, until experience teaches caution, is to respond to these violent rises with an equally violent and hasty strike and the result is a break or missed fish. It is essential to give the fish just a moment to get a good hold on the grasshopper before the angler responds and even then all that is required is a firm tightening. The finest nylon will stand the most astonishing pressure from a fish when it has been hooked but it will not stand fierce sudden strains. The grasshopper should be fished with a minimum of lead, in fact it is best fished without lead at all whenever this is possible. The reason is that the bait's attractiveness lies in its vigorous kicking on the surface of the water and if lead is added to the cast the grasshopper is soon dragged below the surface and drowned. If conditions are such that shot have to be used then they should be put on the cast about 18 in to 2 ft from the bait so that they will not be so likely to draw it under.

My best fishing with grasshopper has been had in the quieter runs and eddies around rocks and tree stumps. The quiet pools, which are too still for many methods, will yield trout of surprising size to the vigorous grasshopper and such places are well worth a trial. A rewarding dodge is to carefully drop the bait into the little revolving eddy in an otherwise lifeless pool. These places are frequently very small and not easily spotted and a careful and continuous watch has to be kept to ensure that they are not passed by. A useful point to remember is that there are often pieces of white foam near them, built up by the current and washed into the back eddy from which they are unable to escape.

Grasshopper fishing requires considerable attention to detail and a delicate hand if the best results are to be obtained. Time spent in the careful selection of the best places is always time well spent, especially where grasshopper fishing is concerned. Only a dozen or so good spots may be available in any given stretch but it is far better to fish only these and move on rather than waste time flogging unsuitable water. If the amount of fishing is limited or you come to a place which you consider well suited to another method, by all means change over and give it a trial. To come back to grasshopper fishing, never fish with anything except a really lively bait. Remembering this point increases the chances of success by about fifty per cent.

Bushing (or dapping)

Because of the small dimensions of the water and the fact that the banks are frequently overgrown, brooks are the ideal place for the method of fishing known as bushing. In fact it can be fairly said that they are the only places where it can be successfully carried on to any extent. Quite a few baits can be very easily used for this method but the three which I have found most successful are grasshopper, caddis and worm. Thickly overgrown banks with fairly steep, slow-moving water beneath, provide excellent places for beginning operations. It will be remembered that great care must always be exercised when getting into a casting position but for bushing the need for care

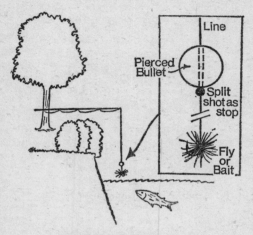

FIG 33. Dapping or 'Bushing'.

is doubled. There must be no trace of a shadow thrown on to the water, so the sun should always be in front of the fisherman. If bushes have to be parted to allow the rod point to be pushed through, make sure that the bush does not hang down into the water otherwise it may disturb the surface and frighten any fish lying below.

Method

Let us imagine that we are going to try bushing with a worm. We shall require a much shorter cast than usual; 2 ft 6 in or

3 ft will be quite long enough and the nylon should not be heavy, not much over 2 lb breaking strain. The single hook is put through the worm but no lead is added, a last careful look to choose the best spot before we approach our objective and we are ready to begin. As we peer cautiously over the top of a bush a nice trout rises unconcernedly immediately below us so we have at least got as far as the water's edge without disturbing the fish. We ease smoothly and gently back behind the bush and carefully push the rod forward with only the cast and a few inches of line hanging from the rod top. Another cautious look to pinpoint the position of the fish, yes, there he is, still rising.

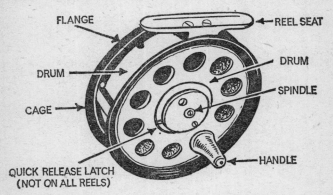

FLANGE

REEL SEAT

DRUM

DRUM

SPINDLE

CAGE

QUICK RELEASE LATCH
(NOT ON ALL REELS)

HANDLE

FIG 34. Fly reel. Standard sizes: 3 in by eighths to 4 in.

This time we stay motionless and wait for the next rise. As soon as we see the ring we begin to move and the next instant we drop the worm gently into the centre of the expanding ring. A flurry in the water is followed by a sharp pull and we raise the point of the rod to hook the fish. Dropping the worm into the ring is a very deadly way of taking trout and they take the bait so confidently, even in the slow water, that the strike should be made at once.

If we had not actually seen a fish rise then we should have carefully fished the water within reach before moving on to another likely looking place. The method then is to quietly drop in the worm and let it writhe its way out of sight towards the bottom. Allow the worm to stay on the bottom for a few moments then gently raise the rod point a few inches and allow the worm to go to the bottom again. With the help of any slight current, and by moving the rod around, the bait can be worked slowly and attractively along for a few feet. Don't forget to try right in under the bank where there are probably good trout sheltering and waiting for food to come near. It has been my experience that this searching type of bushing requires that more time be given to the fish before striking otherwise it may be found that it has not properly taken the bait.

I always fish the grasshopper as though I were dropping it straight on to the nose of a rising fish, even though there may not be a sign of a rise. Being such a lively bait it awakens interest from many fish which would not stir an inch for a worm and they will come quite a long way for such a tasty morsel. A slight hesitation is all that is necessary before the rod point is raised.

Bushing is often referred to as dapping, a word also used for a totally different style of fishing, on lakes, with a fly on a line blown out by the wind (see pages 129 to 131).

Appendix

TACKLE AND KNOTS

Rods

MOST modern fly rods are made either from split cane – strips of cane, usually six, glued together – or from fibreglass tubes.

The most popular lengths lie between 8 ft and 9 ft for general fishing. For mountain streams, brooks and other narrow waters, a light 6–7 ft rod is desirable, especially if the banks are overgrown.

The angler who does most of his fishing from the shores of lakes or reservoirs, where long casting can be an advantage, may prefer a longer wet-fly rod (say up to $10\frac{1}{2}$ ft), with greater casting and lifting power.

Rods are made for dry-fly fishing and for wet-fly fishing, the difference lying mainly in the delicacy of the action. A dry-fly rod will do practically everything you want for wet-fly fishing on rivers and brooks, but it is difficult properly to cast a dry-fly with a wet-fly rod.

Reels

The standard fly reel (Fig 34) is between 3 and 4 in in diameter. It has a permanent or optional ratchet check.

It should be filled nearly to capacity. To do this, attach one end of the fly line lightly to the empty drum. Reel on the fly line. Carefully attach the backing line to the fly line and reel on sufficient backing nearly to fill the reel. Pull off all the backing and line, fasten the free end of the backing securely to the drum, and wind on the remainder.

Lines

Fly lines are made of braided silk, braided nylon or other types of man-made fibres.

They are made as floating lines or sinking lines. Silk lines must be treated with a floatant (nowadays usually a silicone preparation) to make them float. There are several types of 'guaranteed to float all day' lines, including the popular plastic lines. These float well and pick up easily because they do not 'grip' the surface of the water as do other lines.

Lines can be level, tapered, double tapered, forward taper, or shooting (or torpedo) head.

Level lines are relatively cheap but their use is practically limited to wet-fly fishing with the wind.

Double taper lines are the most popular for general fly fishing. The standard length is 30 yds, tapered from the fine ends to the bulky centre. The increasing bulk of the rear half can have a steadying influence in long casting, but the main idea is that the line can be reversed when the forward end gets worn through use.

Forward taper lines have the bulk of the weight concentrated in the front part of the line. This aids long casting and casting into the wind.

Shooting heads consist of a single tapered line, usually 30 ft in length, which finishes bluntly at the thick end, where there is a loop or other device for attaching it neatly to the 'shooting line' (or running line). Monofilament of 20 lb bs is as good as anything for this, though fine diameter floating lines are made specially for the purpose. Shooting heads are used by those who want to make exceptionally long casts and are of little interest to the general trout fisherman.

Fig 35 shows, in telescoped form, these various types of line. This illustration, originated by Scientific Anglers Inc, the American makers of Air Cel floating lines, was taken with permission from *The Truth About Tackle*, a booklet by Dermot Wilson which anyone buying trout tackle will find invaluable. It is obtainable for 25p direct from the author at Nether Wallop Mill, Stockbridge, Hampshire.

Line specifications

Until recently fly lines were described by letters indicating *size*. The system has not been entirely discarded. Diameters were lettered thus:

A	0·060 in	F	0·035 in
B	0·055 in	G	0·030 in
C	0·050 in	H	0·025 in
D	0·045 in	I	0·022 in
E	0·040 in		

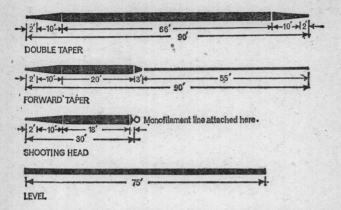

FIG 35. Anatomy of a line. *NB*. Remember that the first 30–40ft of line (at the left of the diagram) is the part that most affects casting. This is the only part which you normally 'aerialize'. (*Reproduced by courtesy of Dermot Wilson*).

Thus an HDH line would indicate a double tapered line with a diameter of 0·045 in in the middle and 0·025 in at each end. HCF indicates a forward taper line, with a diameter range 0·025, 0·050, 0·035.

The point of any line specification is to match a line to a particular rod. The letter system was satisfactory when only braided silk lines were in use, but diameter became insufficient when lines of man-made fibres of different specific gravities came into common use. The Association of Fishing Tackle Makers has adopted the following system, which is based on the *weight* in grains, of the forward 30 ft of line, expressed as a number preceded by the symbol #.

No	Weight	No	Weight
1	60	7	185
2	80	8	210
3	100	9	240
4	120	10	280
5	140	11	330
6	160	12	380

Acceptable tolerances range from 6 grains each side for the lightest weights (ie No 1 can be anything from 54 to 66 grains) to 12 grains each side for the heaviest.

All fly rods should be marked with the AFTM symbol and number to indicate the lines considered suitable for use with them.

A simple code of lettering shows the type of line.

    L = level
DT = double taper
WF = weight forward
 ST = shooting taper

These letters precede the # number.

    F = floating
    S = sinking
    I = intermediate (ie a line that will sink in its natural state but which will float when floatant has been applied)

These letters follow the # number.

Examples: DT-8-F indicates a floating double taper line the forward 30 ft of which weigh 210 grains. In a standard braided silk DT line the size would be GAG.

WF-7-S = a No 7 weight forward sinking line (HDG).

Casts (or leaders)

The cast connects fly to line. It is normally from 6 ft to 9 ft in length.

Silkworm gut is still in use but it has been almost entirely superseded by nylon monofilament or similar chemical products.

A tapered line needs a tapered cast. These can be bought in one tapered length or they can be made up from any lengths of monofilament of different diameters (see page 50 for examples). The butt end of the cast should be roughly the same diameter as that of the tip of the fly line. Many of the ready-prepared casts are too thin at the butt end.

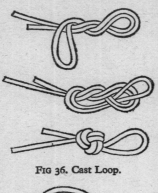

FIG 36. Cast Loop.

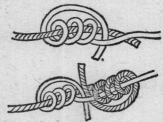

FIG 37. Blood Knot: for joining cast and point.

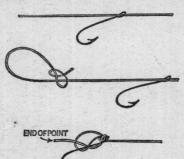

FIG 38. Turle Knot: for attaching fly to point.

249

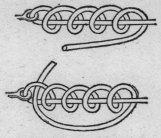

FIG 39. Half blood Knot.

FIG 40. Sheet bend for joining line and cast.

Hook scale

Old (Redditch) Scale No	New Scales No
8	7
9	6
10	5
11	4
12	3
13	2
14	1
15	0
16	00
17	000

INDEX

251

253

Edited by Kenneth Mansfield
Coarse Fishing 60p

Seven authors, each well known for their writing on angling topics, provide the complete handbook on coarse fishing for every angler.

All the main species are dealt with individually, together with full descriptions of tackle and techniques. Baits – how to find, clean and use them – are covered in the same comprehensive manner, and there is a wealth of other useful information.

Trevor Housby
Boat Fishing 60p

An experienced professional charter-boat skipper describes the most productive boat fishing techniques for saltwater species, described here, together with a wealth of practical hints.

T. C. Ivens
Still Water Fly-Fishing 80p

'Another great classic . . . Long regarded as the standard work on still water fly-fishing . . . confirms its position as one of the world's best textbooks on angling' SCOTSMAN

'A very good book by a good, experienced and thinking fisherman. It contains much of value for the skilled and novice alike, from flies and tactics to boat handling and clothing' THE FIELD